OCCULT PHENOMENA

IN THE LIGHT OF THEOLOGY

ALOIS WIESINGER

Published by Left of Brain Books

Copyright © 2023 Left of Brain Books

ISBN 978-1-397-66998-8

First Edition

All rights reserved. No part of this publication may be reproduced, distributed, or transmitted in any form or by any means, including photocopying, recording, or other electronic or mechanical methods, without the prior written permission of the publisher, except in the case of brief quotations permitted by copyright law. Left of Brain Books is a division of Left Of Brain Onboarding Pty Ltd.

Table of Contents

INTRODUCTION 1

GLOSSARY 7

PART I THE PRETERNATURAL GIFTS 11

   I Body And Soul 12

   II Pure Spirit 21

   III The Body-Free Soul 29

   IV The Partly Body-Free Soul 38

   V The Twofold Nature of the Soul's Activity 68

   VI Body And Soul of our First Parents 79

   VII The Fall 94

PART II OCCULT PHENOMENA EXAMINED IN DETAIL IN
THE LIGHT OF THE AUTHOR'S THEORY 101

   I Natural Sleep 102

   II Pathological Sleep And Somnambulism 116

   III The Phenomena Of Artificial Sleep 135

   IV Certain Special Aspects of the Phenomena of Artificial Sleep 180

   V Searchings by Mankind to attain to the Contemplation of Spiritual Truth and to transcend the Material 247

   VI Mystical Sleep 257

INTRODUCTION

The number of books that have in recent years been written on the subject of occultism is very large indeed, and the number of its adherents and of the periodicals concerned with it grows continually; this is a sign that it has become a serious problem, one which disturbs men's souls like a spiritual epidemic. Professor Feldmann, to whom the writer is obliged for many valuable suggestions, states in his *Okkulte Philosophie* that a second-hand bookseller in Munich sent him a catalogue of books on occult sciences consisting of four volumes, each of which contained between 600 and 800 titles. A number of firms are engaged in the printing and distribution of publications on the occult both at home and abroad. The causes of this general widespread interest reside first of all in the great hunger for the preternatural which the various philosophical systems are unable to assuage, however high-sounding their names; this epidemic, however, is also a violent reaction against the materialism which "holds matter to be the sole reality and the mother of all living things", which assumes no difference between spirit and matter, and refers to man simply as "a digestive tract open at both ends".

The religion of Christ satisfies this hunger; but many have forsaken God, the fountain of living water, and have built unto themselves "cisterns that hold no water" (Jer. 2. 13). They have no knowledge of the means of salvation, and, although they consider themselves educated, are ignorant of Christian doctrine. They stand in particular fear of the Catholic Church because of her moral code, live like heathens and are ready to accept any superstition that in some slight way promises to lead them beyond the material.

Others seek the occult because of the childish curiosity which the unusual inspires, or because of the astonishing cures which, as they believe, could not be explained if there were not an element of truth in Spiritualism. Others again concern themselves with it in order to acquaint themselves with the behaviour of the soul when it is in certain unusual states and to learn its hidden nature, characteristics and powers, possibly also to assist in the development of man towards a new species, towards the superman.

The explanations of occultism are as varied as they are numerous; the materialists seek to explain it in terms of matter and its movements, by a theory of "waves", the exact nature of which is not yet known. Others believe that we are dealing with reappearances of the dead, with "rebirths", or with a "perispirit" which is not truly either spirit or body but is what is called an astral body. The majority of learned Christians fall back on the devil, who is supposed in these cases to misuse human powers and so to deceive us. Admittedly they try increasingly to ascribe as many of these phenomena as possible to natural powers. So far, however, they do not appear to have arrived at a satisfactory explanation.

Writers who ascribe everything to demoniac intervention, or, at any rate, do this in the case of transcendental phenomena (supersensual manifestations) such as "spiritual suggestion", perception of objects that are not present to the eye, movement of objects at a distance, etc., argue as follows: there are certain manifestations for which there is no natural explanation, and since they cannot be ascribed to the intervention of God or the angels or to the dead, there remains only one possible author, and that is the devil.[1]

At first sight this seems sensible enough, but it rests on the supposition that the soul has no powers save those which it ordinarily displays; it is thus essentially a superficial view, and those who hold it seem unaware of the fact that they are opening the door to precisely that kind of demonomania that for some five hundred years caused the West to have witches on the brain. Moreover, to call on the devil as though he were a kind of *deus ex machina*, every time we cannot think of some natural explanation for a thing, is really a little unscientific.

The teaching of the Church is equally far removed from either extreme, from materialism as from demonomania. The Church does not deny the possibility of diabolical possession and even has a special ordination conferring powers of exorcism for the casting out of devils, but she enjoins us to treat everything as natural until the contrary is proved, a rule that she applies with particular strictness when alleged miracles are cited in a canonization process.

---

[1] Dr Arthur Lehmkuhl, *Theologia Moralis*, I, 1902, n. 363; Adam Göpfert, *Moraltheologie*, 1922; Lapponi *Hypnotismus und Spiritismus*, Leipzig, 1906 (German translation of the Italian).

In these circumstances it is surely legitimate to present in the light of theology and of Christian philosophy an explanation which seems to come closer to the truth. It is not suggested that the theory here advanced is wholly new, for its essential features are to be found in other Catholic writers, but so far it has not been presented as a consistent whole. One could call this theory the theory of the spirit-soul, and its basic assumption is that the depths of this spirit-soul are as yet insufficiently known to us.

It is a curious thing that until recently man had much neglected to explore the depths of the human soul. Myers draws attention to this remarkable fact in the following words:

> In the long story of man's endeavour to understand his own environment and to govern his own fate, there is one gap or omission so singular that, however we may afterwards contrive to explain the fact, its simple statement has the air of a paradox. Yet it is strictly true to say that man has never yet applied to the problems which most profoundly concern him those methods of enquiry which, in attacking all other problems, he has found so efficacious.
>
> The question for man most momentous of all is whether he has an *immortal* soul, or—to avoid the word immortal, which belongs to the realm of infinities—whether or no his personality involves an element which can survive bodily death.... I say then this method (of modern scientific enquiry) has never yet been applied to the most important problem of existence: the powers, the destiny of the human soul ... in most civilized countries there has been for nearly two thousand years a distinct belief that survival has actually been proved by certain phenomena observed at a given date in Palestine. And beyond the Christian pale—whether through reason, instinct or superstition—it has been commonly held that ghostly phenomena of one kind or another exist to testify to a life beyond the life we know.
>
> But nevertheless neither those who believe on vague grounds, nor those who believe on definite grounds that the question might possibly, or has actually been solved, by human observation of objective facts, have hitherto made any serious attempt to connect and correlate that belief with the general scheme of belief for which science already vouches. They have not sought for fresh corroborative instances, for analogy, for explanations, rather have they kept their convictions on these fundamental matters in separate and sealed

compartments of their mind, a compartment consecrated to religion or to superstition, but not to observation and experiment.[2]

To devote one's powers to the exploration of the human soul seems therefore to be both a lawful and a necessary undertaking. Admittedly people like Flammarion, Crookes and Moser have in the past repeatedly referred to something they called "psychic power", but none of them has so far been able to indicate its sources or explain it more precisely. The reason for this is that there is only one person qualified to do this, and that is the theologian, for the theologian knows the powers of the soul from other sources and is thus able to make the necessary inferences and deductions.

Men today are everywhere concerned with scientific progress. They seek for knowledge about minute microbes and even about electrons, they enter the depths of the sea and the heights of the stratosphere. If they do all these things for the sake of increasing their knowledge, it is surely permissible for us to explore the depths of the human soul and thus to learn more of those rare qualities and powers which are the cause of so many astonishing manifestations.

The phenomena of occultism are very remarkable, but they are not unlike certain manifestations which occur in sleep, under hypnosis, in magic, in the delusions of witchcraft and even in lunacy. Perhaps we can find a common cause for all of them in the fact that under certain conditions the soul is freed from the bonds which bind it to the body and from the restrictions thus imposed, and that when in this state it may be capable of extraordinary activities.

It is most necessary that when we are trying to define the extent of the natural powers of the soul, we should remember that we do not actually know the limits of this same human soul at all. Let the disciples of Kant in particular recall that the Königsberg philosopher assumed a metaphysical basis for the soul lying beyond the phenomena accessible to us in the normal way. Theology teaches us that in Paradise man possessed powers which were afterwards lost to him. The question is, which powers were lost completely, which were merely weakened, and whether certain of these powers, which

---

[2] *Human Personality and its Survival after Bodily Death*, Preface.

may have remained latent, might not in certain circumstances be capable of revival.

There are two truths which people today have almost completely forgotten. The first is that man is a fallen creature, which means that he once possessed certain spiritual powers that can now only be present in him in a weakened state; they can thus only become effective under certain exceptional conditions, and even then only in a very imperfect way. The second truth is that, although it is connected with the body, the soul is a spirit which may sometimes loosen that connection, and may thus be able to achieve things that would ordinarily be impossible. The writer is acquainted with those veritable mountains of objection that can be raised against such a theory; he is nevertheless prepared to defend himself

If we can succeed in throwing new light on the two truths to which reference has just been made then the way is open to a better understanding of certain acts of the soul which it has hitherto been thought necessary to ascribe to the intervention of an alien intelligence. The writer knows well enough that the task is difficult, and that, as may always happen when one follows a path that none other has trod, there is danger of a false step. He does not by any means despise the somewhat different approaches made by others to this problem, and he expects that the consideration which he extends to others should be shown to himself. At least he hopes to be credited with the good intention of wishing to serve the cause of truth.

To effect a comprehensive survey of the subject, it will be necessary to refer to a number of departments of knowledge, such as scholastic philosophy, dogmatic theology, the psychology of the normal, psychopathology, and finally parapsychology. This can obviously only be done somewhat sketchily, nor can there for the present be any question of detailed scientific work, though the latter will become much easier when this Ariadne thread has led us out of the labyrinth of occult phenomena into the daylight of modern mental science. If the present attempt to break open a door succeeds, it will perhaps prove possible to treat the whole question in a more sober and serious spirit than has hitherto been the case.

There is yet another purpose that is served by this work. The findings of modern research into matters pertaining to the soul often shed a quite surprising light on to many of the truths of the Faith, which indeed, according to the medieval view, is the real purpose of scientific enquiry, so that every increase in our scientific knowledge is really a stage in the progress of our knowledge of God and of his Revelation; thus "religious belief may obtain a (new) scientific basis and our knowledge may become a continuous and unbroken progress from the things of this world to those of the next", while the facts we thus discover may provide "an experimental demonstration of survival after death and bring about a fusion of religion and science" (Moser).

Science and religion should never be at enmity; they should assist, complete and illuminate each other, and in the present publication the concept "spirit" (which implies a complete absence of matter) will be introduced from theology into occult science, where so far it has not had the place it truly deserves; as against this it is hoped that a certain amount of new light will be shed on the teachings of the Faith, a light that will necessarily be lacking when there has been no experimental demonstration of the faculties of the purely spiritual soul.

If the reader has no great interest in purely theological exposition, he had best skip the first part of this book, though such expositions are necessary for anyone wishing to examine occult phenomena in the light of theology. For the rest the writer can but treat the words of the astronomer Flammarion as though they were his own:

> If I had the time, I would gladly pursue this study of occult phenomena with greater intensity, though it is a good thing not to devote oneself to it exclusively, else one is liable to lose that independence of mind required for impartial judgment; it is best only to occupy oneself with such subjects by way of exception, and to treat them as an interesting and attractive diversion. There are certain forms of food and drink that should be enjoyed in small doses. I only wish to study a part of these secrets. What one man fails to do is done by another, and each modestly adds a stone to the proud edifice of knowledge, ... so every writer has his own sphere of responsibility; we live at the centre of an unseen world, which we cannot explain by means of our earthly knowledge alone; possibly the knowledge vouchsafed to us through theology may bring us a step nearer to it.[3]

---

[3] *Riddles of the Life of the Soul* (German translation of the French, Stuttgart, 1908, p. 427).

GLOSSARY

ABSTRACTION: Leaving aside the accidental, non-essential qualities and considering only the essential.

AMNESIA: Loss of memory, forgetting.

ANAESTHESIA: Loss of sensation.

ANTHROPOSOPHY: Like Theosophy: immediate, intuitive knowledge.

APPORT: Bringing (objects) near.

ASTRAL BODY: A living form, ghost or wraith originating in the world of spirits.

AURA: A fine emanation surrounding the body.

AUTOMATISM: Involuntary self-movement.

AUTOSUGGESTION: Influencing of self.

BHAGAVAD GITA: Indian sacred book.

BODY-, OR CORPORAL, SOUL: The soul in so far as it works through the body.

CHIROMANCY: "Hand-reading". Used here in the sense of reading the history of a person's life from an examination of the lines of the hand.

CHRISTIAN SCIENCE: Claims to heal by the power of the mind.

CLAIRVOYANCE: The power of seeing things not present to the senses.

CONTROL SPIRIT: An intermediary between the medium and the "spirit".

CRYPTAESTHESIA: Perception of what is hidden.

CRYSTAL-GAZING: Clairvoyance by means of a bright sphere.

CUMBERLANDISM: Thought-reading by observation of the involuntary movement of the muscles: "muscle reading".

DIPSOMANIA: Alcoholism.

DUALISM: Philosophical system that assumes two essentially different elements.

ECSTASY: Being "out of oneself", i.e. without sense perception.

EIDETIC: An imaginary seeing of things.

ESP: Abbreviation of "Extra-sensory perception".

ETHEREAL BODY: A body of fine, subtle matter.

EXORCISM: Driving out of a devil.

FAKIR: Indian ascetic.

GNOSIS: Knowledge: used especially of mystical knowledge.

GRAPHOLOGY: Science of reading the character of a person from his handwriting.

HALLUCINATION: Perception of things with no external existence.

HOROSCOPE: Prediction of the future by observation of the position of the stars.

HYPERAESTHESIA: Extremely heightened power of perception.

HYPERMNESIA: Extreme power of remembrance.

HYPNOSIS: Artificial state of sleep.

HYSTERIA: Action influenced by the subconscious.

IDEOMOTOR: Of the theory that every thought produces a movement.

ILLUSION: Erroneous interpretation of what is perceived.

INTUITION: Immediate sight (without the agency of the senses).

MAGNETIZE: To produce electro-magnetic effects by stroking the body.

MEDIUM: An intermediary between man and the "spirit".

MONISM: Philosophical system that assumes only one principle in explaining the world.

NOOPNEUSTIA: The mutual influence exercised by two spiritual beings.

occasionalism: Theory that soul and body do not influence one another but that the operation of one is only the "occasion" of the working of the other.

OCCULT: A happening the cause of which is unknown.

PERISPIRIT: The ethereal body able to leave men.

PHANTOM: A spirit ("ghost") appearing in a body.

PSYCHOMETRY: Divination or prediction while touching a lifeless object.

RAPPORT: The connection established by which the hypnotized hears and is influenced by the hypnotist.

RUDIMENT: Vestigial, unusable organ

SECOND SIGHT: The power of seeing what is removed in space and time.

SPIRIT-SOUL: The soul in so far as it reaches beyond the body.

SPIRITUALISM: Ascribes occult phenomena to the action of the souls of the dead.

SPÖKENKIEKER: "Ghost-seers".

SUGGESTION: Hypnotic influencing.

SYNTERESIS: Knowledge of the supreme principles of being, thought and morality.

TELACOUSTIC: Hearing at a distance.

TELAESTHESIA: Perception at a distance (includes clairvoyance).

TELEKINESIS: Motion at a distance.

TELEPATHY: Feeling, perception at a distance (includes thought-reading).

TELEPLASMA: A bodily substance separated from the body.

THEOSOPHY: Knowledge by immediate spiritual communication.

TRANCE: A state of insensibility.

TRICHOTOMY: View that man consists of three parts: body, soul, spirit.

WHISPER-THEORY: Theory that direct transmission of thought is really a faint whispering that is heard by another.

PART I

THE PRETERNATURAL GIFTS

I

BODY AND SOUL

[It is the author's contention that occult phenomena, such as telepathy, second sight, the production of sounds (raps), and the movement of bodies otherwise than through muscular action, are due to the activity of a part or element of the human soul which he calls spirit-soul, and that in so far as this element is active, the soul is simply behaving after the manner of a pure spirit and showing a pure spirit's characteristics. It is the author's ultimate contention that this mode of action is a vestigial remnant of the preternatural powers with which our first parents were endowed before the Fall.

The author's first task is clearly to show that this element in the soul actually exists, and he sets about doing so deductively. According to scholastic philosophy body and soul are a unity, and the soul without the body is an imperfect substance. Nevertheless this imperfect substance lives on after separation from the body, and when doing so can only exist as a pure spirit. It follows that the soul must have within itself, potentially or actually, the attributes of a pure spirit.]

Occult phenomena astonish us because they appear to pass beyond the powers of our living body and seem, as it were, to take place miraculously outside the framework of the laws of nature. We must therefore first acquaint ourselves with the nature of man, and learn something of the powers both of the body and the soul and of the mutual interdependence of these powers as, under the guidance of Catholic teaching, these things are presented to us by scholastic philosophy.

In order to understand what follows we must keep before our minds the scholastic doctrine that the body consists of both matter and form. This doctrine goes back to Aristotle, and the findings of science afford no grounds for amplifying it further save in a few insignificant particulars. Matter is an indeterminate substance without extension, it is a real potential which cannot become a concrete body save through conjunction with another principle of being, that of substantial form. Today our minds would turn to those quite indeterminate waves whose mutual intersections and mergings form the wave packet (electron, neutron, positron, etc.), and by means of this first form change' from a state of wholly indeterminate being into a concrete thing.

Primary matter, which is only a "reality in posse" (a potential reality), becomes through the addition of a form, a real thing. Scholasticism conceives of all bodies as so constituted, and applies this conception to man itself. In this last, however, a bodily substratum existing by virtue of a subordinate form receives a higher form of being, the soul. The reasoning soul is the substantial form of the human body, and this after such a fashion that it comprehends within itself the lower forms, namely the vegetative and the animal soul. Body and soul are incomplete substances which only in combination make a unitary substantial being—man.

This unity is not merely a unity of common dynamic effect, as was thought by Plato, Olivi, Descartes and more recently by Klages, but a unity of nature and being which forms one principle of action, one nature, and only falls apart in death. The reasoning soul is the immediate form of the body and contains within itself the vegetative and sensitive souls, much as a polygon contains a triangle; all three are interdependent and are adjusted to one another.

Man therefore consists of a body and a soul. The body contains the material elements and substances of the earth; it is the material part, it is extended, inert and made up of a number of cells, molecules and atoms, all distributed according to a marvellous pattern. Of itself, however, it is incapable of an independent movement.

As against this, the soul is the immaterial part, simple, endowed with reason, and active; together with the body it forms the natural entity, man. The ancient philosopher Aristotle defines the soul as "the first principle of the vegetative, sensitive and spiritual functions" (*De Anima*, II, 2).

The vegetative life, with its functions of nutrition-intake of matter (without its form), of growth and procreation, is dependent on the soul which unites the various parts that are separated as to time and place. The vegetative life, however, is confined to the purely physiological processes.

The sensitive life activates essentially different processes in which the organs of sense exercise specific functions that are peculiar to themselves and receive the various sensible forms without their matter. We usually reckon with five senses, those of touch, taste, smell, sight and hearing, though modern philosophers add certain others; these senses are all receptive to the stimuli proceeding from matter and duly transform them. These transformed stimuli are carried on to the brain, where in mysterious fashion they release sense perceptions; these last are again closely bound up with the vegetative life; they are weakened, for instance, when we are hungry or overfed, a proof that they are dependent on the same essential principle, the soul.

Our intellectual and spiritual life is in its turn bound to these sensual perceptions and to the images that are based upon them; it apprehends their content, that is to say the substantiated forms of their being, without their substance, and thus penetrates into the nature of the sensually apprehended objects and grasps the relation between them; in this way also it forms general ideas and can recognize the nature and norm of the good and with it that of evil. It therefore extends far beyond the senses, which can only apprehend isolated material things.

The reason passes beyond the reach of sensual perceptions, it discovers abstract and non-material concepts and general supersensual ideas, and thus raises the world of sensual cognition on to an essentially higher, spiritual and non-material plane. Even at that level, however, it still remains dependent on the apprehensions of the senses for so long as the soul is bound to the body. Nevertheless such dependence does not imply that the soul can in no circumstances be free of the senses, or is incapable of regaining at any time its purely spiritual nature. A distinction must therefore be made between the body-soul, which possesses the faculties described above, and the spirit-soul which, in its activities, reaches out beyond the material (cf. St Thomas, I, q. 76, a. 4, ad 1).

The principle of this vegetative, sensitive and spiritual life is the soul, which forms a single nature, a single substance with the body, its instrument to which it is essentially united; this soul is, though of a spiritual nature, an incomplete substance and is designed for this union with the body; it is only through that union that it becomes a complete substance, and it is from the body that it receives the elements by means of which it can develop its own spiritual attributes.

From this unity of being there results the ability of soul and body to influence each other, and it is this that makes it possible for the two modes of cognition to act upon each other. Perception takes place by means of the senses, which are the living body's organs and instruments. Physical damage to any of the senses or to any other bodily organ can impair their ability to apprehend the outer world or to make representations of it to the mind. A physiological process which disturbs the functions of the sense-organs also changes the quality of their perceptions, since these are conditioned by chemical and mechanical processes. The air waves that strike our ear occasion sound, while light waves cause the picture in our eyes. A fault in the eye can cause colour blindness or make us see flashes, while damage to our auditory mechanism may produce a buzzing in the ears or may cause us to become tone-deaf or completely deaf Physical condition may also influence our intelligence, for the body is the instrument of the soul, and from this arises the necessity for the care of our bodies; from here also comes that inheritance of character among families and races of which there is so much talk today.[1]

The vegetative life influences the life of the senses, as we can see for ourselves whenever we please, by observing the quality of our mental activity after a meal; as the scholastics put it: *una actio, quando fuerit intensa, impedit alteram* (if one act is intensive, it hinders another); this is why we are unable to do any work immediately after a meal, at least not any mental work—as indeed that somewhat crude proverb tells us: *Ein voller Bauch studiert nicht gern* (a full belly is reluctant to study). We also know the effect of intoxicating drink on our mind and on our senses, and the disturbance caused in our sensual perception by hunger, thirst and anaemia of the brain; we know the effect of opium and other narcotics which often bring about the most remarkable hallucinations (see the remarks on witches below).

In recent times this fact has been rather more thoroughly exploited than before. Mesmer already believed that in "animal magnetism" he had found a power that enabled him to make men as pliable as wax in his hands. Later this method was further developed in hypnotism and psychoanalysis. But modern man was not satisfied with this additional key for the opening up of the subconscious; he began to use the crowbar of narcoanalysis, inducing "somnolence" in the patient with barbituric acid, whereupon "a certain euphoria and freedom from inhibition and often a protracted urge to talk would become observable and conscious control appeared to relax". In this state a man will report and confess anything, a fact of which the unscrupulous do not hesitate to make full use.

---

[1] See *Salzburger Hochschulwochen*, 1937, p. 95.

Even more drastic effects can be produced by certain drugs which have been in use over the past thirty years; these are derived from mescalin, which comes from the juice of a certain Mexican cactus, or from marihuana.

The criminologist A. Mergen writes as follows[2]:

> It is a well-known fact that mental functions can be influenced by drugs; we can even induce genuine functional psychoses in this way. It is known, for instance, that mescalin can produce a quasi-schizophrenic state and that adrenalin or actedron can produce a depressively coloured psychosis. We know that in a depressive psychosis the sufferer relates all misfortunes to himself, that in his manic state he feels himself to be loaded down with the most terrible guilt, that with the uttermost contrition he begs for punishment, even for death. The depressive psychopath is profoundly convinced of his wickedness. He displays remorse and asks for punishment for purely imaginary crimes that he has never committed at all. He brings accusations against himself, and his remarks and confessions are subjectively correct, for his guilt is something of which he is firmly convinced. His basic mood is one of sadness and fear; he is slack, lacking all impulse, and the little spark of energy that he can muster is devoted to the accusation of himself as the supposed author of all the suffering and misery in the world and to asking for a "just" punishment for his alleged misdeeds. There is in such cases a constant danger of suicide.
>
> This psychopathic condition can be induced in people by drugs that act on the sympathetic nervous system (ephedrin, adrenalin, actedron, etc.) and can be maintained by the continuous administration of the drug in question. These sufferers, with their sad and anxious faces and general appearance of slackness and fatigue, with eyes starting out of their sockets and reflecting the terror inspired by a creeping uncanny "something", accuse themselves and ask for punishment in most contrite fashion. They dig their own graves in which they hope at last to find forgiveness and redemption. There is nothing very remarkable about this behaviour if one has regard to the fact that the entire personality has undergone a change which causes the patient to exhibit the symptoms of depressive mania. These refined modern tortures, which are much more horrible than those of the Middle Ages, are quite useless for clarifying any question of actual fact but knowingly falsify it. Truth is indeed,

---

[2] See *Hochland*, 1952, p. 245.

to those who employ them, an irrelevancy. Their only purpose is to exact confessions.

It has been reported that such confessions on the part of helpless prisoners are relayed directly to an unthinking public. For the scientifically trained observer, however, they merely furnish another example of the influence which that part of us which belongs to our body and our senses can exert over our mind. The latest development is that narcoanalysis has been abandoned in favour of surgical measures, the nerves between the frontal lobes and the brain stem being severed. Since this operation can actually be performed through the eye-socket, the conversion of political opponents into obedient dummies without a will of their own can be achieved without scars and concentration camps—and without any scream of pain penetrating into the records of history.

If the influence of the body on the mind can be as disastrous as this, the converse is true in an even greater degree, for the mind most certainly can react upon the body, or to be more precise, the intellectual can influence the vegetative life. Some people cannot think of things that are repulsive to them without vomiting, or at least without losing their appetite. The mere thought of tasty dishes can activate certain glands; also intensive mental work tires our bodies and uses up our nerves. "The soul builds up the body—*Die Seele erbaut den Körper*" (Schiller), spiritualizes the features—or bestializes them—and every thought leaves its marks upon the body. There are people who profess to be able to read the whole life history of a person in the furrows of his face or the lines of his palm (chiromancy) or in the tremors of his handwriting (graphology). Dr Victor Naumann, whose pseudonym is "Spectator", was able to tell what were the special subjects taught by the teachers at a certain high school by simply examining their faces.

Recent experiments in suggestion have also shown that the soul can produce sense perceptions, for which there is no real external stimulus at all—as in hallucination—while the mere act of thinking about an action tends to produce the actual muscular movements necessary to call that action into effect. This is the law of ideodynamics, which is the basis of "Cumberlandism" or "muscle reading".

In hysteria the subconscious controls the vegetative life to such an extent that the body can be sick or well according as the imagination dictates, and in abnormal states a distribution of the blood and of the juices of the body can be attained which will cure a diseased part by causing hyperaemia to occur there. However, more of all this hereafter; for the moment let it suffice that we have shown the interdependence of the vegetative, sensitive and mental life, and so given proof of the unity of the soul.

If it were true that there exists, as some people maintain, a third element, a perispirit which directs the functions of our vegetative-sensitive life, then the thinking subject would be unable to feel, or indeed to live, since these activities would depend on another principle—and this goes counter to our actual experience. The various functions of the soul are immanent and take effect within the same subject from which they proceed; if the subject that thinks also lives and feels, then this proves that there is no trichotomy, and when Holy Scripture uses different names for mind, spirit, etc., namely νοῦς, πνεῦμα and ψυχή the purpose is to indicate natural and supernatural life (Lercher, *Dogmatik*)—or possibly the soul's two modes of existence, as a spirit-soul and a corporal soul; the soul is of course in each case the same soul, but it has a dual aspect, that of a pure spirit and of something that has combined with the body. Similarly the mystics have one and the same soul in mind when they speak of the "ground of the soul", or of the "spark of the soul", or of the "soul's point".

The corporal soul is also dependent on sense perceptions for its highest activities, for the formation of non-material concepts, in accordance with the principle that *Nihil est in intellectu quod non fuit in sensu* (nothing is in the intellect which has not previously been in the senses), for it is impossible to have any real idea of a thing of which there has never been a sense perception, A blind man can never form any proper notion of the nature of light or colour, and none of us has really any conception of non-material or supernatural things, since we have never been able to apprehend them sensually and only from the senses could the soul abstract immediate notions. Whether the soul during its period of conjunction with the body can engage in activities that are wholly divorced from the body will be discussed in Chapter IV below.

Most people know Raffael Santi's fresco in the Vatican, "The School of Athens", in which the philosophers and learned men of antiquity are depicted. The artist has placed the two greatest ones, Plato and Aristotle, in the centre, with the former pointing his finger skywards, while the latter points down to earth. By depicting them in these attitudes the painter indicated the nature of their respective philosophies and the manner in which they conceived universal ideas to have originated. Plato thought that they came from heaven, and that the soul had lived with them there before its union with the body. Later, when it has been united with the body, it remembers them, and that is how the knowledge of universal ideas is acquired.[3]

As against this, Aristotle believed that universal ideas are formed by abstraction from the perceptions of the senses. These perceptions must always have prior existence if any concept is to be formed; when this is not the case, the concepts are very imperfect and are negative, and are in the nature of similes or symbols, and it seems that experience has shown that Aristotle is right. Moreover Aristotle seems to make the unity of the soul much clearer than Plato, who seems to overemphasize the element of spirituality and thus to dissolve this unity. Plato, however, is a better teacher of that other truth which today tends to be so widely forgotten, namely that the soul does possess an element which is pure spirit and nothing else (see page 32).

We know, however, that this union of soul and body must one day cease with death; indeed death consists in this very severance; the question now before us is whether the two parts can exist and function in separation.

When the body no longer possesses its form, the soul, which makes of it a complete substance, it disintegrates; it is true that, as philosophy says, it receives a transient form as a corpse and still has the attributes of matter, namely weight and extension, but this transient form can no longer hold the constituent parts together but permits them to fall apart.

And the soul? The soul continues its life, for it is spiritual and therefore immortal, but it continues its life as something essentially incomplete and naturally experiences an urge to reunite with the body. It therefore leads an extra-natural and extra-ordinary life until at the resurrection of the dead the reunion with the body can be effected.

Now what is the nature of the life of the soul during this phase of separation? Since the soul is a spirit, we must first acquaint ourselves, if we are

---

[3] Cf. Wiesinger, *Zur Auffassung Platos heute*, in the jubilee publication on the occasion of the 400th anniversary of the Gymnasium in Kremsmünster, Wels, 1949.

to answer the question just posed, with the nature of pure spirits. This is all the more necessary in so far as we have reason to believe that even during its time of union with the body the soul can in certain circumstances, such, for instance, as those of the mystic state, act after the manner of a pure spirit.

II

PURE SPIRIT

[So far we have inferred that the soul possesses within itself, potentially or actually, the attributes of a pure spirit. What then are those attributes? Here theology can enlighten us—at least to some extent, for it can tell us much concerning these attributes, in particular it can tell us what is a spirit's mode of knowledge. This is different from our own, in so far as human knowledge is built up out of sense perceptions while a spirit's is not, a spirit's mode of knowledge being wholly intuitive.]

There is scarcely a concept of philosophy that has been less perfectly clarified than that of spirit. The inevitable result of this has been that in all cases in which we are dealing with the effects of a spirit's activity people go so widely astray, that they search for and excogitate explanations possible and impossible, set up hypotheses and invent so-called working methods, and all the while get ever deeper into the mire. One of the reasons for this is that it is in the nature of profane philosophy to proceed inductively from the phenomena themselves, and to endeavour to infer from these the actual concept of spirit. But this is at best a very unsatisfactory procedure and cannot yield any good result, since it is only the manifestations of the corporal soul that are taken into account. Where the purely spiritual is concerned, those engaged on these enquiries are usually devoid of all knowledge of such a thing and flatly deny its existence even where it is to be plainly inferred; for exact science will only recognize a "closed natural causality" and rejects the findings of all other categories of knowledge—that of theology, for instance. The men who take this attitude are only too well aware (as we shall see on pages 136-137) that the whole proud rationalist edifice would have to submit to revision, if the force of evidence were to compel them to assume the existence of a non-material power.

Now the phenomena of occultism are simply not to be understood unless we can take cognizance of a cause that lies outside the purely material, and actually the researches carried on for over sixty years at the University of Durham, U.S.A., very strongly suggest that such causes do exist—as we can see from Professor J. B. Rhine's book *The Reach of the Mind*. It is therefore necessary to find out whatever we can concerning the essential nature of the powers in which these causes are to be found.

Actually the researchers in question are most anxious that their findings should have light shed upon them and possibly be confirmed from other departments of knowledge. "The bearing of our work upon religion", Professor Rhine wrote in a letter to me, "is to me its primary significance"; and certainly such men stand to gain if the results of their research can be confirmed by the undisputed findings of another department of learning, and one might add that it is equally satisfactory when the truths proclaimed by religion and philosophy are confirmed by the findings of exact science.

In all the circumstances, then, we need have no hesitation in using the concept of spirit as finally developed by the Scholastics as a means of explaining occult phenomena, even if that concept seems somewhat strange and its employment unusual to profane science. I use the words "finally developed" advisedly in this connection, for there were those among the Fathers who ascribed a fiery or "ethereal" body to the angels, basing themselves on Psalm 103. 4, while certain Scholastics assumed some combination of matter and form. Today the completely incorporeal character of angels, as also of the human soul, is accounted a firmly established doctrine. That being so, it is well worth our while to study the scholastic concept of spirit which radically rejects any kind of material attribute and draws its conclusions accordingly.

The scholastic idea of spirit is of course very different from that of the "spirits" and "controls" of spiritualism, which are all supposed to have a delicate astral body, and which have been invented because their existence seemed necessary for the explanation of occult phenomena. The concept of spirit here employed, however, is not a thing that I have been forced to invent under the pressure of necessity, nor the expedient of scientific bankruptcy, but a doctrine taught by the greatest philosophers of mankind, and one that has lasted for thousands: of years—even though it may be unknown to many and ignored by many more.

The ethnologist Fr Wilhelm Schmidt, S.V.D., tells us that the oldest peoples of the earth have always ascribed a kind of spirituality to the supreme being, God, though they were not always able to express very clearly what was in their minds. Comparisons such as "He is like the wind" represent crude attempts at such a description.[1] It was the task of human culture and learning to clarify this concept of spirit and to trace it in different beings.

In man we can see two substances, spirit and matter, united in a single nature, although each is completely different from the other. Matter exists separate in the bodies surrounding us. From this it would seem to follow that spirit may also exist separate from matter. Spirit is the name given by the philosophers to a substance that is neither matter nor dependent on matter for its existence or its activity. God is a spirit, as are the angels, the devils, as are also human souls. The philosophers say that it is the nature of a spirit that it should uninterruptedly possess itself. One can only possess something that one recognizes as such and appropriates to oneself; this activity is an unbroken transition from possibility to actuality by means of thought and will. It is not an organic process—since a spirit has no organs—but a spiritual one and consists of acts of the understanding and the will which are the two basic faculties or accidents of the spirit. The intellectual memory is not a special faculty, but merely the natural effect and development of the intellectual power according to habit and disposition.[2] In order to get to know the nature of the life of a spirit, however, we must explain its activities.

The intelligence of a pure spirit is essentially higher than that of human beings, for the latter can only apprehend the phenomena of matter through the senses, and it is only thus that they can arrive at a knowledge of tilings themselves and of their nature. This means that men must first learn the nature of material things, and that this knowledge serves as a means whereby they can most imperfectly grasp things that are nonmaterial, spiritual and supernatural.

The spirit on the other hand first knows the nature of purely spiritual things, doing so directly; it first of all knows spiritual substances and, as St Thomas teaches us (I, q. 84, a. 7), through these the material (the actual object

---

[1] *Ursprung der Gottesidee*, VI, Münster, 1935, p. 394.
[2] Cf. St Thomas, I, q. 79, a. 6, and Stöckl, Mayence, 1910, *Grundzüge der Philosophie*, p. 466.

of the divine intelligence is the nature of God in which he knows everything that is knowable). The spirits first apprehend themselves, and after this the other spirits, and by this means arrive at a knowledge of (God and) matter; their way is thus the opposite to that of man.

Moreover the actual mode of apprehension is different. In order to recognize an object the spirit must have the thing within itself, that is to say, it must have its form without its matter; this is what the philosophers call a "species impressa" or "vicaria".[3] Human beings must gradually acquire these "species" through study and experience, and must always arrive at universal ideas by means of an abstraction from phenomena, whereas a spirit receives all species at once at the time of its creation. Thanks to these inborn species the spirits first recognize non-material things and only after this the material ones, but even the latter are more perfectly apprehended by them than by man, despite the fact that man apprehends them directly; this is so because their means of apprehension, namely the inborn species, are more perfect than those of man, the means in man's case being the acquired species. Similarly the knowledge of God is the most perfect of all, being infinitely more perfect than that of any spirit, because it has at its disposal the most perfect means, which is the divine nature itself, and the infused species are always more perfect than those that have been acquired.

Nevertheless even infused knowledge is sometimes less perfect than acquired, a fact that St Thomas (I, q. 55, a. 3) explains as follows: Much knowledge, he tells us, is already given to the angels by a single species; even so the less perfect among them may need more than one, much as a talented human being can grasp a thing more quickly than a less talented who may need numerous explanations of detail. Since even among the spirits there are numerous degrees of perfection, it follows that the lower angels have need of a greater number of such species, while the human soul, which is a rather less perfect spirit than any angel, requires a greater number still. From this it follows further that when it functions as a pure spirit, the knowledge acquired by the soul always has something vague and general about it, unless by a special grace God raises it to a higher level of clarity. This makes St Thomas think (I, q. 89, a.2) that it is better in this respect for the soul to be united to the body,

---

[3] Cf. Schiffini, *Disp. metaph. spec*, p. 272.

although circumstances may arise in which its intuitive knowledge may be much more perfect than that which is acquired.

For all this the cognition of a pure spirit is much more perfect than that of man, for man acquires his knowledge by slow degrees and with some labour, and he is inclined all too easily to forget anything that has not been very thoroughly impressed upon him, or anything that knowledge subsequently acquired has pushed into the background of his mind. Moreover men's energies are often diverted by other forms of work, so that the knowledge that such men have acquired may become useless to them. Or again they grow tired, need sleep, fall sick, or are for some other reason not in the right frame of mind, or they suffer from the weather, from heat and cold, etc. Spirits on the other hand experience nothing of all this; they receive the species at their creation, they forget nothing, are not subject to fatigue, and even if they are incapable of thinking of everything at once, they have nevertheless no difficulty in turning their thoughts towards whatever thing they please, however distant that thing may be, so that one may say with St Augustine that they see things that are far away as from the top of a mountain and so are wiser than man, who, like one who looks out through a chink in his prison, sees but little.

The theologians therefore tend to represent the knowledge of angels somewhat after this fashion. "Let us imagine", they say, "that an angel has directed his attention on to the species of natural science. He can then not only read the main outlines which are revealed to ourselves through experience, but also all the details of geology, astronomy, botany, zoology, or of archaeology . . . or of the animal kingdom. He not only recognizes the different kinds of living creatures, but also each individual one that exists, or that ever has existed within each kind, its individual attributes, modes of activity, etc.[4] All this seems clear enough.

Even so there are limits beyond which the knowledge of spirits does not extend. Though they know the nature both of spiritual and material things, as also everything towards which they direct their attention and which has actual existence, they seem, according to revelation, to be ignorant of all those things that are dependent on free will and which the other wishes to conceal from

---

[4] Lepicier, *Il mondo invisibile*, p. 37.

them, that is to say of the secret thoughts of others and of the undetermined future (Mat. 24. 36). The same is true of the sacred mysteries of religion.

Pure spirits can associate with one another, which means that they can speak to each other and their manner of speaking is very simple. All that is needed is that a spirit "should be prepared to reveal its thoughts to another spirit, and that that other spirit should give its attention to them" (Lepicier, *op. cit.*, 42). Notice that it is the nature of communications between spirits that is in question here—and the soul is a spirit.

Although Catholic writers, following St Thomas, say much about the angelic intelligence, they say little of the angelic will, and this despite the fact that it is certainly one of the spiritual faculties. Let us therefore examine this angelic will a little more closely. First of all it is clear that the spirits have free will through which they can conform themselves to the will of God. The freedom is an active one—which means that they can act or refrain from action in any particular matter in regard to which the possibility of acting exists. Freedom therefore does not consist so much in the fact that an act can be performed when all the factors which would lead to such action are present, for this would apply equally to any physical or chemical cause. Rather does freedom consist strictly in being able to refrain from action, when action is possible. In so far as freedom consists primarily of a negative act, of a negation, that act can have its origin in the free will of the creature, for it is only all positive things that necessarily have their primal cause in God. Actually, however, pure spirits do not refrain from performing any act which God enjoins, although they have the ability to do so, but always willingly obey.

One might well ask what is the origin of this willingness, and the answer is as follows. First of all such obedience is easy for them, it needs no effort, a fact which distinguishes them from ourselves. Further, the action takes place in an instant, so that there is never any lack of the time necessary to carry it out. Moreover, because of the goodness of God and of the good spirits, the whole effort of pure spirits is directed towards good, and an evil deed would be something that would be quite alien to a pure spirit's character. There are other reasons for this willingness that are adduced by the theologians, but we will not go into them here.

When theologians deal with the powers of knowledge possessed by angels, they like to talk of something called "illumination", noopneustia, which represents "an act by means of which an angel of a higher order transmits a piece of knowledge concerning supernatural things to one of a lower order. This piece of knowledge will have first been received by the highest angel by way of divine revelation and will have been passed on by him to the inferior orders of angels in a form which the latter can understand" (Lepicier, *op. cit.*, 39). An influence similar to that exercised on the intellect exists with regard to the will. The higher orders of angels and those nearest to God himself partake supernaturally in his holiness by conforming themselves as perfectly as possible to his will and then in their turn pass on this will by means of spiritual inspiration (the power of which we on this earth cannot conceive) to the other spirits. This noopneustic power strengthens all spirits in the love of God, so much so that a deviation therefrom is morally impossible, though the physical possibility of such a thing admittedly remains.

The persistence in good of the spiritual will is strengthened by yet another angelic quality, by virtue of which a decision once taken remains firm and unchangeable. We ourselves frequently change our decisions, because they depend on motives the quality and wisdom of which we may come to reassess in the light of subsequent judgments and deeper insight; we may in fact realize that we have erred. With spirits this does not happen. By reason of the species infused at their creation they immediately know the whole truth intuitively without error or imperfection. Their decisions are therefore unchangeable, which is what St Thomas teaches when he says (I, q. 64, a. 2) that the angelic intelligence apprehends first principles unchangeably, even as men do. From this follows also the obduracy of the evil spirits in so far as they are responsible, and it is this that makes their redemption impossible. With men those fixed ideas which so often trouble souls and which they cannot shake off are something very similar. (No attempt is made here to touch on the purely theological question whether this obduracy is due ultimately to a lack of God's saving grace.[5])

With the same readiness therefore as that with which pure spirits receive a piece of knowledge, they also receive a command, when something is suggested to them by another spirit; this capacity for being influenced is a very

---

[5] Cf. Joh. Stufler, *Die Heiligkeit Gottes und der ewige Tod*, Innsbruck, 1903.

important principle, which can explain much to us, as we shall see in a moment.

By all their obedience, however, and all their good works the angels acquire no merit whatever, nor do they earn for themselves any higher glory as a just recompense for good works, for they are no longer *in statu viae* and can perform these works without any effort or difficulty. Merit only accrues where there is effort and sacrifice and to the spirits these things are unknown (cf. St Thomas, I, q. 62, a. 9).

The theologians treat of many other questions concerning spirits, of which only the following two need concern us for the present.

A spirit is present at that point where its power and energy is made effective; it cannot be in two places at once, nor, in so far as the categories of space and time are applicable at all to spirits, can two spirits occupy the same place. Of more importance to us here is the power of spirits over matter, a power by virtue of which they can move bodies, for since "a thing of a lower order is subject to the influence of a being of a higher order" (Lepicier, I, c. 68), spirits can move bodies and transport them from one place to another, can bring about inward changes in them both in regard to their substance and their accidents, though the degree of their ability to do this varies in accordance with their position in the spirit hierarchy.

This power of the spirits extends to man, giving them influence over his body, as we see in cases of possession, over his senses, which are also a material element, and his imagination, which in its turn guides his reason. Theologians, however, differ in their views of the manner in which his reason is influenced. Some lay stress on sensual images and on the imagination, while others are more inclined to think of direct illumination (noopneustia) of the kind that takes place between pure spirits. This latter opinion seems preferable.

It is plain from all this that the spirits, both good and evil, are great and mighty beings—and indeed that is the way the Bible represents them to us, and this in its turn goes to show how mistaken it is to depict them as a child might fancy them, as things with a gay and slightly sentimental charm about them, though that is precisely what we all too often find in holy pictures and in the more degenerate forms of art.

III

THE BODY-FREE SOUL

[We have studied briefly the characteristics of pure spirits as they have been described to us by theology, and somewhat later in this book we shall see that the characteristic mode of action of pure spirits bears a striking resemblance in its results to certain occult phenomena brought about by, or through the apparent instrumentality of, human beings. Before drawing any inference from that, however, we can continue to proceed deductively, and, by drawing a more complete picture of the nature of pure spirits, gain by inference a fuller conception of the powers latent in the human soul. In this chapter we deal further with a pure spirit's mode of cognition and also with its manner of communicating with, and influencing, other spirits. We also observe two further characteristics of pure spirits, namely their immunity from forgetfulness and fatigue, characteristics which we shall later rediscover in the human subconscious.]

We have already shown that the soul and the body constitute a single nature, a single substance which is man. We have also seen that it is a natural thing for the soul to be united to the body, since it is itself only an incomplete substance; this has as its result that, when separated from the body, the soul is continually moved by a desire for reunion with it, so that it may complete its substantiality. Nevertheless we know that after death it must live in separation from it until the resurrection of the body on the last day, and this state of the soul is connatural to it, since even while the state of separation obtains, the soul can engage in certain activities which we will now discuss.

It is instructive to observe how those authors who ascribe all spiritualist and occult phenomena to the devil seem concerned to minimize the powers possessed by the soul when it has become separated from the body; they seem determined that this whole territory shall remain strictly reserved for the powers of evil which alone are assumed to be capable of these activities. We should therefore really submit the facts to a calm examination, and take note of what the masters have to tell us so that we may attain clarity in this important question. Certainly it is misleading for Fr Lacroix to say[1]: "The soul, when separated from the body, has no power over the body", or when Alessio Lepicier continually speaks of an essential difference that exists between a spirit on the one hand and the soul that is freed from the body on the other.

Admittedly the soul belongs to a different species of spirits than those to which the term spirit usually refers, but that is no reason for denying that it possesses any of the powers which usually belong to spirits, all the more so since according to some writers every angel belongs to a different species but all have the powers proper to spirits. Naturally, as an inferior spirit, the human soul possesses these advantages in a less degree than the angels, but in essence it does possess them in one form or another.

It may now be objected that it is immaterial for us to know what powers the soul may possess when freed from the body, since in this life we invariably find it united to the body; we come across it, that is to say, under circumstances where these spiritual powers are necessarily fettered. Yet it is precisely in order that we may learn to know and appreciate better the faculties and powers of the human soul during its union with the body, that it is desirable to understand its spiritual powers generally—powers which the soul should never have lost, unless we assume, as some people do, that its union with the body is a form of punishment, powers which are identical—let us state this here and now—with the preternatural gifts given to man at the time of his creation. These powers were lost by man through sin, or were at best only retained by him in a feeble rudimentary form.

In regard to these powers the following principle holds good. We must ascribe to the soul, when freed from the body, all the qualities that we have predicated of pure spirits, even though it may possess them in a lesser degree. So that there may be no misunderstanding in the matter, let it be explicitly stated that the soul is not a pure spirit in the same sense as we use that term of the angels, since it is an incomplete substance which was essentially created for union with the body. For all that, however, it is a spiritual substance, though of course it is one dependent on matter, matter being a joint cause of the vegetative and sensitive activities, and being in intellectual life a condition of

---

[1] *O Espiritismo a luz da razão*, p. 301.

its function, which means that even where the mind forms spiritual concepts, matter is the basis and point of departure of the abstraction.

Yet as a spiritual substance the soul reaches out beyond matter, so that it survives and is active even after separation from the body. This activity can only be that of a spirit and of a pure spirit at that. It is only in this sense that the words "pure spirituality" or "pure spirit" are to be understood in what follows; it is not intended to imply that the soul as such is a pure spirit; it is, to be perfectly accurate, a spiritual substance. Yet this spiritual substance, when separated from the body, cannot in its manner of acting behave otherwise than as a pure spirit. It must therefore possess a higher intelligence, the objects of which are non-material things, i.e. the purely spiritual nature of these things, their recognizable substance (St Thomas) that is separated from the body; it therefore apprehends directly and intuitively everything that during its union with the body it apprehended imperfectly by means of abstractions; it is merely debarred from those forms of activity which are dependent on the body such as the vegetative and sensitive life the intellectual life, however, remains to it, since this is not inwardly dependent on the body.

Thus, as St Thomas says, the soul can apprehend all things, happenings and acts which are "actual" (*entia actu*). Admittedly this holy teacher asserts (4 Sent. d. 45, q. 1, a. 1; q. 3c) that the souls cannot have knowledge of the happenings on this earth, though he gives a reason for this: *Quia sanctorum animae perfectissime justitiae divinae conjunctae nec tristantur nee rebus viventium se ingerunt, nisi secundum quod justitiae dispositio exigit* (I, q. 89, a. 8)—because the souls of the saints are perfectly united to the justice of God and so are neither made sad nor concern themselves with the affairs of the living except in so far as divine justice demands this. In this way this fact of non-apprehension is adequately explained, for nobody, not even the most perfect angel, can apprehend anything if God's command does not permit it; ultimately it is the will of God that determines whether they should have knowledge.

Duns Scotus puts the matter thus[2]: *Anima ergo separata potest acquirere notitiam non solum abstractivam sed etiam intuitivam, non solum sensibilium sicut postea (post resurrectionem) conjuncta, sed etiam quorumcumque*

---

[2] Opus Oxoniense 4, d. 45, q. 4, n 2.

intelligibilium proportionatorum et proportionaliter presentium; proportionatum autem est sibi quotquot intelligibile creatum. Ergo orationem viatorum sive vocalem quam et conjuncta potest nosse per sensus corporeos, sive mentalem, quae tunc erit sibi proportionata, potest tunc intuitive. The separated soul can not only acquire an abstractive but also an intuitive knowledge, and this not merely of all things that can be perceived by the senses (as is the case when it is reunited to the body after the resurrection) but also of all things that are intelligible and proportionate to itself and are present in a proportionate measure; but all created intelligible things are proportionate to it. For this reason it can become aware intuitively of the prayers of those on the way, both of vocal prayer, which when joined to the body it can know through the bodily senses, and also of mental prayer, which will then have become proportioned to it. This is precisely my own contention.

It might be held, as it seems to be held by St Thomas, that the saints in heaven, or the souls in purgatory, would be saddened if they knew what was happening in the world, but this is not the case, for such souls conform absolutely to the pattern of God's will and are content when they see the holy grounds of his actions. Certainly no theologian has found any difficulty in believing that the angels are aware of what is happening on earth. Why then should such difficulty arise in the case of the souls of the departed?

In order to possess such knowledge, souls must be possessed of certain means, namely of two kinds of species. There are first of all the species which are infused immediately after the soul's separation from the body, the species which the angels receive at the time of their creation, as things belonging to their nature. Then there are other species that derive from the time of the soul's union with the body, and are retained by it by virtue of that spiritual memory which, as part of its powers of knowledge, it retains after separation from the body. Through these species, which mutually strengthen one another, the knowledge that has been acquired becomes sufficiently clear, definite and perfect. The old knowledge, which derives from the ability to distinguish the general from the particular, combines with the infused species and so becomes more lofty and perfect, so that the soul's capacity for knowledge is much greater than before. This new form of knowledge comes easily to the soul. It is acquired, in so far as the soul acts as a pure spirit, by a simple act of the will.

The spirit-soul neither tires nor forgets. Before separation from the body much knowledge had necessarily to sink into the subconscious by reason of the weakness of the bodily organs. Such knowledge in fact became unconscious knowledge, but was not lost. The soul's acts of knowledge, however, occur in an instant of time. Thus after separation from the body it sees as by a lightning flash whether it is or is not in a state of grace, it sees its Judge and the just grounds that must weigh with him, it sees its past life, the benefits it has received from God, the opportunities for good which it has used or failed to use, and in seeing all this, it judges itself, for it cannot appear before the face of God, nor does it desire to do so, so long as its sins have not been purged by penance.

Souls that are released from their bodies can speak to one another. All that is needed is that one soul should have the will to communicate something to another and that that other should give its attention to the first. Such speaking is based on noopneustia, the nature of which can be dimly apprehended by us in its degenerate form of mental suggestion, and here theology gives us a certain basis for accepting the latter's possibility.

Even so there are limits to what souls or indeed spirits in general can know. Anything dependent on a free act of the will, anything lying in the future that is undetermined, remains hidden from them, but there is nothing to prevent a human being from communicating to them the nature of such free acts, nor is there any reason why God should not by a special grace (prophecy) reveal the future to them. Whether God does this for pagans is disputed.[3]

If the faculties of the soul are the same as those of other spirits, we must assume that it has a power over bodies similar to that of the angels (St Thomas, I, q. 117, a. 4). It is true that St Thomas appears to say the opposite when he asserts that a limb separated from the body no longer obeys the spirit, *naturali sua virtute* (by reason of its natural power), but the holy doctor here only refers to what usually happens in the case of a soul that is still fully united with the body, and says nothing of what could happen in exceptional circumstances when the soul is free of the body, and it is only this last with which we are here concerned.

---

[3] Cf. Friedlieb, *Die sibyllinischen Bücher*, 1852, and Nostradamus.

Incidentally such mutual influencing of one another by spirit and matter is continually taking place—even when we lift our hand. The act of the will is a spiritual thing and a physicomaterial action is carried out. Contrariwise when somebody speaks, sound waves are created which means that matter is set in motion, and this in its turn calls forth the spiritual activity of thought. This mutual influencing of one another on the part of matter and spirit is so familiar to us that we take it for granted. There is no new principle here that we need establish. Certainly there is a difference between such mutual influencing when it occurs within a life-process and when it occurs outside of it. Yet we understand as little of the real nature of the thing in the one case as we do in the other.

Modern medicine teaches us that our mental life influences our bodies—in neurosis, hysteria, compulsive actions and complexes, in psychotherapy and even in abnormal states. Here we have the influencing of matter by the spirit—admittedly by way of the bodily organs, but for all that the influence is a fact. From here to direct non-organic control is only a step. That is why theologians speak of such an influence over matter—for instance Heinrich (*Dogmatik,* X), Gutberlet (*Katholik,* 1901, II) and Lercher (*Dogmatica*, IV, p. 703).

Souls in the next world can be influenced by material fire, which seems to suggest that a reverse process is possible.

> We can think of spiritual beings who have no kind of natural relation to anybody. Such are the pure spirits, and in heaven the angels have precisely this character. Yet where the angels are concerned there is no reason for supposing that they cannot by means of their natural powers act directly upon material objects and move them from one place to another. If this were not so, then according to St Thomas any connection between the body and the world of the spirits would be impossible, for every influence upon the bodily world is connected with the movement of bodies from one place to another. As Aristotle teaches, such movement from place to place is the first of all movements and is connected with all bodily changes. Without the power to move bodies the spirits would have no power of putting themselves in touch with the physical world at all. Yet it would be unnatural if the orders of being that are subordinate one to the other, as the physical world is subordinate to the world of the spirit, were without the power to establish any connection

with each other. St Thomas therefore concludes that by virtue of their natural powers the spirits of the next world are capable of moving bodies in this one.[4]

All this applies equally to souls that are wholly free of the body and to those that are partly free, nor can we here speak of an *actio in distans*, since the spirits are present there where their will is effective (cf. St Thomas III, *Contr, gen.*, c. 103-107). To be absolutely accurate, St Thomas says (I, q. 110, a. 3, ad 3) that angels can move material bodies, but that the power of the soul does not extend beyond its own body. I do not quarrel with this at all. St Thomas, however, is speaking of the soul in its normal state, when it is completely united to the body, not of the soul when it is partly separated from the body, for according to the measure of that separation it enjoys the powers of a pure spirit.

It is in the light of all this that we can, among other things, explain the reappearance of the dead; unhindered by the body the soul seeks to follow its natural connections and appears to persons who are closely connected with it. Dr Robert Klimsch (*Leben die Toten?*) reports many such cases, while Emil Mattiesen in his three volumes *Das Überleben des Todes* has collected a large number of well-authenticated cases of reappearance on the part of the dead, including some where an actual body was visible that could be seen by animals.

An example from Schneider may be quoted here:

A most remarkable and moving short story [he writes] is to be found in Sebastian Brunner's *Woher? Wohin?* Brunner received it directly from the mouth of the man to whom the incident happened. This last was a man called J. K. Weber, a pupil and a favourite of Bishop Sailer. He was at that time chaplain at Mittelberg im Allgäu. It was a cold, stormy, winter day. Weber was seated at dinner with his parish priest when there entered to them a poor ragged boy who begged pitifully for alms. He was admitted and given food. He thanked them and wanted to go, but felt so weak and ill that he could not move from the place. Weber suggested that a room in which Capuchin monks used sometimes to pass the night should be put at the boy's disposal. The parish priest agreed, and Weber put the child to bed and called a doctor. The doctor declared that a violent fever was developing. The good chaplain nursed

---

[4] Feldmann, *Okkulte Philosophie*, p. 73.

the child most lovingly, and when the fever abated, became more intimate with him. He learned that the lad had neither father nor mother and was wandering about the world without any one's being responsible for his welfare. He instructed him in the Faith and the boy showed himself very receptive and eagerly drank in the instruction that was given him, so that Weber had much joy in imparting it. The illness, however, grew to a raging fever which ended in the autumn with the boy's death.

During the following winter Weber had to visit a sick person at a place an hour away from where he lived. It was night when he returned, and snow had fallen, covering the roads and making them unrecognizable. The priest lost his way. Suddenly there was the sound of a crack beneath him, and he found that he was in the middle of a frozen pond. The ice had broken and Weber sank up to half his height into the water and could find no ground beneath his feet. He vainly sought to save himself in this dangerous situation, and was giving himself up for lost when he suddenly saw a bright light. The boy whom he had nursed, and whose eyes he had closed, was floating in the air above him; he offered Weber his hand, drew him out of the water and brought him back to firm ground. Then with outstretched arm he pointed in the direction that Weber was to go, and disappeared. The rescued man followed the directions he had received and came safely home. Next morning he went out to the pond where he had been in such danger. His footsteps were visible in the snow. He saw the broken ice and found that it was at the deepest part of the pond. Brunner speaks of the profound impression that the event had made on Weber, as it did on himself when it was thus related to him.[5]

(Other examples are cited below when the subject of ghosts is dealt with, p. 217.)

Let us nevertheless draw attention again to the fact that these powers occur in a lower degree in human souls than in angels, since human souls are spirits of a lower order. Further, it should be noted that I am predicating these powers of the soul, not to furnish proof for the genuineness of apparitions of the dead at spiritualist seances, but to demonstrate stage by stage the powers of pure spirits, of souls that are freed from their bodies, and finally of the soul that is still joined to the body but in certain exceptional cases achieves a partial freedom therefrom, a state in which such acts as these are possible, at least in an imperfect form.

---

[5] *Der neuere Geisterglaube*, p. 537.

Souls that are free from their bodies also resemble pure spirits in the matter of the will, particularly in the firmness of their decisions and in the matter of noopneustia. This influence which spirits can exert upon one another is immediate and direct, and arises from their character of pure spirits; it is so great that theologians have sometimes been impelled to deny its existence, because they thought that by reason of it spirits would forfeit their character of free and independent beings. Fr Gredt, O.S.B., writes:

> This influence could only occur knowingly and deliberately. If therefore a created spirit could thus act on the understanding (and on the will) of another, that other would be directly subject to the will of the first which could move its understanding and its will in any way it pleased. It is, he's ever, a contradiction to suppose that a being endowed with understanding could thus be subjected to another creature.[6]

Even so there is nothing contradictory in the idea that in the spirit world, both in regard to illumination (see pp. 26-27) and to movement (Lepicier, p. 53), there should be an ordered hierarchy, or that within that hierarchy the higher should continually influence the lower, for the result of this is that a great harmonious whole comes into being, one elevating the other rather than subjecting it, strengthening it, not enslaving but confirming and perfecting it. It really will not do to deny the existence of this power simply because it appears so overwhelmingly great; if that power did not exist, all intercourse between spirits, all interchange of thought and communication of the will, such as there must be in an ordered multitude, would become impossible. The theologians definitely tell us that the angels speak, and it is a fact of much the same kind that the wills of spirits can be influenced. This explains many religious mysteries to us, it also explains a number of phenomena which we cannot understand in any other way—telepathy, for instance, and other facts of the superconscious.

---

[6] *Die aristotelisch-thomistiche Philosophie*, I, 390.

IV

THE PARTLY BODY-FREE SOUL

[One activity inhibits another, and precisely as an intensification of the vegetative life of the soul impedes its other activities, so a diminution of that part of the soul's life that is connected with the body and the senses makes for greater activity on the part of the soul's purely spiritual element. Even when this last named process has not actually taken place, however, we find (A) that the soul does on occasion act after the manner of a pure spirit and that its will and understanding can be influenced otherwise than through the senses and otherwise than by the employment of concepts built on sense perception.

There are, however, (B) abnormal states in which the life of the senses has been diminished, or cut out altogether, in which the life of the spiritual part of the soul is greatly intensified. In these it acts increasingly after the manner of a pure spirit, and can receive communications from other spirits, such, for instance, as the angels. The fact that, while in this state the soul may still make a limited use of concepts built up on sense perceptions does not alter the fact that its mode of behaviour is radically different from that which it practises in its normal state, and that in this abnormal state it acts wholly after the manner of a pure spirit.

From time immemorial (C) men have been aware of these potentialities in the human soul. Plato and Aristotle knew of them, as did also such writers as Posidonius of Apameia, Plotinus and the Neoplatonists, and they are discussed by St Thomas. In more modern times Swedenborg aroused keen interest by his feats of clairvoyance, while Kant, Schopenhauer, Fichte and others all dealt with the phenomenon of extra-sensory modes of knowledge, Kant endeavouring to explain it through the essential oneness of the immaterial world. Today a host of writers have observed these things and sought to classify and explain them. It is the author's contention that all can be explained if we simply recognize the fact that the soul in certain circumstances acts as a pure spirit, remembering always that, according to theology, our first parents were endowed with the faculty of acting and knowing after this fashion, though these gifts were lost through original sin and now only survive in a rudimentary and vestigial form.

All this makes it desirable that we should here examine (D) how actually the human soul is organized, and what is the exact relationship of this purely spiritual element with the other elements within it. Here the author follows Catholic teaching, according to which the soul is a unity with the body and is its form; nevertheless the soul is not wholly submerged in the body (*non totaliter comprehensa*) but reaches out beyond it. In other words there is a part of the soul that is, so to speak, not actually wedded to the body. Modern writers have tended to relegate this part of the soul (if one may thus employ—as of necessity one must—a purely spatial terminology) to the subconscious, and it is therefore necessary that we should here (E) briefly examine this concept. Such an examination reveals that though this concept, which has now been current for about half a century, is a useful ideological tool and a means of grouping certain phenomena, it is far from self-explanatory, and in the last resort we are driven to assume the existence of some carrying agent behind it.]

We have now reached the point which is probably the most disputed of all, and which so far has not been examined as thoroughly as it deserves. Since, however, it is more or less the centre of this whole exposition, we must give it rather closer attention.

We already know that when it is in its normal state, one intense activity of the soul impedes another; for instance, when the vegetative life is strong, mental activity becomes weak and is difficult for those attempting to engage in it. But the converse of this is also true; when the soul withdraws its activities from one field, its faculties become sharper in another. In blind people the sense of touch tends to be strongly developed, and the deaf often have sharper sight. The same thing takes place as the normal mental life becomes weaker in the various states of sleep when a certain dimming takes place in the sense perceptions. On these occasions a very abnormal mental life begins to develop that is peculiar to the state of the soul when half removed from the body. Let us call it the state of the partly body-free soul. To prove that the soul can indeed act after this fashion, and that it can thus dispense with the assistance of the senses, let us call the following to mind:

(A) Normal Activity of the Spirit-Soul

Certainly no Catholic theologian has till now expressed any doubt on the fact that the soul possesses the faculties of the body-free soul when it receives impressions and acquires knowledge without the help of the senses, as in the case of the efficacious graces whereby the understanding is directly illuminated or the will directly influenced. Nobody has yet suggested that such a direct influencing of the soul was contrary to the nature of man, or that it impaired the natural unity of soul and body. This immediate influencing of the soul is even more in evidence when we are dealing with the revelations which God vouchsafes from time to time to man and in which he speaks to man without any mediation of the senses. *Deus etiam sine signis externis in homine producere potest speciem intelligibilem et quidem mediante phantasia vel immediate agendo in intellectum* (Lercher, *Dogmatica*, I, p. 40)—God can produce acts of the understanding in man even without external signs and that through the imagination or by directly influencing the understanding (noopneustia). *Locutio interna divina qua divina interdum ex ejus indole certissime cognosci potest ab illo, quem Deus alloquitur. Profecto nequit a priori Domino et Creatori negari facultas modo mere spirituali ita colloquendi cum anima humana, ut haec maxime certior fiat se familiariter conversari cum Deo* (I, c)—The inner speaking of God can with the greatest certainty be recognized as such by the person to whom it is addressed. For no one has the right arbitrarily to deny to our Lord and Creator the power to speak in purely spiritual fashion with the human soul (i.e. noopneustically) and in such a fashion that the soul is quite certain that it is conversing intimately with God. God gives the infused species which man uses to perform his acts of knowledge. *Locutio Dei per ministerium angelorum dicitur immediata; angelus enim ut purus spiritus et civis regni coelestis se tenet intra ordinem ipsius revelantis* (I, c)—The speaking of God with the help of the angels is called direct speech; for the angel as a pure spirit and a citizen of the heavenly kingdom is accounted as being within the order of the revealer. God and the angels can therefore communicate with the human soul as with a pure spirit, that is to say noopneustically; those therefore are in error who reject every such intercourse that takes place without the mediation of the senses as being contrary to human nature.

Into this category also falls that synteresis which is generally accepted by the theologians, as also the knowledge of the immediately evident first principles of being (see p. 51 and Fr Viktor Cathrein, *Einheit des Sittlichen Bewusstseins der Menschheit*, Herder, 1914, III, p. 563 ff.).

(B) Abnormal Activity of the Spirit-Soul

These powers of the soul gradually pass over into abnormal activity. We find them in the exceptional graces of the true; mystics, when the senses are stilled and the soul rests in the contemplation of God and of the truths of the faith, and at times receives new revelations—as occurred at Lourdes, Parayle-Monial and elsewhere. In the case of the true mystics, at any rate, the theologians assert this without any qualifications, and in recent times this contention has been advanced with particular force by Fr Mager in his various writings; these last have now been gathered into a fine volume, *Mystik als Lehre und Leben* (Tyrolia, 1934), and in them the author speaks continually of an activity which the soul exercises as a pure spirit while the life of the senses and of the body recedes.

> If this is so, however [he says on p. 51], we must see in this curious behaviour the essential matter of the mystic life. Once we see this, we are possessed of the solution of all the most difficult problems with which the scientific treatment of mysticism has to contend. If Christianity from its earliest days, if indeed the whole tradition of the Church all testify to the fact that there is such a thing is an immediate experience by the soul of the life of the spirit and of grace, then this is only psychologically possible or conceivable on the assumption that the soul can and does act as a pure spirit. There is no other way in which the testimony of the mystics can be explained that in their mystical experiences they have contemplated God and his attributes, the Holy Trinity and so on.

The activity of the senses is cut out as though the soul were separated from the body (p. 167). In the mystical life we can observe how the soul separates itself by stages from the body; this applies to its activities, not to its being (p. 170). This is like "the manner of knowledge of the souls in purgatory" (p. 210).

It is not my intention to identify the phenomena of occultism with the mystical state that has been granted to certain persons as a special grace, but merely to demonstrate that the soul is capable of purely spiritual activities even while it is still joined to the body. From this we may conclude that the residue of such activity, or echoes of it, are part of the very nature of the spiritual soul and are to be found outside the mystical state, though only in exceptional conditions which bear, psychologically speaking, nothing more than a degenerate resemblance to the genuine mystical states described above.

Among the mystical phenomena here under review we may include the speaking by God and the angels to men during sleep—as, for instance, in the case of St Joseph when he was commanded to flee to Egypt with his holy bride in order to save the divine Child from Herod. If the objection is now raised that in all these cases we have to deal with exceptional graces, we must admit that this is true. Nevertheless such things prove that this kind of communication can take place without human nature being thereby destroyed; just as the infused virtues do not destroy those that have been acquired, and the supernatural does not destroy nature, so the preternatural does not infringe on the nature of man. It is not contended that it is usual for the soul thus to act in freedom from the body, or that the powers normally held enable it to do this, but merely that it does possess these purely spiritual faculties and can activate them in extraordinary cases.

There are writers who, while not denying the existence of these faculties, nevertheless put such a construction on them as to render their existence almost illusory. Let Fr Alessio Lepicier serve as an example. In his book[1] he treats quite correctly of the angels and their intercourse with one another, but then continues:

> This form of intercourse is also maintained when human beings communicate with pure spirits, for the body is no obstacle for the latter; if therefore we desire to reveal our thoughts to an angel, the desire to do this suffices, so long as the angel directs his attention to us. The same cannot, however, be said of the thoughts of angels in regard to human beings. Man cannot directly read the thoughts of angels, even if these wished to reveal them to him. In this life there can be no act of knowledge without the mediation of material images, which we speak of as acts of imagination by our spirit (*Geistesvorstellungen*); these produce specific alterations in our brain which correspond to the mental picture of the object we are to know (p. 150).

The author here asserts the contrary of dogmatic theology, according to which God and the angels can communicate with us directly. It is true that in his case the mistake would not do very much harm, since he ascribes the power

---

[1] *Il mondo invisibile*, p. 42.

to the angels of producing in the brain the necessary images, with the result that they do communicate with the soul after all, though by a circuitous route. The difficulty increases, however, in cases where body-free souls are conceived as seeking to communicate with us. They can communicate with the angels and with one another, because in this respect they are like pure spirits, but they cannot communicate with living persons, since "they have no power over the images of our imagination" (p. 157) and cannot, like the angels, act on matter.

Here one sees clearly how a mistaken theory can prevent people from recognizing the facts, the mistaken theory being in this case the insistence that the powers possessed by souls are less than those of spirits and the mistaken idea that even pure spirits can only communicate with us through the medium of matter, that is to say, by means of material stimuli. Moreover once a man has got on the wrong road, the conclusions he draws deviate ever more widely from truth, so that this writer is ultimately driven to call on the aid of the devil. When asked whether we can communicate our thoughts to body-free souls, the learned Servite answers "No", although he had previously answered that we could communicate them to the angels. With the latter he admits the possibility of a purely spiritual intercourse, but he does not admit that possibility with souls—neither by means of signs, "for souls have no knowledge of the sensual phenomena of this world" (p. 158), nor spiritually, since our thoughts are accompanied by cerebral modifications, which mean nothing to body-free souls, "because they lack the key, that is to say, the consent of our will" (p. 162). If we ask whether the consent of our will is not always the key when we will to communicate something, we receive no reply.

Here we see into what difficulties authors get when they first belittle the capacities of the soul, then seek to explain all the communications it may receive in purely material terms to which they then say the key is missing. They first of all get on a wrong road and then have only verbiage left with which to circumvent the truth when a critic touches the delicate kernel of the matter.

There are other authors who also only go half-way. Thus, for instance. Professor Fischl insists that for every act of knowledge the "gateway of the senses is indispensable",[2] and cites St Thomas in support of his view (I, q. 89,

---

[2] *Christliche Weltanschauung und die Probleme der Zeit*, Graz, 1941, p. 217.

a. 1): "So long as the soul is united with the body, it cannot form a single thought except by turning to its mental images", and he continues:

> According to such a view a direct contact of soul with soul of the kind Hans Driesch assumes in the case of clairvoyance is impossible. Any such action upon the soul of ideas in the Platonic sense, or any irradiation of spiritual ideas in the sense of St Augustine by the divine light, is wholly without confirmation by experience, and is therefore fundamentally rejected by such sober thinkers as Aristotle and Thomas Aquinas.

However, a more careful study of St Thomas will show us that the matter is not quite so simple. First of all the text quoted above is somewhat inaccurately expounded; what St Thomas says is that, in so far as it is united with the body, the soul can form no thought except with the aid of the mental pictures created by the imagination: *Animae secundum istum modum essendi quo corpori est unita competit modus intelligendi per conversionem ad phantasmata corporum* . . . . But he also indicates in q. 76 (a. 1, ad 4) that the soul is not a form of the body that can be completely submerged in matter, and that because of its perfection; there is therefore nothing that stands in the way of certain of its faculties not being acts of the body. This is elaborated in greater detail in q. 86 to the effect that the soul can in particular more easily apprehend universal truths and spiritual causes when it frees itself more from the senses. From this it is plain that in the normal way an action "from soul to soul" may well be impossible but that exceptional conditions may occur in which the activity of the soul is more or less free of the senses and becomes purely spiritual. In such circumstances the soul becomes capable of extraordinary performances, though such feats need in no wise be accounted a miracle from God.

Whether such knowledge comes by means of imaginative mental images or not is irrelevant; probably it does, as in the case of concepts and words. These are figurative and transferred, such as one must use when he wishes to form images of the supersensual which eludes all imagery. In particular he is under the necessity of clothing divine revelations in images which do not fully express the matter they contain, since *omnis comparatio claudicat* (all comparison is deficient). It is the same with the mental images conjured up by the imagination; these too are borrowings from sensual perception and perhaps do not go to the root of the matter. For it is all too true that our knowledge becomes dim and indistinct in proportion to the paucity of perceptual images that accompany it, but we must not reject these because of their insufficiency or because of the difficulty we experience in making them convey spiritual truths; indeed, as we have seen, St Thomas speaks of the matter in very definite terms.

Moreover it is not necessary for the attaining to direct spiritual knowledge that we should reject imaginative mental pictures altogether. Driesch does not do this when he speaks of communications "taking place from soul to soul" for even where the impulse to an act of knowledge is purely spiritual, the soul, in order to obey the impulse, can hark back to the images that it has built up out of sensual experience, and with them give expression to something purely spiritual. That is why, as has already been noted, these acts of knowledge always have something dim, vague and symbolic about them. Let us freely admit that it is only of things that are sensually perceptible that we can form exact concepts, and that when dealing with things supersensual we can only form concepts that are really not proper to them; when, however, we leave the normal roads to knowledge, it becomes still more difficult. Here such knowledge becomes still less adequate to its object, yet not absolutely impossible. All experience of clairvoyance confirms the view at which we have here arrived by pure theory.

Other writers again who admit such direct communication between souls, explain it in material terms, that is, by means of certain material waves. Such men fail equally to do justice to the facts. Fr Heredia (*O Espiritismo e bon senso*) is a case in point, although this author is the most progressive and intelligent of all. The same applies to W. Schneider, Fr Donat, Feldmann, Malfatti and others, the one exception being Fr Mager, O.S.B.

I have dwelt on these matters because this is the central point of my thesis and I therefore wish to be particularly clear. People have forgotten that the soul is a spirit and that it does not cease to be a spirit even when it is united to the body, and that it requires no material connecting links (radiations) for its activities.

(C) ANTICIPATIONS OF ABNORMAL ACTIVITIES OF THE SPIRIT-SOUL

As proof that the opinion here expressed is correct, we can adduce the names of many learned men from the philosophy and spiritual erudition of the past who in some cases speak specifically of direct activity on the part of the spirit-soul and in others suspect the existence of this activity but cannot see the truth clearly enough because of faulty philosophical assumptions—though the facts before them should have driven them to the correct conclusion. The fact that this conviction has been so generally spread among men is itself a ground of congruence for the theological thesis. There have always been men who have been accounted as seers and have performed extraordinary feats, which seemed to go beyond ordinary human powers. Since these things were undoubtedly facts, the philosophers were under the necessity of explaining them, and they sought to do this in a number of books which they wrote on dreams, visionary powers and magic. In these we can today discern a certain kernel of truth, though it is enclosed in the philosophies and general opinions of the time, and this becomes increasingly apparent if we regard the whole matter in the light of Christian philosophy.

Thus Plato tells in his *Phaedrus* how men "through divine madness become partakers of true prophecy" and can foretell the future correctly at the oracles of Delphi and Dodona; also in the Republic he speaks of true dreams coming in the state of sleep, when the soul has loosened its connection with the body and can cast glances into the future. In his book concerning prophecy in dreams he seems already to assume the existence of telepathy.

In the same way Aristotle knows of an exalted state of the soul in sleep, in which it withdraws into its own nature and has power over the future.[3]

Somewhat later the Stoic Posidonius of Apameia (135-51 B.C.) in his book on prophecy (in Nestle, *Die Nachsokratiker*, II, Jena, 1923, p. 63) says this:

> There is, however, yet another method of prophecy that proceeds from nature; this proves how great is the power of the spirit, when it has been released from the sensual organs of the body. This occurs especially in sleep and in ecstasy. For as each of the gods knows what the other is thinking

---

[3] Gf. Feldmann, *Okkulte Philosophie*, p. 169.

without the mediation of eye, ear or tongue—which is why men do not doubt that the gods hear them if they only make a silent wish or vow—so also the souls of men, when they are sunk in sleep and loosed from the body or when rapt in ecstasy and wholly free from their appetites, are thrown back upon themselves, behold things which, while bound to the body, the soul cannot see. But when the soul is in sleep released from its connection and contact with the body, it remembers the past, sees the present and can contemplate the future. The body of the sleeper then lies there as one dead, but the soul lives in the fullness of its power. This is much more true after death when it has completely left the body. That is why at the approach of death its divinity (=spirituality) is shown forth in a still higher degree, for men who are sick unto death see the approach of death, so that images of the dead appear to them, and it is just in that moment that they seek to be recognized for what they are, and those who have lived otherwise than they ought to have lived, now more than ever repent of their faults. In its condition of waking the human spirit is the slave of the needs of life, it is bound by the fetters of the body and separates itself from communion with the divine (=the spiritual). . . . In three ways human beings are vouchsafed certain dim forms of knowledge at the instigation of the divine. The first is when the spirit itself foresees a certain thing because it is under the spell of a divine relationship, the second kind derives from the fact that the air is full of immortal soul-spirits upon whom, so to speak, clear indications of the truth are perceptible; the third kind occurs when the gods themselves speak with the sleeper.

Rarely indeed did a philosopher in the time that was to come see as clearly as Posidonius saw one hundred years before Christ, even though everything he says is still coloured by the views of his age.

Eudemos says in his work on prophecy: "The (lower) soul is indeed not immortal, but partakes of the divine in ecstasy and in dreams." The Delphic high priest Plutarch (d. 120 A.D.) declares the *daimonion* to be the guardian spirit which, unlike the soul, is not completely united to the body, but reaches out beyond it and sometimes loosens its connection with it to wander abroad and communicate immediately with gods and spirits, whence it derives the gift of prophecy. This *daimonion* is our spirit-soul.

Somewhat later the Stoic Artemidorus (135-200 A.D.) declares in his book *Oneira Kritica* that the word *oneiros* signifies "declaring what is", which implies that the very word itself conveys the meaning of dreaming the truth, a faculty which the body-free soul attains—Philo also accounted clairvoyance as among the special powers of the human spirit.

What was vaguely perceived by these philosophers was brought to its conclusion and rounded off in Neoplatonism, for Neoplatonism, following straight along the line of Plato's doctrine of ideas, made efforts to contemplate the spiritual, and this in its turn postulated a receding of the body and the senses. We have no reason for doubting Plotinus when he tells us that he contrived four times to attain to this state:

> Always when I awake out of my body into myself, I leave all else behind me and enter into myself. Then I see a most wonderful and powerful beauty and am confident in such moments that I belong to a higher region; the highest form of life then becomes a reality, I am one with the divine and rest on that foundation, for I have attained the higher reality and have taken my stand above all else that is spiritual. After thus standing still in the divine, when I then step down out of the spirit into reflection, then I must always ask myself: "How is it possible for me thus to descend? And how is it possible for my soul to have its habitation within my body, seeing that this same soul, despite its sojourn within my body has, even now, when it was wholly alone and by itself, shown me its higher nature?"[4]

When the body had withdrawn itself, the soul could function as a pure spirit, could contemplate God, and apprehend truths to which others were blind, could prophecy, experience second sight and act upon material things, as is the nature of pure spirits. This corresponds with the views of all Neoplatonists such as Philo, Porphyrins, Iamblichus, Proclus. All these ascribed second sight, true dreams, and apparitions to the special powers of the human soul. Indeed this is the consistent *teaching* of antiquity, and it was from this starting point that Christian writers such as Tertullian, Augustine and Gregory the Great proceeded, though in the time that followed the doctrine was more and more allowed to lapse into oblivion; a confused belief in demons and magic took its place.

In the Middle Ages it was the leading figures of scholasticism who sought to escape from the clutches of a wild belief in demons, as, for instance, St Thomas, who, as already mentioned, speaks in his Summa Theologica (I, q.

---

[4] From Richard Harder's German rendering.

86, a. 4) of the soul's power of clairvoyance and states that the soul becomes free in sleep, or when the mind is disturbed and in general when there is the maximum of detachment from the senses. (*Hujusmodi autem impressiones spiritualium causarum magis nata est anima humana suscipere, cum a sensibus alienatur; quia per hoc propinquior fit substantiis spiritualibus et magis libera ab exterioribus inquietudinibus.*)

In much the same fashion that St Thomas speaks of the higher powers of the soul when it is partly freed from the body, Roger Bacon (d. 1294) speaks of the influencing of souls for the purpose of healing disease, and does so in a manner that suggests the methods of Coué. Mystics like Bonaventure and Meister Eckehart, however, incline to give supernatural explanations when dealing with exceptional states of the soul.

Men in later times were well acquainted with the existence of such states, but did not seem inclined to seek a preternatural explanation for them. Thus Abbot Johann Tritheim (d. 1516) once says in one of his letters: "I am able to communicate my thoughts to one a hundred miles away, who knows this art, and to do so without writing, words or signs; I do not need a messenger at all. It can be made as clear and explicit as may be required, and that by natural means without the aid of spirits or any other kind of superstition."

In his explanations he identifies his views with those of his contemporary, Cornelius Agrippa of Nettesheim (d. 1535), who in his work De Occulta Philosophia ascribes all this to certain "sympathetic powers" which cause like to be drawn to like and unlikes to repel each other, and which are supposed to explain everything that cannot be explained in any other way.

Tritheim's pupil, Aureolus Paracelsus, is more specific when he informs the world that many a supposed piece of witchcraft was really something perfectly natural:

> It is possible for my spirit without help from my body, without a sword but by a fervent word alone, to stab and wound another. Similarly it is also possible for me to bring the spirit of an adversary within an image and then to cripple or lame him according to my pleasure. You should know that the operation of the will is an important point in medicine. By this means one can do harm by cursing both to man and beast, causing illness, and this does not take place by means of virgin wax or inscriptions, but the imagination alone is the means of

accomplishing one's will. It is a mighty thing where the human mind is concerned.[5]

The physician and natural philosopher von Helmont declares with a touch of inspiration:

> That magical power lies hidden in the inward part of man; it sleeps and moves within us after the manner of a drunkard; it has been put to sleep through sin; that is why we must reawaken it; for in the inward part of man, in the kingdom of the soul there is the kingdom of God, and that secret power which enables us to act outside ourselves at will and to communicate a similar power to others, a power that can act on the most distant objects.... If therefore this power has been shown to be a natural one, it was absurd to believe till now that the devil was concerned in the matter ... the power that is hidden in man is an ecstatic one that does not operate unless it has been awakened by the imagination, which in its turn must be kindled by a burning desire; it is a spiritual power ... which proceeds from man himself as a spark comes out of the flint (*op. cit.*, 453).

Something of this kind seems to be perceived by those authors who speak of a dual personality and of a magical ego, as do Baader, Flammarion, Daumer, Wipprecht: "The faculties that have been lost in our struggle for existence are still present in our subconscious."[6]

In 1848 E. Freiherr von Feuchtersleben published a book that was frequently republished, called *Zur Diätetik der Seele* (*Concerning the Dietetics of the Soul*), in which he cites the most numerous examples of the power of the soul over the body, all of which serve to make the latter's essentially spiritual nature plain. A pupil of Boerhave's went through all the diseases which his instructor described in the lecture hall; "ultimately he was compelled to abandon his studies, which would have 'studied' him into his grave". Doctors tell of ailing women who during a time when they feel too weak to move across a room find no difficulty in waltzing through half the night with a favoured dancer; the mute son of Croesus cried out when he saw the drawn sword of his father's enemy hanging over that father's head; "Man,

---

[5] Schneider, *Der neuere Geisterglaube*, p. 452.
[6] Staudenmaier, *Versuch einer Experimentalmagie*, p. 366.

do not kill Croesus!" etc. We thus see that for centuries there has been an awareness of the fact that there were other modes of cognition than the purely rational.

Now scholastic philosophy had spoken of knowledge and will as the two fundamental faculties of the soul, but there came a time when men began to add something else to these, the thing we call "feeling". But what exactly is feeling? P. J. Donat, S. J. (*Psychologia*, p. 257), answers the question as follows: "The somewhat vague expression 'feeling' denotes quite frequently an act of our conative powers and often also a sense perception; yet it can, in addition, refer to a dim awareness on the part of our understanding". Mercier, too,[7] struggles hard to find a definition of feeling "whose principle is the imagination" but which "is rooted in the conative powers"—and which in actual fact represents the uprising of the purely spiritual will and of purely spiritual memory out of the subconscious; for it is in this manner that we apprehend the supreme principles of morals and of thought (synteresis), it is thus that we obtain the "natural certainty" in aesthetics, and it is thus that we become aware of knowledge and experience gained in the past; *"und wecket der dunklen Gefühle Gewalt die im Herzen wunderbar schliefen"*.

This is also what the philosopher Friederich Heinrich Jacobi (d. 1819) really seems to have had at the back of his mind when he spoke of "feeling" and "heart". "Man learns to know the good directly from the heart and in no other way" (*was gut ist sagt dem Menschen unmittelbar und allein das Herz*).[8]

Let us examine the matter under a slightly different aspect. Every body of knowledge rests on certain principles or "prejudgments", postulates, as Kant called them, which are selfevident and on which we build. Scholastic philosophy called them synteresis (synteresis: συντηρέω=to preserve together). They imply a knowledge given to us by nature of the governing principles of morals and philosophy. The knowledge rests in the soul, and, as St Thomas clearly shows (I, q. 79, a. 12), does not require any new radical power in the soul. Nevertheless there is still one question to answer, and it is a question which the schoolmen never posed—how does the human mind come to possess this knowledge?

---

[7] *Psychologie*, II, p, 180.
[8] Works, V, 115.

Yet the answer to that question is not so very far to seek. Professor Raymond Paniker of Madrid has shown in an exquisitely reasoned enquiry[9] that this same "feeling" is nothing less than a direct contemplation of truth. It is the thing that Bergson called "super-rational intuition": Dilthey, "intuitive experience", Keyserling, "irrational and mystical imagination"; Husserl, "direct contemplation of being"; Scheler, "direct experience of feeling and love"; Volket, "intuitive and super-logical grasp of the outer world"; Roland Gosselin, "direct sight"; Maritain, "abstractive intuition"; Jolivet, "rational intuition", etc.

Jacobi felt the insufficiency of intellectualism,[10] because the facts pointed everywhere to knowledge that did not derive from any form of direct apprehension and could not be traced back to exact perceptions of the senses and intellect. It was a form of knowledge given us directly with our nature. Kant certainly went too far with his "innate forms of sensual perception" his "forms of knowledge of the reason and the understanding," and was justly criticized and refuted on this account. But there is still a residuum, as is admitted by the schoolmen and by Catholic theology in general, and the existence of that residuum must be taken as self-evident and as based on this indefinable element called feeling—so much so that the theologian can write: "Feeling, that is to say 'Gemüt' (which can be loosely translated 'sentiment' but for which the English tongue has no exact equivalent), is fundamentally nothing other than the first dawning of the soul and the first intimation of its existence as a pure spirit" (Mager, *Mystik als Lehre und Leben*, p. 171).

Consideration of such super-rational and intuitive modes of knowledge necessarily leads to a discussion of the powers possessed in high degree by certain individuals, powers which enable them to have cognizance of events taking place at a distance and to know what is passing in the minds of others and to do this wholly without any mediation on the part of the senses. Swedenborg, who was perhaps the most important "ghost-seer" of modern times, had great influence on his age and was the cause of considerable speculation on this subject. Kant, though he ridiculed Swedenborg's adherents, showed in his *Dreams of a Ghost-Seer* how keenly his interest in this

---

[9] "F. H. Jacobi y la Filosofia del Sentimiento", *Revista Sapientia*, La Plata-Buenos Aires, 1948.

[10] See Bishop Prohászka in *Hochland*, 1910, II, pp. 385 ff.

field had been aroused and that he too felt the need for some kind of an explanation. Kant believed in the direct communication between one soul and another on the ground that the immaterial world was a single whole. Thus immaterial beings were able to act directly on one another without the mediation of matter. Indeed where this latter circumstance obtained, it should be treated as fortuitous and incidental, nor does the fact that they may use material means to act upon one another mean that they do not have, in addition, a continuous interconnection of a different kind through which they mutually influence one another. "It will one day be proved, I do not know when or where, that even in this life the human soul stands in indissoluble connection with all immaterial beings of the spirit world, that it both acts on these and receives impressions from them, of which it is not conscious as a human being so long as all goes well"—that is to say, so long as the soul is not in an exceptional state.

Schopenhauer[11] assumes in his *Essay on Ghost-Seeing* the existence of a special dream organ which is supposed to make true dreams possible; these last only differ from ordinary dreams in the matter of degree. The whole thing, however, is said to be explicable purely psychologically and in terms of the will.

This brings us right down to modern times, and even in these the idea of a direct communication between souls, though these may still be united to the body, refuses to leave mankind, sunk though mankind may now be in monism and materialism. This last causes them to seek explanations, which are often tortuous and forced, but accord with their philosophical preconceptions.

Eduard von Hartmann, the philosopher of the unconscious, has written a special book on *Spiritualism*, in which he expresses his conviction that "there are more powers and faculties in the human organism than our present exact sciences have contrived to discover or explain". He calls the psychic power which mediums display in a state of trance, a power which often transforms itself into physico-physiological formations proceeding from the nerve power of the brain, the umbilical cord which binds every creature to the all-mother nature. "If all individuals of a higher order have their roots in the absolute, then they have in this, at one further remove, a connection with one another,

---

[11] In *Parerga und Paralipomena*.

and all that is necessary is that an intensive interest on the part of the will should establish the 'rapport' or telephonic connection in the absolute between any two such individuals, for the unconscious spiritual interchange of thought to be established between them without any mediation by the senses" (p. 78).

A somewhat similar explanation is given by Immanuel Hermann Fichte (d. 1879) of the transference of thought. This takes place because the active life of the senses disappears in certain organic conditions of the body and the "vision" of the spirit is thus freed from its fetters. The background which till then had been hidden, an unconscious or preconscious something wakens into life; it is then that the individual spirit can be influenced in what is actually a quite natural way by a being similar to or higher than itself.[12] Other philosophers who have concerned themselves with this subject speak in a similar vein. Dr Friedrich Zur Bonsen, a high-school teacher, writes that the soul, even in this life—while it is still united to the body, that is to say—can attain a state of partial freedom from the body, in which to a greater or a lesser degree it is endowed with the faculties of a pure spirit and so can perform abnormal feats (see below, p. 118)

Dr Bruno Podlasky, an Evangelical pastor of Garstedt, Hamburg, writes in his review of the first edition of this book: "To me as a Protestant the fundamental idea is both noteworthy and surprising, that not all the faculties of the soul were lost in the Fall, but that a 'Paradisal residue' remains. This thesis recalls the views of E. Dacqué concerning man's original faculty of seeing into the nature of things (*Natursichtigkeit*) which throws light on occult faculties and phenomena." When I wrote to him that I could not accept Dacqué's views, he replied that these might perhaps not accord with what we know of the human spirit, but he was glad to believe that something other than evil could still be attributed to man after his fall, namely this same "Paradisal residue", from which there might well flow prophecy, the possibility of love, of sacrifice, etc.

I myself follow up this idea to its ultimate limits and draw the final logical conclusions from it. In addition to the proofs already adduced, I can refer to theologians who have seen the truth of at least part of my contention. Fr

---

[12] See Feldmann, *Okkulte Philosophie*, p. 88.

Heredia[13] seeks to explain the phenomena of spiritualism by telepathy, that is to say, through "the fact that the spirit of one man can communicate with the spirit of another", although he gives a materialist explanation of such communication, as was shown above.

Hans Driesch[14] comes very near to my own view. He sets up a mental parapsychic theory which only takes account of the souls of the living (p. 113). Admittedly his theory is incomplete. Animism must be exploded when "no living person remains who knows anything of the content of knowledge" (p. 121). I myself declared this above, but Driesch did not go so far.

Let us here especially note the views of Charles Richet[15] who applies the term parapsychology to that science "which has as its subject mechanical and psychological phenomena which are called into being by apparently intelligent forces, or by unknown powers lying dormant in the human intelligence". Richet is also one of those who believe that there are powers of knowledge of another kind than our ordinary ones, and that there are movements of objects in ways other than those to which we are accustomed. In regard to the explanation of these phenomena he distinguishes five periods, the mythical one (going up to Mesmer, 1778), the magnetic one (up to Fox, 1847), the spiritualist one (up to Crookes, 1872), the scientific one, represented in particular by the Society for Psychical Research. He himself would like to open the classical period in which spiritual powers are assumed in man which he, Richet, does not wish to define because he does not know them (p. 486). Occultism will ultimately develop into parapsychology much as chemistry developed from alchemy. It seems then that the intimations of men of science have tended to move in this direction.

If we listen to what the mediums themselves have to say concerning their art, we find that they are unanimous in their opinion. Once the phantom Katy King (or more correctly, Florence Cook) was asked by the physician Dr Gully whether it could give any explanation of its powers; it answered: "What people say about electricity is all nonsense. . . . The origin of the phenomena is the power of the will."[16] Similar views are expressed by those theorists who, at least

---

[13] *O Espiritismo e bom senso*, p. 160.

[14] *Parapsychologie*, Munich, 1932.

[15] Richet, *Outline of Parapsychology*.

[16] Schneider, *Der neure Geisterglaube*, p. 176.

in part, accept the animist theory—men such as Aksákow, Bruno Schindler and Maximilian Perty. According to Aksákow the soul can, in certain people, perform feats which reach out beyond the periphery of the human body. It does this by reason of laws which so far are unknown to us. According to this view the anima, conceived as Plato conceived of it, as an independent substance wholly different from the physiology of the body, is the sole and ultimate cause of telepathy.[17] Later he returned to spiritualism. It is said of Hieronymus Cardanus that he could deliberately put himself into an ecstatic state "in which he experienced the feeling of separation from the body: he felt as though a door was being opened and he was leaving his own self... and entering the realm of the spirits".[18]

Many authors seem at least to have had intimations of the theory expounded here by the present writer. Thus, for instance, Bishop Schneider[19] says:

> There are a number of instances of exhibitions of power which are supposedly of a magical nature, but which like certain abnormal phenomena connected with sleep and dreams, can be referred to a heightened activity of the inner sense... and instinct. If science were capable of giving a truly accurate account of the nature of sleep, dreams, sleepwalking and so on, other obscure phenomena of our spiritual life, in particular the trances of spiritualist mediums, would be powerfully illuminated. The soul itself as a living substance and as an active reality can never rest. If the functions of the outward senses are inhibited, then the inner sense develops all the livelier an activity... a healing instinct that is very greatly heightened in deep sleep as in the temple sleep of the Egyptians and the Greeks..., a heightened faculty of perception..., an ability to apprehend more widely in regard to space and time..., hidden regions of the spirit are opened up and the soul delves into unknown depths, etc.

Feldmann[20] voices a similar view:

---

[17] Feldmann, *op. cit.*, p. 85.
[18] Schneider, *op. cit.*, p. 486.
[19] *Der neuere Geisterglaube*, p. 488.
[20] *Okkulte Philosophie*, p. 119.

What is remarkable is that these occult processes seem to take place between comparatively few people and are facilitated if they have their starting point in the unconscious part of the transmitter's psychological life and are received by the subconscious of the recipient. Actual mediums, when they receive telepathic influences, are normally in a state of trance —which means that the ordinary waking conscious life has been partly or wholly suspended. The full waking consciousness seems to be a positive obstacle to telepathic communications. This would explain why we are markedly susceptible to these things in dreams and under hypnosis, a fact which ... has been observed over thousands of years.

It is with a view to illuminating this same fact that has been observed for thousands of years and bringing it into harmony with theology that I have introduced the concept of the partly body-free soul. There are many who have experienced a real sense of relief when this idea has been put before them, if, as is so often the case, they have hitherto been confronted with an ever-growing and infinitely varied body of phenomena which admitted of no natural explanation and which they have been instinctively reluctant to ascribe to the devil. "A whole cargo load of mysticism and of nonsense about spirits has now been jettisoned as a result of this discovery (of purely spiritual activity). Imagination has taken the place of supposedly magical power and the influence of an alien spirit has proved itself to be nothing more than the fantasy of our own. The phenomenon of 'long-distance magnetization', which had previously set us marvelling, has wholly ceased to be a mystery".[21] This same Wilhelm Schneider dwells particularly on the cases of dying persons, from whom the soul was beginning to separate itself and who were thus able to attain to certain kinds of knowledge which they had often striven for—though that knowledge now came too late. Mohler said before his death: "Ah, now I have seen it, now I know; now I would gladly write a book, but now it's all over."

Something of this kind is also indicated by the French physician Lauvergne (in Daumer's *The Kingdom of the Wonderful and Mysterious*, 1872, p. 298):

> I have known people to whom the hour of death, which reveals so many things, brought a divine illumination about things which till then had been

---

[21] Schneider, *op. cit.*, p. 117; *Das andere Leben*, 1919.

obscure to them. They claimed that they had found the answer to the problem which they had vainly been puzzling over for thirty years "and that if they were to remain alive they would show that it was real".

This heightening of the powers of the spirit in the hour of death strongly resembles what takes place in sleep and dreams, particularly during the abnormal states of sleep, which means that it recalls those manifestations of our spiritual life which occur when cerebral activity is suspended, or at any rate greatly diminished.

We look upon the states in question and the phenomena connected with them, at least in their manner of beginning, as enormously—or, better, abnormally—intensified manifestations of the natural powers of the soul.

As its nature causes the soul, while united to the body, to have need of the co-operation of the inner and outer senses, so that some nature endows the soul, once it has been separated (or partly separated—A.W.) from the body, with powers of direct spiritual knowledge.

If the soul possesses, as it seems, even in this our bodily life, potentialities of higher illumination which in our normal state the bonds of our sensual nature prevent from unfolding, and which can only break through these bonds in rare and quite exceptional circumstances, and then only for brief periods and at the expense of other powers, then how profound in its depth and all-penetrating in its clarity must be the vision of that soul, once it has passed on to the shining heights of the next world.

How concerned is Dr Franz Schmid[22] to explain the powers of knowledge possessed by the human soul when it has attained freedom from the body. He speaks of soul-sleep, he asserts that the soul is not a pure spirit at all (Gutberlet), he speaks of the soul's pre-existing before it entered the body; but the text Wisdom 9. 15 completely confuses him. He almost has an intimation of the truth when he says that in the Paradisal state the higher spiritual life of man, and with it the life of the senses, were in no way impeded by the body, and that it was only as a result of original sin that our spiritual energy has become so feeble and so dominated by evil desires. But his grasp of this does not seem to influence the conclusions he draws. He utterly fails to perceive that the soul must have as clear a knowledge of itself and of its actions, after death although he is utterly unable to explain the nature of the punishment of the damned, if it is not in the nature of the soul to know God.

---

[22] *Zeitschrift für kath, Theol.*, 1898.

The best proof of the correctness of my thesis is its simplicity, for not only does it make intelligible all that theology has to teach us concerning our first parents, and their fall; it also provides a thoroughly plausible explanation of the phenomena of occultism, which have so disturbed men's spirits. Before discussing the matter further, we should like to quote the objections of Fr Alessio Lepicier (*Il mondo Invisibile*, pp. 308 ff.), who is not ignorant of my solution of the problem. He writes:

> Certain authors assume the existence of a purely spiritual intercommunication between persons who are at some distance from one another, in order to furnish an explanation of the phenomena of telepathy and telaesthesia that rejects the mediation of spirits. They say "We do not know the form in which one spirit exchanges its thoughts with another, or one soul with another, such as whether this occurs by means of ether waves or from soul to soul without any kind of physical means, or through the putting forth of some kind of psychic power. We know nothing of the process by which the transmission from sender to recipient is brought about. All we know is the result. Yet most certainly whoever argues after this fashion mistakes the whole character of thought and the manner in which we human beings communicate with one another in this life. Whoever is acquainted with Catholic philosophy knows how frivolous it is to speak of a projection of thought or will by means of some kind of psychic or other power, and how such an hypothesis goes counter to the rational nature of the soul. That is why the attempt to dispose, by a simple stroke of the pen, of the co-operation of the angels in bringing about direct communication between the spirits of two human beings, is an arbitrary and childish method of procedure."

My reply to this is brief. My endeavour has been to explain direct intercommunication between souls, not by a stroke of the pen, but by the use of the most meticulous care. I have avoided all talk of ether waves and psychic power and have based myself on the authority of theologians and of a long list of philosophers, who have been named above and who all affirm the existence of such influence. Being acquainted with Catholic philosophy, I am aware that ordinarily such intercommunication does not exist, but there are exceptional states, states of sleep, during which the bodily fetters of the soul are loosened and its purely spiritual nature can take effect. To assume that in such states intercommunication can take place without the mediation of a devil is neither childish nor arbitrary, but a matter of plain common sense, as the weight of evidence furnished by the above examples most decisively demonstrates.

(D) THE PSYCHOLOGY OF THIS ACTIVITY
OF THE SPIRIT SOUL

Now if one ascribes to the soul after it has departed from the body the powers of a spirit, and if sleep is the brother of death, one can assume that the state of sleep to some extent foreshadows our condition after death.

When we refer here to the "partly body-free soul", we must, if we are not to fall into error, take note of the definition of the Council of Vienne (1311), according to which the thinking soul is directly and by virtue of its nature (*per se et essentialiter*) the form of the body. This definition was at the time directed especially against the Franciscan, Peter John Olivi, who held that the vegetative and sensitive soul informed the body but that the intellective or thinking soul was only externally connected with it and did not enter with it into a union of being but only into a dynamic union, such as the director or mover of an instrument has with the instrument concerned.[23] He had thus repeated Plato's error, who speaks of man as a spirit that uses a body, an idea expressed by Descartes in the words: "*L'homme est une intelligence desservie par des organs*" (man is an intelligence using bodily organs).

As against this the Council stressed the fact that the soul forms with the body a unity of nature and being, in that it directly informs the body, which it makes human by the communication of its being. Yet for the learned there still remained this intellectual difficulty: how can the spiritual soul enter into such a close conjunction with matter without itself becoming a material form? This difficulty disappears if with St Thomas[24] we take the view that this higher form contains the lower one within itself, as a polygon contains the square, the triangle and the pentagon, and that the human soul is not wholly submerged in the body (*immersa*) nor completely enclosed by it (*totaliter comprehensa*), a thing which because of its higher degree of perfection is

---

[23] Cf. Bernhard Jansen, *Wege der Weltweisheit*, p. 130.
[24] I, q. 76, a. 1, ad 4.

inconceivable, and that in consequence there is nothing to prevent it from reaching out beyond the body in its effective power (*dass ihre Wirkkraft über den Körper hinausragt*)—*aliquam ejus virtutem non esse corporis actum*—despite the fact that with its substance it remains essentially the body's form.

What the holy doctor here asserts of the soul in its perfectly normal state can obviously appear in varying degrees with different states of the soul, and can be especially intensified in moments of abnormality, when the thinking soul withdraws itself from the outer organs, thus applying in reverse the principle already quoted: *una actio, quando fuerit intensa, impedit alteram.* Such a partly body-free activity of the thinking soul is therefore to be deduced from principles of theology which have always been recognized, nor does such deduction contradict the unity of being that subsists between body and soul, or force us to believe that this connection is purely dynamic, as Plato, Olivi and Descartes held it to be.

The Schoolmen distinguish between the substance or essence of the soul and its capacities and acts. A child that has not yet attained the use of reason has indeed a soul and the potential capacity for thought, a capacity that is lacking in the animal. When a learned man sleeps, he still retains all his capacities and *potentiae* to carry on his learned work, capacities and *potentiae* which are lacking in the ordinary mortal. They are therefore something different from the soul, but real for all that.

These capacities, according to St Thomas,[25] are more than merely co-extensive with the body. The soul is, as far as its essence is concerned, fully present in all parts of the body, but not in respect of its faculties. The faculty of sight, for instance, is in the eyes, but the soul's capacity for cognition is not confined to any one part of the body; indeed in this respect the soul is not only not wholly present in every part of the body, but not wholly present in the body as a whole, for the power of the soul exceeds in its activity the capacity of the body (*quia virtus animae capacitatem corporis excedit*). When therefore I speak of the partly body-free soul, I am not suggesting that there is a substantial separation from the body, but that its purely spiritual powers reach beyond the body's domain (*ein Hinausragen ihrer rein geistigen Kräfte über*

---

[25] De *spirit, creat.*, art. 4.

den Bereich des Körpers) and that in this way it is empowered to perform feats in which the body has no part, or simply an abnormal one.

The latest psychology treats of the activities of the spirit-soul when it deals with the exceptional states of our psychic life.[26] Sleep, dreams, the hypnotic state, occultism with its physical and spiritual phenomena and even psychic disease are accounted by it as pertaining to the latter, as indeed do I myself. There is, however, a marked tendency to ascribe phenomena to preternatural causes.

I would at this state remind the reader that different philosophies conceive of the connection between body and soul in different ways.

1. *The view of extreme dualism was as follows*

Man consists of two essentially different substances, body and spirit. This dualism goes back to Plato, and its effects are still observable in Kant and among the post-Kantian German idealists. It makes the problem of body and soul virtually insoluble, for it is wholly impossible to imagine how the immaterial spirit is supposed to influence the material body; it leads to false conceptions of the mutual interaction of body and soul (such as occasionalism, and pre-established harmony, as also to the theory of materialist identity and "psycho-physical parallelism") and thus either to spiritualism or materialism.

2. *Materialistic Monism*

The spiritual part of the human personality is always pushed more into the background, until at last it disappears altogether. What then remains under the name of Monism is nothing but crass materialism; cf. Haeckel.

3. *Idealistic Monism*

The same process in reverse; the bodily part is pushed back to vanishing point. What remains is nothing but "Idealism". This view has hardly any adherents today, because it is contradicted by all experience. It is impossible to deny the body's reality. For this reason "Idealism" turns all too readily into materialism: "*les extrêmes se touchent*".

---

[26] P. J. Donat, *Psychologie*, 1936, nn. 478-560.

4. Trichotomism

This distinguishes between soul and spirit as between two different substances. Kauders came near to a trichotomist conception when he pictured the vegetative soul as a psychophysical intermediary stage and contrasted it as a "soul-stratum" with the "spirit sphere". Similarly Frankl, when he speaks of the *psycho-physicum* and identifies this with the *vegetativum*.

5. Anthroposophy

This (like Theosophy and Indian Gnosis) really distinguishes four constituent parts of the personality: the body of coarse matter, the etherial body of fine matter, the astral body which derives from the spiritual sphere, and the spirit. The two central parts interpenetrate, so that that results which can be designated as the soul. The upshot is the same trichotomism as was described above.

6. Scholastic Philosophy

(*a*) Normal state of the soul. The soul penetrates and informs the body down to the last cell, down to the last atom (in this connection we must point to the centrosoma as the dynamic centre of every bodily cell) and normally does not extend beyond the body in its activities. Here the principle applies that nothing is in the understanding that was not first in the senses.

(*b*) Abnormal state of the soul. The soul is in its lower part (the corporal soul) "body-bound" and in this lower part contains the *anima vegetativa,* sensitiva and *intellectualis*, that is to say the living animal, vegetable and intellectual principle, but it rises above these with that part that is designated as the *anima spiritualis* or "spirit-soul" and which can be contrasted with the lower or "corporal" part of the soul. This contrast, however, must by no means be made in a trichoromistic sense—that is to say, in the sense of an essential distinction between soul and spirit, but only in one that affirms the unity and indivisibility of the human spirit-soul. Still less must the spirit be represented as the antagonist of the soul (thus Klages).

The spirit-soul can in certain circumstances partially withdraw itself and its body-bound part from the life of the senses and allow its activity to reach out beyond the body. From this there result phenomena such as we encounter in occultism and to some extent in the mystic life.

The scholastic doctrine concerning the soul is the only one that provides a satisfactory solution for the problems of modern psychology and parapsychology.

In recent times people have located the powers that reach out beyond the body in the subconscious, and have attributed a character to the latter which almost exactly coincides with what has been said above concerning the pure spirit. This therefore seems the place to examine this same subconscious somewhat more closely.

(E) THE SUBCONSCIOUS

The ideas set forth in this chapter must be reviewed from yet another angle. The words "subconscious" and "unconscious" have already been frequently employed, and it is by this term that profane science seeks to indicate the source of a number of mysterious happenings in our psychic life. It was the physician and psychologist Carl Gustav Carus, a pupil of Schelling and a friend of Goethe, who in his book *Symbolik der Menschlichen Gestalt* (Symbolism of the Human Form) first spoke of the unconscious, a word which Fichte and E. V. Hartmann then took over; the latter developed a whole *Philosophy of the Unconscious*. The French psychologist Pierre Janet, on whom Siegmund Freud based himself, coined the word "subconscious" in his examination of the phenomena of neurosis and hysteria. He did so at the same time as F. W. H. Myers in England, and on the whole it is the latter who should be regarded as the author of this technical term.

The age being materialist, this discovery caused an immense sensation. It was disputed and opposed—if for no other reason than that it was like a stone that did not fit into the proud edifice of rationalism and enlightenment; no one knew whence it came or how to fit it into the general plan of knowledge. Yet an attempt to do just this seems very much worth while.

As we have seen, the word "subconscious" appears to be only about half a century old, but a knowledge of the thing itself is really quite old. Even St

Augustine writes in his *Confessions*[27]: "I enter into the wide domain and into the palace of my memory, where vast treasures of all lands are hidden. There slumber all the reflections of the world, the whole of our development, our education, and everything that we have ever learned. Even the act of forgetting and the thing forgotten is still somehow in our memory." Today the word "subconscious" is a word with many meanings, a concept whose significance philosophers have difficulty in determining, Eisler[28] found eighteen different ways of interpreting the word, Schopenhauer looks upon it as an innate instinct with an indeterminate and general object. Fechner calls it a general consciousness that reaches out over all (*ein allgemeines überragendes Bewusstsein*) in which the various individual consciousnesses are rooted, an earth-consciousness or world-consciousness from which the individual consciousness issues forth. Quite recently a Canadian psychiatrist, R. M. Bucke, wrote a book *Cosmic Consciousness*; the American doctor Dr K. Walker has a chapter on this in his book, *Diagnosis of Man*, entitled "Higher States of Consciousness". H. Urban (Innsbruck) translates this last as "Superconsciousness" (*Überbewusstsein*).[29]

The empirical psychologists Janet, Binet, Ribot defined it as something that had split off from the central consciousness, and sought to find in it an explanation of hysteria and psychasthenia. The occultists tend in general to speak of a second ego within us (Perty, Du Prel, Aksákow). The people that seem to have hit the mark are the Anglo-Americans, Myers, James, Schiller and Sandy. These refer to the subconscious as both the source and the continuation of our upper consciousness. Myers, in his book *Human Personality and its Survival after Death*,[30] suggests that there are perceptions in the consciousness that elude all psychology, just as there are vibrations in the ether that we do not see, and light-waves that we experience as warmth; that the consciousness we know is only a tiny part of a greater consciousness with a hidden working. It is like an iceberg, eight-ninths of which is below the surface of the water and only one-ninth above it; this portion represents the consciousness, the part below the water the unconscious. He calls the

---

[27] The quotation is translated from the Kösel edition, VII, p. 233.
[28] *Wörterbuch der philosophischen Begriffe*, 1910, III, 1561.
[29] Cf. *Überbewusstsein* by Hubert J. Urban, 12 vols., in *Blaue Hefte*, Tyrolia, 1950.
[30] Longmans Green, 1920.

unconscious "subliminal" because it lies below the threshold of consciousness. Some, like Paulsen, Sigwart and Donat, dispute the existence of an unconscious, though others, like Gutberlet and Geyser, postulate it as a logical necessity. Very many people, however, today accept Myers' conception and declare that his discovery entitles him to be ranked with Copernicus and Darwin, as one of the greatest geniuses of all time.

Consciousness can, as already indicated, be regarded as the knowledge of the soul in regard to its being and its acts. It is not merely a reflexive knowledge which deduces the cause of phenomena from those phenomena, but a direct and immediate experience. Consciousness is therefore distinct from the soul. The latter is the subject which has consciousness, knowledge, a knowledge that is directed intuitively towards its being and its acts.

The subconscious, however, can be conceived as a sum of functions and activities which remain concealed or "occult" from the normal consciousness (which is also called the upper consciousness) and can at best reach the consciousness reflexively and by a detour with the help of various occult practices. The powers of the subconscious are now described as follows[31]:

Everything that flows towards the soul from the outside first enters into the subconscious, and from here only a small part goes into the upper consciousness at all. The subconscious is therefore much the richer of the two; it leads an independent life, being, so to speak, "busy behind the scenes". It can thus provide an explanation for much that seems to us incomprehensible and surprising. Though everything does not penetrate into the upper consciousness, yet nothing is lost. Experiences may only enter the consciousness after delay, or even not enter it at all, yet they remain effective and condition the freedom of our actions—or they have the effect on us of an alien intelligence. This faculty never tires (*op. cit.*, p. 936) and can thus lead to an actual dissociation of the personality. Since all mental processes result in some kind of physical activity (Swedenborg), it explains pendulum-swinging, psychotherapy, dancing tables and the writings of mediums; indeed, spiritualist methods now become a valuable means of research into the subconscious.

---

[31] Cf. F. Moser, *Okkultismus, Täuschungen und Tatsachen*, Munich, 1935, pp. 147 ff.

A whole series of phenomena is thus made intelligible by this concept of the subconscious. Yet an unexplained residuum remains, and that is why people take refuge in such ideas as animal magnetism "touching and passes", psychodes, psychic power, od, auras, astral bodies, perispirits, vital fluids, biodynamic powers, electricity, skin emanations, magnetoid energy, etc.—all of them postulates by which the attempt is made to explain the phenomena in question.

All this seems to be due to the fact that people did not develop the idea of the subconscious to its ultimate logical conclusion; that they did not search for a bearer thereof, a subject in which it rested. In the same way that we affirm the existence of the body-bound soul in regard to our ordinary consciousness, so we must necessarily assume that of the partly body-free soul in regard to the subconscious, and that in the full sense of the term—that is to say by postulating real spiritual powers for it.

There is no point in talking of the soul and its omnipotence (Moser), if we do not draw the obvious conclusions from such an idea. There must be grounds for such an assumption and it is precisely such grounds that have been furnished by the concept of the partly body-free soul. And indeed one can define the actual circumstances under which the latter can function. The philosophers have from time to time noted that, to give the obvious example, the vegetative functions are unconscious and that nature had presumably made this arrangement ne anima *nimium turbetur*,[32] so that the soul may remain more free for its other functions. The same thing applies to the subconscious, which can best develop its powers when the soul is in some way or other freed from its normal activities. This occurs in sleep, as St Thomas expressly points out (*Summa*, I, q. 86, a. 4).

---

[32] Donat, *Psychologie*, a. 15, § 4 (1936), p. 207.

V

THE TWOFOLD NATURE OF THE SOUL'S ACTIVITY

[So far we have seen that there are certain powers within the human personality which must be accounted as abnormal, and from time immemorial the duality of our psychic functions has been recognized, so much so that two separate terms, ψυχή and πνεῦμα, have been invented to designate these two different aspects of our psychic activity. We are, however, not concerned here with two separate things but with a single entity, though this entity acts differently according to whether we find ourselves in our normal waking state or in one of the different kinds of natural and artificial sleep. To some extent the two merge in the subconscious, which both serves to store our sense perceptions and also records and gives effect to those acts of knowledge and of will which take place otherwise than through the bodily mechanism.]

From the above it is plain that we must assume powers and faculties in the human soul of a somewhat unusual kind. A brief review should make the nature of these powers more clear. We will therefore attempt something in the nature of a psychology of the unconscious and of the occult.

There is a double psychology—that is to say, a double science of the soul and its faculties, and its double character depends on whether we regard its faculties from the point of view of the body, or make our approach to them from the starting-point of the soul itself. In this sense St Thomas wrote a double psychology, one being in his *Explanation of the Three Books of Aristotle concerning the Soul*. This represents his so-called scientific psychology, in which he proceeds from the actual phenomena of our psychological life, and from these deduces the existence of a soul. He begins by determining the various objects which call psychological activities into being, and from these he deduces the faculties of a permanent substratum which he calls the soul, which he recognizes as being insubstantial, spiritual, immortal and personal.

This is very much the way the matter is seen by certain modern authors, e.g. Flammarion, Richet, Myers, Moser, Mattiesen and others. These writers record the phenomena of the occult and deduce from these the existence of a soul; the activities of this said soul reach out much further than the consciousness of the corporal soul. The writers in question recognize that the soul never rests, never grows tired, and never forgets, and that it is not bound by space or time. Nevertheless there remains everywhere a residue which they cannot explain, and they do not succeed in reaching the conception of a spirit, because no analogous concept is anywhere to be found in the other sciences. They are thus driven, like Myers and Aksákow, to accept the spiritualist thesis. That was as far as their particular methods could lead them.

St Thomas,[1] however, travels yet another road than that already indicated. He does this in his capacity of theologian. He makes the soul his starting-point, affirming its spirituality, and since he has defined the powers of spirits—such as the angels, for instance—he deduced from these, proceeding from cause to effects, the powers of the soul. This was in point of fact the way the present writer proceeded above, arriving at the conclusion that the faculties of the soul must of necessity reach out beyond the body.

It has moreover also now been experimentally proved that there exists in man a "something" which is neither matter nor sensually material, but spiritual and personal. Indeed we can arrive at this knowledge quite directly, since the soul can grasp things which are not bound to space or time. It must therefore itself be superior to space and time, an attribute only possessed by a spirit. Admittedly it is at present tied down to the body and its senses, and can normally only engage in an activity proper to the corporal soul. But, as will be seen later, the first man was able to exercise yet another activity, namely that of the spirit-soul.

That is why philosophy has already spoken of a twofold mode of existence on the part of the soul. It has spoken of a bodybound soul (ψυχή) and of a soul that is separated from the body (πνεῦμα, νοῦς). Admittedly, so long as the soul is bound to the body, it can only be active by means of the body. All the artificial distinctions in the world will not get around that fact. For "*agere sequitur esse*"; the activity follows the mode of being. The question which now arises is whether the soul can engage in both kinds of activity together, since a "part" of it (I use the word "part" purely by way of analogy) is not bound to the body. It is St Thomas who urges this conclusion upon us, in so far as he

---

[1] I, q. 7 ff.

asserts (I, q. 76) that a certain separation from the body must be assumed to make thought possible in man, although the soul by virtue even of this power of thought is the form of the body ("*est quidem separata sed tamen in materia*"—I, q. 76, ad 1), and answers the objection that the soul cannot at one and the same time be spiritual and also bound up with the body as follows: *Anima humana non est forma in materia corporali immersa, vel ab ea totaliter comprehensa, propter suam perfectionem et ideo nihil prohibet aliquam ejus virtutem non esse corporis actum, quamvis secundum suam essentiam sit corporis forma.*

(The soul is, because of its perfection, not a form that is completely immersed in bodily matter, nor is it completely contained by the latter; for this reason nothing prevents a part of its power from being something other than a bodily act even though according to its essence it is the form of the body.[2])

The soul, so long as it is united with the body, performs not only its peculiar spiritual functions, but also, by means of the organs of the body, the vegetative and sensitive ones. It is these last which cease completely immediately the soul is parted from the body, while the others continue because of their original and independent quality, by virtue of which they reach out beyond the body. Admittedly St Thomas has not here spoken of any activity of the spirit-soul, for in the ordinary processes of thought the soul uses concepts which derive from its body-bound state.

This much, however, can already be deduced from what he says, namely that the soul is not entirely absorbed by its function of informing the body, but, though it remains the body's form, reaches out beyond its imprisonment in the latter. "The spirit-soul is not claimed by the body in its totality; in part it reaches beyond it, and one can designate the part that does this as the spirit (*spiritus*), while that part which is more closely bound to the body can be designated as the soul (*anima*). Soul and spirit are nevertheless an inseparable unity (spirit soul); and this last is capable of two modes of acting and being."[3]

From this it would appear that the soul as a spirit can already be active in this present life, as indeed is indicated in St Thomas (I, q. 86, a. 4) when he discusses the question whether the soul can know the future. This is indeed possible for the soul when higher spiritual powers make impressions on it to

---

[2] I, q. 76, a. 1, ad 4.
[3] Nidermeyer, *Salzburger Hochschulwochen*, Salzburg, 1937, p. 96.

which the soul can only react purely spiritually. *Hujusmodi autem impressiones spiritualium causarum magis nata est anima suscipere cum a sensibus alienatur, quia per hoc propinquior fit substantiis spiritualibus et magis libera ab exterioribus inquietudinibus* (I, q. 86, a. 4, ad 2).

In so far as St Thomas here already expresses the opinion that the soul, when it withdraws itself from the senses in sleep, can more easily perform the functions proper to the spirit-soul, then he is saying exactly what this book is seeking to establish.

Earlier theologians had also argued in dissertations *De anima et spiritu* (e.g. Alcher of Clairvaux) that when, instead of allowing sensible objects to act on the soul, God acts upon it directly himself, then it is only by means of an activity proper to the spirit-soul that the soul can answer. It is the conviction of such men that God acts thus upon the soul when it is in the mystical state, or when he communicates revelations and other supernatural forms of knowledge. It is also their conviction that sleep is the brother of death, and if during the latter the soul, being free of the body, has powers of spiritual knowledge, then it is to be inferred from this that in sleep also some kind of freedom from the body or pure spirituality is present. A pure spirit, however, can never be inactive; if it is not in a mystical state in which God speaks to it, it must of necessity experience some kind of feeling or subconscious knowledge, or be the recipient of a true dream or be engaging in some activity in the department of natural mysticism (Plotinus, Buddha) or even in thte mysticism of hypnotism, trance or of some other state in which the senses are confused.

If we have recognized the fact that the soul is made free towards its spiritual side when the senses withdraw, the conclusion lies to hand that when this occurs the soul must in some way be active. In its normal state consciousness, or rather self-consciousness, is the way in which the soul becomes approachable. When the spirit-soul is active, a different kind of consciousness comes into being, and actually there is a split between the pathological and mediumistic element and the mystical consciousness. In the latter there comes into being a consciousness of a higher kind (maximum tension), in which the soul knows itself and also the spiritual substances directly. In the ordinary states of sleep or half-waking, however, this activity remains hidden in the subconscious (maximum relaxation). The connections between this last and the actual consciousness are few, yet it brings the psychogenic activities into being, and without direction by intelligent thought and will, it becomes the cause of our erratic dream-life, sets our imagination into motion, begins in its somnambulistic processes to carry out activities that have been the subject of its thought, governs the life of our feelings, and in hysteria the activities of the body till we reach epileptoid states, clownishness and delirium.

Thus, to recapitulate, we arrive from the side of theological psychology at the conclusion that the activities of the soul partly reach out beyond the purely bodily into the sphere of pure spirit and so take on the character of the activities of spirits. Moreover, according to St Thomas, this occurs when, and in so far as, the sensual and bodily is withdrawn in sleep and the soul thus remains left to act as a pure spirit. The faculties of pure spirits, however, and their method of acting—and this includes the spirit-soul—are, as we showed above, precisely the same as those recorded by experimental science (by Moser, for instance) in the case of the subconscious.

If modern science and occultism, in so far as this last may be ranked as a science, have established the existence of the subconscious, then we must assume a carrying agent for it, and we have discerned such a carrying agent in the soul that has become partly or wholly free of the body.

It is possible to compare what has been stated above concerning pure spirits with what modern science has established in regard to the subconscious; it will be found that the two things are exactly the same. The only difference between the two concerns things that cannot be experimentally established at all, e.g. immortality; but in so far as traces of the subconscious are discernible, they exactly coincide with the spiritual powers of the soul. To give but one example, there are the pieces of knowledge which man is able to acquire when in an abnormal state, and which come from sources that are not accessible to the soul in its body-bound state; these are, however, open to the soul when it has been freed from the body, and lie stored up in the subconscious, and it is only in the state of trance that, as through a slit, they become apparent.

Quite recently Dr Hubert Urban, professor of the University of Innsbruck and president of the neurological and psychiatric clinic of that university, occupied himself in his work *"Cosmic Consciousness" according to Bucke and*

Walter (Innsbruck-Vienna, 1950) with the great question of the subconscious and finally remarked as follows:

> It is very desirable that other sciences should co-operate in the solution of these problems so that we might again restore the conception we have lost of man as a whole. This has actually been done quite recently by the theologians (e.g. Wiesinger, *Okkulte Phänomene*, Styria, Graz, 1948). In accordance with a tradition that is thousands of years old, these distinguish between the "corporal soul" and the "spirit-soul", i.e. between anima and spiritus, between ψυχή and πνεῦμα. Since it is only the latter (spirit-soul=spiritus=πνεῦμα) that can be regarded as the carrying agent of the powers that are wholly independent of the body, it must necessarily be that with which "Cosmic Consciousness" or "Superconsciousness" (*Überbewusstsein*) is connected. It thus seems to be identical with what the mystics called the "point of the soul" (*apex mentis*) or the "spark of the soul" (*scintilla animae*). The state in which the soul is "partly body-free" seems to be one of the necessary conditions for this.

Here then we have a meeting-point between the most recent researches of medicine into the depths of the soul and the deductions of theology from the great treasuries of Revelation.

The fact that "extra-sensory perceptions" (ESP) are unconscious in man has led many scientists to the conclusion that they would be particularly certain to find them in the lower forms of life which do not possess consciousness. In this connection many have drawn attention to the instinctive actions of animals. Thus many animals have a sense of direction which remains quite unaffected by distance, and this, they argue, is not very different from the power of human beings in trance to become aware of things that are far removed in space or time. The American J. B. Rhine[4] has written on this subject and laid stress on the migration of birds which have often flown to distant parts of the world long before these had been discovered by man; he also lays stress on the migration of fish at breeding time in the great oceans of the world, and on the sense of direction in pigeons and dogs, which can find their way home from great distances. These facts, together with the

---

[4] "The Present Outlook on the Question of Psi in Animals", in *The Journal of Parapsychology*, Durham. N.C., U.S.A., 1951, pp. 230 ff.

skill shown by birds in the building of their nests, a process in which not inconsiderable mathematical problems are often solved, and in which a knowledge of construction is displayed that man only acquired after prolonged study, might possibly suggest to us that a spirit-soul is also present in animals. Since this supposition can hardly be entertained, it might well be thought that the foundations had been knocked away from under the whole thesis of this book.

When it fell to theology to consider these instinctive actions, it regarded them as a proof of the existence of a supernatural Creator who had endowed living creatures with faculties designed for special ends that are activated unconsciously and without any knowledge of their purpose. Nevertheless the question still remains unanswered: why do we in this respect view men and animals in two such widely differing ways? Why do we in the case of man regard the spirit-soul as the seat of the ESP, and trace them back to the Creator in the case of animals? Would it not be better to use the same approach in both cases? Would it not be better, that is to say, either to assume the working of an alien intelligence in the case of man or to ascribe a spirit-soul to animals?

Yet the different treatment of these two groups of living creatures seems really to be in the nature of things, for in animals the faculties in question are possessed in equal measure by all members of any particular species, whereas in man they are only observable here and there. For thousands of years birds of passage have sought the same territories and for thousands of years humming birds have built the same kind of nest, and during all that time there has, in the case of the birds, been no sign of change or progress, whereas in man the occult or mystical faculties tend now to develop and now to be lost. Further, such faculties in man relate to all the things with which his intelligence concerns itself, whether it be such a matter as the diagnosing of a disease or the deciphering of an inscription, or whether it be a matter of having supranormal knowledge of something taking place at a distance, or of undertaking ESP tests. In the animal all instinctive actions are directed mediately or immediately towards the survival of the species or of its individual members. One might add that if their actions originated ultimately from within themselves, one would have to attribute to them a degree of wisdom often far surpassing the wisdom of man. This would make it all the more remarkable that their mental life should have remained utterly stationary and one-sided.[5]

We can thus see that in animals these faculties are gifts with which their creator has endowed their nature, and that they operate with equal force in all members of a species, doing so with blind necessity, even when they do not achieve their purpose at all. In man, on the other hand, they manifest themselves in certain individuals as the natural extension of their spiritual life, and in doing so extend over every kind of field; they develop and dry up again according to inward and outward circumstance, and have nothing whatever to do with the survival of the individual concerned or of the species. In the case of man, therefore, these faculties pertain to the individual spirit-soul, of which we can trace no sign in the ordinary behaviour of animals.

These observations, which are made from the point of view of theologically orientated philosophy, are in no way intended to discourage the collating and observing of facts in the manner practised by the University of Durham under the initiative of Rhine.[6] Indeed such activities may help us, by means of a long and painstaking process of observation and comparison, to create a broad and exact basis for the establishment of man's true nature and place in the universe. This kind of enquiry has been too much neglected till now, to the detriment of our culture and of mankind as such. We can anticipate such researches with both interest and calm, even though certain intermediate results may appear to contradict our traditional opinions. The disastrous thing would be to content ourselves with half knowledge: "Dig deeper and you will everywhere encounter Catholic soil" (Görres).

It is often contended that the fact that animals dream disproves the whole existence of a spirit-soul, since animals obviously do not possess one. However, even in man most dreams are the dreams of half sleep (p. 102) which derive from incorrectly interpreted sense perceptions of the corporal soul. Finally it would be hard to prove that a dog has a purely spiritual intuition when it barks in its sleep.

It now remains for us to discover the sources from which the subconscious gains its knowledge. These are first of all the knowledge acquired by the understanding which, owing to the weakness of our physical organs, has been

---

[5] Savicky, *Die Wahrheit des Christentums*, Paderborn, 1921, p. 72.
[6] *Loc. cit.*

forgotten, but remains stored up in the two milliard cells of our brain. It would appear that the soul, when it uses the powers of the human organism, can only remember the things that lie on the surface of the organ; the rest lie buried and forgotten, covered over like the greater part of an iceberg in the water, and it is only to the extent that the part above the water melts away that, as a result of some disintegration, of sleep, illness, injury or emotional disturbance, the other part can come to the surface. This, then, is the knowledge that derives from our ordinary mental life.

A second source is both more important and further reaching. The soul is, as I have already shown, a spirit. It is therefore able, when it is at least partly free from the body, to cognize things that are distant, everything in fact to which it directs its attention and which represents a fact. When in this state, it can read the thoughts of others, even those concealed in the subconscious, can know what has occurred in the past, can diagnose disease, it can have visions, such as those of Madame Guyon (1646-1712), who, while in a state of trance, wrote entire books on quietism (a religious system condemned by the Church). It can reveal things that are hidden, as is done by the spiritualist mediums, who thus create the belief that they are receiving revelations from the dead or from demons; it can also, after the manner of pure spirits, move bodies at a distance (telekinesia) or give shape to matter (teleplastia) as do the angels when they make themselves visible. It can therefore bring about all the phenomena of materialization, which today so astonish us. We know that the soul once possessed, as a preternatural gift, greater power over matter, and that of this there only remains a part, a rudiment, which serves to perform the astonishing "miracles" of spiritualism, as the modern epidemic is called. For this second kind of knowledge the soul would first have to use the infused species, which would then enable it to take over the imagination pictures from its normal activity, as was indicated earlier.

Perhaps there is yet a third source, of which T. K. Oesterreicher seems vaguely aware when he speaks of a telepathic transmission.[7] The same applies to Fr Gatterer, S.J., when he falls back on the idea of an "all-telepathy" as an explanation of metaphysical phenomena. Further, we know that our first parents most certainly had great preternatural spiritual power by means of

---

[7] *Der Okkultismus im modernen Weltbild*, 1923.

which they were able to communicate their knowledge and their will to their posterity. The power of suggestion, which in a very limited way intimates that other power, as far as there is still anything left of it after the Fall, is something faintly similar. The influence which our first parents were able to exert was something incomparably stronger, and it could act on their immediate posterity. This last could then influence its own posterity by suggestion, though rather more faintly, and could thus communicate knowledge to them as a world heritage—and who knows whether such knowledge of past generations did not leave some kind of traces behind which though only rudimentary, could in exceptional occasions revive. This might provide an explanation of certain instances of psychometry, such cases as that of A. Catherine Emmerich, who saw those gigantic white animals in Paradise whose existence could only later be confirmed when the remains of mammoths were found in the ice of Siberia. Another case is that of Theresa Neumann, who is not only herself present at the historic passion of Our Lord, but hears Aramaic words, such as until our own day even the learned did not know, but have since found to be correct, and also legends which people had at one time or another invented. Such rudimentary powers would certainly explain all the phenomena of modern mysticism with which both ordinary curious people and despairing men of science seem to be preoccupied.

After Myers used his simile of the iceberg, nearly all authors that dealt with this subject began to employ it. In doing so they are endeavouring to make plain that the submerged, the subconscious, part of the mind is much larger than the waking consciousness and reaches down into cosmic depths, into secret things which escape our ordinary cognizance, it is only in so far as the upper part melts that the rest comes to the surface. The same applies to the consciousness of our corporal soul; this must more or less disappear if the powers of the subconscious, which pertain to the spirit-soul, are to manifest themselves. This, however, also shows us the danger in those powers and the price we have to pay for them. It is necessary for them to remove the consciousness until it is ultimately "deranged", so that the mind is clouded and actual madness can ensue. All this is not made any different by the circumstance that a few mediums were able to produce phenomena without going into a trance, and suffered no particular harm from doing so.

Der Mensch versuche die Gotter nicht,
und begehre nimmer und nimmer zu schauen
was sie gnädig bedecken mit nacht und grauen.

Let man not tempt the Gods,
nor desire ever to see
what they mercifully cover with night and horror.

Der Taucher, SCHILLER

VI

BODY AND SOUL OF OUR FIRST PARENTS

[Whereas today the spiritual element in the soul can only function fully when the rest of the human personality is put out of action, this was not always so. In our first parents the preternatural endowment was fully present and active without the rest of the personality suffering any impairment. This was true both in regard to (A) the preternatural modes of knowledge and (B) the firmness of the preternatural will.]

(We have so far endeavoured to make plain the nature of the faculties of the human soul, and have proceeded from the world of spirit, and from that starting-point have endeavoured to deduce its endowment. In doing so we made use of the findings of theology in order to shed light on this occult territory. Despite the fact that secular authors talk quite freely of uncontrollable spirits, of od, spirit-controls and all manner of things of that kind, exception has been taken to our own strictly scientific manner of procedure, because people have simply not taken the trouble to examine the arguments to their ultimate foundations. The whole of Chapters VI and VII, which here follow, are a further purely theological extension of what has already been said concerning the body-free soul. They can therefore be passed over by those who are unacquainted with Catholic theology, or who find that theology unacceptable.)

I have spoken of the pure spirituality of the soul. It is now proper that I should produce an example of a human being who experienced the state described without his human nature suffering any hurt thereby. Such a man was Adam before the Fall. We know that it is very difficult to tell from a broken machine how its various parts are intended to operate. One can only learn that by seeing a sound machine in actual operation. The same is true of man, particularly when we are concerned with the most important part of him, namely his soul. In order to become acquainted with all its attributes and functions, it is necessary to study it in its sound condition; it is only by making this our starting-point that we can infer where the malady lies, and what rudimentary powers remain that are still working in secret and thus giving rise to much confusion because of the strange effects that they produce. It is only thus that one can recognize the cause of these strange happenings, and ignore all devils, reincarnations, perispirits, od waves, astral bodies, leaders, materializations, spirit-controls and the rest.

We must therefore visualize the sound condition of our first parents in Paradise, as the Faith reveals it, and also study the vast devastation wrought by their first sin. In order to ensure a better understanding of all this, we must first acquaint ourselves with the technical terms of theology.

What is it that we understand by nature and the supernatural? We call all that "natural" which constitutes a substance, or derives from it or which demands it. This means:

1. All that inwardly constitutes the specific essence of a thing, whether it be an essential or an integrating part of its being.

2. Everything that proceeds spontaneously from the nature of a thing, such as aptitudes, talents and powers, and everything that can proceed from it under the influence of some other being, such as proficiency in some art, skill or craft.

3. Everything which, while lying outside the thing itself, is nevertheless necessary for its continued existence (nourishment, light, air), for its activity (the God-given will for survival), for its development (instruction, society, state) and for the attainment of its goal (knowledge of God, free will). The theologians group all these together under the term "demands of nature" or of things due, the things that God had to allow men to have, assuming that he desired to create men at all.

What goes beyond this is something that is not actually due, it is an addition to that, something which is over and above nature, which is supernatural, or at least preternatural.

The supernatural is of two kinds: the first is a perfection which transcends all created nature, as does, for instance, sanctifying grace, which gives man a divine nature, something to which no creature can have a claim. This is what we mean when we speak without further qualification of the supernatural. The second kind is the supernatural *secundum quid*, and consists in the participation by our nature in a higher created" nature than our own. If for instance a man makes an act of knowledge without the mediation of the senses and after the manner of the angels, then he transcends his own nature and is permitted to partake in the higher nature of the angels. We call this category of the supernatural "preternatural", and again there are two kinds of the preternatural; the first is the preternatural "according to the matter" (the thing done), and is a perfection to which we have no claim; the second is the preternatural "according to the form" (the manner of doing—receiving—it), that is when we have no claim to the form. Thus when, for instance, we make an act of knowledge after the manner of the angels, then that is preternatural according to the matter, but if someone has the science of medicine infused into him, then that is preternatural according to the form, for that a man should acquire this science is natural, but the manner of acquiring it through infusion is not.

Our first parents were created by God and received in addition to all that was proper to their nature—in addition, that is to say, to the talents, powers, aptitudes, which were necessary for their survival, activity, development and for the attainment of their goal—the wholly supernatural gift of sanctifying grace, which raised them up from the condition of nature to a much higher one to which they had no claim and which made them into children of God, so that they shared the same nature with God. With this grace they received the infused virtues, so that they might act in such a manner as would merit them Heaven.

Apart from their nature and these wholly supernatural graces, they also received a number of preternatural privileges, such as freedom from concupiscence, from suffering and from death, the power of higher knowledge, the faculties of pure spirits which were natural to their spirit-soul as such, but were nevertheless not its strict due, in so far as it was bound up with the body and the body was its instrument. Yet God permitted our first parents to enjoy both, so that they possessed both the powers of an angelic nature and also those deriving from connection with the body. And it was in this that the extraordinary, the preternatural character of our first parents consisted, namely that the soul was not a complete substance in itself, but needed the body for that. Even so, they received spiritual powers by which the natural qualities and capacities of man were perfected.

If we proceed very carefully and ask how these preternatural gifts are to be understood, our attention is drawn to those faculties of the soul which reach out beyond the purely bodily (cf. St Thomas, I, q. 76, a. 4, ad 1). St Thomas says (*De Veritate*, q. 18, 1): there are three ways of knowing God: (1) After the Fall, we know God only in the mirror of his creatures. (2) In Paradise, God was known by virtue of a spiritual light which he infused into the human spirit. This light was an expressed similarity (*expressa similitudo*) of the uncreated light.[1] (3) In the *visio beatifica* God is known by the light of his glory. St Thomas says the same in his Summa (I, q. 94, a. 1), namely that Adam did not see God according to his true nature (except *in raptu quando Deus immisit soporem in Adam*—Gen, 2—"in a transport, when God allowed sleep to come over Adam"), yet knew him with a higher form of knowledge than that with which we know him now, so that his knowledge stood half-way between the knowledge that we possess on earth and that of God in the light of glory, in which God is beheld according to his true nature. Thus the knowledge of God possessed by our first parents stands midway between our present knowledge and that of eternity.

If we ask further and enquire how exactly we are to visualize Adam's manner of knowledge, he replies that it was similar to mystical contemplation, and explains the idea of the spark of the soul (*scintilla animae*) by telling us that "as the spark, being a part of the fire, leaps upward out of the fire, so a part of the soul reaches upward out of the purely human and receives a small participation (*modica participatio*) in the kind of knowledge possessed by the Angels" (Comment in Sent., 31, 4), while in the Summa (I, q. 94, a, 1) he refers us to the passage in St Augustine[2]: "Perhaps God spoke to the first human beings as he does to the angels, by illuminating their spirit with the unchanging light, although not with such communication of the divine essence as the angels can receive."

From this the theologian, while adhering strictly to dogma, can draw the necessary philosophical conclusions that will enable him to understand the spiritual powers of our first parents as being proportioned to the degree of their knowledge. It is most certainly not true that the first man was a pure spirit. No, he had a body and a soul and the latter was the form of his body. His knowledge, like our own, was by means of abstractions from his sense perceptions; but we can conclude from certain indications in divine revelation

---

[1] Cf. Fr W. Schmidt in vol. 6 of his grandiosely conceived *Ursprung der Gottesidee* (10 vols, have so far appeared, Münster, Westphalia). This author shows (pp. 491 ff.), on the basis of an immense body of facts which he adduces, that God directly revealed his nature and actions to men.

[2] *De Genesi ad litt.*, XI, c. 43.

that the powers and faculties of his spirit-soul, which even in his present condition often reach out beyond the body (St Thomas, I, q. 76, a. 4), were also present and enabled him to act after the manner of a pure spirit, in so far as their essential connection with the body permitted this. This reaching out of his spirit-soul beyond the body was bound to show itself both in the quality of his knowledge and in the acts of his will. When therefore in what follows here the expression "pure spirituality" is used, then this is to be understood as meaning that in addition to the natural powers of the corporal soul (which is bound up with the body and acts through the body) the powers of the spirit-soul are also present in man, and that these sometimes reach out beyond the powers of the body even in this life. This tends particularly to occur in the exceptional states of the soul such as those experienced by our first parents and residually by the mystics. It would also appear to occur in a rudimentary form in the mysticism of the occult. If, however, such purely spiritual cognition took place in our first parents, then we must attribute to them a corresponding mode of being, for "action follows being". This mode of being we call the state of semi-freedom from the body, and in Adam this was present as a normal condition.

In one respect therefore our first parents performed their acts of knowledge in the same manner as we do ourselves, but they also performed them directly after the manner of pure spirits. Also they possessed an openness and decisive quality of the will such as is only to be found in pure spirits. Through this their understanding was perfected, so that they had a better knowledge both of God and Nature and were free from everything that could hurt their happiness, their health or even their life; also their will was perfected and was kept superior to matter and remained free from concupiscence. It seems desirable to deal individually with such matters as preternatural knowledge, the inability to suffer, immortality, freedom from concupiscence and the preternatural will.

These gifts are, according to theology, preternatural both "as to substance and manner"; they constitute a partaking in the nature of pure spirits and co-exist with our human nature. If therefore theology affirms that preternatural gifts existed in our first parents, it thus indicates that, apart from human nature, they also received certain angelic powers, thus participating in the nature of pure spirits.

For this reason it is clear that those scholars are in error who hold that a radical inconsistency in human nature would be implied, if, apart from its normal methods of cognition through the senses, the soul were also to possess direct means of knowledge without the mediation of the body. The preternatural gifts of our first parents did not impair the union of their bodies with their souls; rather did they serve to strengthen and perfect it. The soul was not punished by its union with the body, but was thereby endowed with a new form of knowledge and will which, as a pure spirit, it would not have possessed.

From this it is plain that it is inexact to say that "the angelic powers of our first parents were wholly bound up with their bodies", since this is philosophically impossible: *agere sequitur esse* (action follows being). If the powers are wholly bound up with the body, then they are not angelic, that is to say, purely spiritual. There must be some kind of liberation from the body, or rather, a reaching out beyond the body. In this connection another question remains to be discussed, namely whether it is a punishment for the soul to be bound up with the body. Speaking generally, the theologians are inclined to look upon the state of the soul when it is separated from the body as a perfection thereof (Mager) and regard its powers of knowledge as much more perfect than those possessed by it when it was bound up with the body (Donat, *Psychologie*, V, 2). Others, however, do not agree; they say that if this were so the soul would have to free itself from "its entrapped and enmeshed state and escape into pure spirituality".[3]

In reality the truth lies half-way between these two positions. Undoubtedly it was originally an advantage for the human soul that in addition to its purely spiritual nature which it shared with the angels, it should also possess a body by means of which it could acquire a new manner of knowledge and perform meritorious works. After man had sinned, however, the body became a burden upon the soul (*Quis liberabit me de corpore mortis huius?*—St Paul); so that the state of being freed from the body was a preferable one. Yet the reunion of the soul with a glorified body is again a further stage of progress beyond the mere freedom from the body which has just been mentioned. It is, as has already been shown, an upward development.

---

[3] Weber, ZKT., 1950, p. 105.

(A) THEIR PRETERNATURAL MODES OF KNOWLEDGE

All that we know of Adam's powers of understanding shows that his knowledge surpassed the wisdom of modern man, despite the latter's very considerable progress and development, a thing we can only explain if we ascribe to Adam the powers of a pure spirit.

1. Actually we read that while he was creating woman "God cast a deep sleep over Adam", a sleep which in actual fact represented a great release from the senses. Theologians have been at some pains to explain the condition that is indicated by the word *Tardemah*. Though this word does not really mean "ecstasy", which is the Septuagint rendering (the Septuagint was a translation into Greek carried out by *seventy* scholars), it can nevertheless be rendered as an ecstatic sleep, that is to say, a state of being in which the soul dwelt outside the world of sense and was active after the manner of pure spirits. (The word itself is connected with the Semitic *radam*=keeping in check, i.e. making the senses recede. According to St Thomas (I, q. 94, a. 1) Adam, while in this state, knew God in His essence.) "Adam's mystical life, however, was not to be a mere psychological experiment, as it is with us, but a personal and direct contact with God".[4]

This personal contact did not only last during this mysterious state of sleep, but in a slighter degree was (St Thomas, I, q. 94, a. 1) the actual life of Adam; it was an intimacy with God such as is enjoyed by the pure spirits. Adam heard "the voice of God walking in Paradise at the afternoon air" (Gen. 3. 8) and had spiritual intercourse with God, for it would hardly be appropriate to suppose that God made use always of the air waves for this intercourse, during which Adam was taught by him (Eccl. 17. 4-12).

From this the holy Fathers have deduced the doctrine that Adam, like the mystics, intuitively beheld God, the creation of the world and the purpose thereof, the principles of law and morals and all that was necessary for him as head and instructor of the human race. "To interpret this divine revelation in the first chapter of Genesis as an indirect revelation which is not to be literally interpreted would be equivalent to supposing that the greater part of the stories of Genesis (1-3) were only allegories, and this would be in

---

[4] Fr Joh, Mehlmann, O.S.B., *Rev. Eccl. Bras.*, 1943, p. 359.

contradiction to the decrees of the Bible Commission of 30th June, 1909" (Mehlman, *op. cit.*). St Bernard says quite plainly: "It was only through sin that reason was thus imprisoned in the senses; once man also had a spiritual eye, that did not need the senses in order to know God, but this has now been clouded and darkened by sin (*intricatus caligat oculus*) and can only be cleansed for contemplation by asceticism."[5]

2. From this it is plain that Adam possessed an angelic intelligence; his genius, however, shows itself particularly in the fact that he gave names to the animals, an act that was very highly rated by St Augustine as an act of the highest wisdom—much as the ancient Greek philosopher Pythagoras accounted that man the wisest who first gave names to things.[6]

In order to appreciate the significance of this act, we must understand something of the mentality of the ancients. In their view, the name indicates the nature of a thing. In order therefore to give a thing a name, one must know fundamentally its nature. Now there are two ways in which one can grasp the nature of a thing; one is by abstracting the non-essential phenomena, a process that necessitates protracted study and experience; the other is the intuitive understanding of pure spirits. No doubt Adam had several centuries to obtain a knowledge of things by abstraction from sensual perception; for the rest, we can only suppose that he cognized things intuitively by the light that God had infused into him at the time of his creation.

This ecstatic intercourse with God and his profound knowledge prove that Adam, in addition to the powers of understanding based on his sensual perceptions, also had an angelic intelligence by means of which he was able to know God and the nature of things. This purely spiritual understanding also aided him in obtaining ordinary knowledge by means of the senses. Understanding therefore came very easily to him, a fact on which St Augustine lays great stress (*against Julian*, V, 1). He was free from the obstacles caused by passion, untroubled by an undisciplined imagination or evil disposition, free from the necessity of providing for his own support and from the weakness of forgetfulness—in a word, free from the body as an impediment to the soul (Wisdom, 9. 15).

---

[5] *Op. cit.*, cf. Linhardt, *Mystik des hl. Bernhard*, p. 48.
[6] Cf. J, Pohle, D*ogmatik*, I, 1907, p. 465.

3. This spiritual power that Adam enjoyed had one very important consequence, since by reason of it Adam was able to avoid all dangers to his health and so achieved the freedom from suffering, the happiness and immortality, which is so astonishing to us "for God created man incorruptible" (Wisdom, 2. 23). This immortality was not that of the blessed in heaven, who can no longer die; it was simply the possibility of not dying (*non posse mori et posse nan mori*). Our first parents, thanks to their spiritual powers, were able to avoid the causes of death, which are either external, like the mischances of nature, or internal, like sickness, age and the like. Adam was able to avoid the former and could protect himself against the latter by means of the fruit of the tree of life (Gen. 2. 9). Such knowledge could only be possessed by an angelic intelligence which understands anything to which it directs its attention.[7]

Thus there existed two kinds of knowledge in Adam. On the one hand he derived it by means of abstractions from his sensual perceptions; on the other he gained it by means of that spirit-soul which reached out beyond his body, and this last is not only probable, but is what in actual fact the theologians have always held, though they may not always have expressed it so clearly. Nevertheless, it is most certainly true, and the truth of it is still further confirmed for us if we observe the quality of the will in these first members of the human race.

(B) Their Preternatural Will

1. Apart from their freedom from suffering and immortality, which were consequences of the angelic quality of their understanding, the theologians also account among the preternatural gifts vouchsafed to our first parents their innocence and freedom from concupiscence, qualities which originate from the preternatural character of their will and which have now to be explained. Given the qualities of understanding already described, it is really only to be expected that our first parents should also have been privileged in the matter of their will, and that this will should have been firm and

---

[7] Cf. Lepicier, *Il Mondo invisibile*, pp. 36 ff.

unconquerable, and that it should have been the complete master of matter and body.

Concupiscence is a sensual desire that has gone ahead in advance of considered thought and of the commands of reason. It is a desire that seeks its object in a manner that is contrary to reason. When sensual desire is subjected to reason, it is not in itself evil, and can aid the natural powers in attaining their object. Yet if this subjection is lessened or removed, it can only cause ruin, for the moral and even the physical order is then bound to be subverted.

Freedom from such evil desire is known as innocence. In the state of innocence, man's reason keeps the lower part of his nature, namely his body and its senses, so much in subjection that the latter can never interfere with the free deliberation of the mind, but continues to be wholly subservient to it. Reason can then activate the powers of the will, and, when they are excited, curb and suppress them. The first human beings had a nature that was pure and strong, and they had powerful and healthy bodies, nor were they denied the delights of sense, though these were always kept under control and subjected to the reason (St Thomas, I, q. 98, a. 2). Holy Scripture shows this very clearly when it tells us that our first parents, though naked, were not ashamed, and only became aware of this circumstance after the Fall, This was not due to the fact that after sin they developed a more tender conscience, or that before it the purpose of marriage had been unknown to them; while they were free from concupiscence, the body with all its powers remained subject to the soul. It was only after sin that they became aware of a confusion, a weakness of the soul and the degrading fact that the lower part of their nature had dominion over the nobler part, that is to say, over the soul and its reason.

2. By reason of this innocence they held in restraint not only their fleshly desires, but also all others, their love of pleasure, of possessions and of power; all remained in peace and in order and subject to the will which was united to God. The soul directed the body, while, for its own part the latter, like a good and obedient instrument, gave them its support. Although they had an animal body, they experienced nothing in the nature of rebellion; right order brought it about that even as the soul obeyed God, so the body obeyed the soul and was subject to it without any kind of opposition.[8]

---

[8] St Augustine, *De pecc. mer. et rem.*, 2, 22.

3. The spiritual will not only dominated the body but also matter, so that it could avoid suffering and death and make work easy. God had ordained: "Of the tree of knowledge of good and evil thou shalt not eat, for in what day soever thou shalt eat of it thou shalt die the death", or as Symmachus, Theodoret and St Jerome translate: "thou wilt be mortal". By his angelic intelligence Adam knew how to avoid the causes of death and disease and by his will he was able to direct the fluid and solid substances of this world, so that they not only did him no hurt but greatly contributed to his happiness. "Man lived happily in Paradise, so long as he desired that which God ordained. Food was there for him so that he suffered no hunger, and drink, so that he suffered no thirst; the tree of life was there so that he should not be wasted by old age. No disease was to be feared from within and no blow from without. There was for him perfect health in body and soul, no fatigue, and no sleep against his will."[9]

4. He knew no fatigue; his work was itself a pleasure for him. Today one asks how it was possible for work to be a pleasure, for there was work in Paradise even before the Fall. "And the Lord God took man, and put him into the Paradise of pleasure, to dress it and to keep it" (Gen. 2. 15). As we see things today such "dressing" could not be accomplished without toil and sacrifice. Some theologians explain the ease with which this work was performed by the supposed fact that the labour of our first parents was like that of the earlier stages of civilization, as the ethnologists describe them for us, in which men lived by hunting and the gathering of fruits, activities which can sometimes be agreeable and can even be sources of pleasure. Yet this only holds good if there is a sufficiency of game and fruits, and when these can be obtained with comparative ease. When, however, the population increases and the game becomes more scarce and a man has often to stalk a quarry for days before killing it, and when in similar fashion it becomes difficult to get in a harvest, then this labour is no longer pleasurable and "without sweat". We know how arduous is the toil of getting in a harvest even in cultivated territory; how much more must this be the case where the fruits of the earth have to be gathered in a wild state. Nevertheless the labour of man would always have been pleasurable despite the shortage of game and the heavy toil

---

[9] St Augustine, *De Civ. Dei*, 14, 26.

of the harvest, if man had never sinned. How could this have been brought about? Nobody till now has given a satisfactory answer to this question, though for us it is not difficult to find one. Our first parents possessed the preternatural gift of a spiritual will which reached out beyond the body, a will which gave man the power of acting on matter and moving it without any kind of effort, even as pure spirits can act upon it and move it. We may thus suppose that Adam performed bodily work for so long as this gave him pleasure and redounded to his health. When, however, it threatened to become wearisome, he used his angelic powers over matter, as he required them. Nearly all peoples retain some memory of a golden age at the beginning of the history of man "*Aurea prima sata est aetas*" (Ovid). Golden was the first age.

5. Although we have now shown sufficiently clearly that a pure spirituality was present in our first parents which perfected and strengthened the ordinary human powers of the soul, we are nevertheless anxious to attempt a further proof, and for this it will be necessary to enter upon a fairly detailed explanation of the great dogma of original sin; in doing so it is by no means the writer's intention wholly to deprive it of the element of mystery, but, following modern scholarship, to make it somewhat easier to understand.

Original sin, the sin of our first parents, inherited by all their posterity, consists formally in the deprivation of sanctifying grace with which man had been endowed by God and which he lost both for himself and for the whole human race—as indeed is plainly stated in St Paul (Rom. 5. 12): "As by one man sin entered into this world and by sin death . . . so death passed upon all men in whom all have sinned."

Let us pause for a moment at these words "all have sinned". (The Greek aorist ἥμαρτον denotes the beginning of an action and not a state.) The difficulty, as it seems to me, is not that all men should be punished, for it often happens in the world that posterity is punished because of the guilt incurred by an ancestor. In the case of original sin, however, we are not only all punished, but we are all guilty. We have all committed the sin and incurred the guilt and all are in a state of sin and have accordingly been robbed of grace, so that not even children can be saved without baptism.

The difficulty becomes even greater when the theologians tell us—and quite rightly—that original sin must be for us a free act of the will (when theologians such as Bartmann[10] or König[11] tell us that it is not a free act, they would seem to be in error). It must be a free act of the will if it is to be a real sin at all, even if it is only an habitual state of fallen nature, because sin is a free and knowing transgression of a divine command. How then can it be that original sin is a free act of the will for us?

The theologians are well aware of this difficulty, for the element of free will cannot simply derive from the fact that Adam is the physical principle of the human race. That is why certain other theologians believe that a contract subsisted between God and Adam according to which God would only grant grace so long as Adam remained obedient.

But apart from the fact that there is no proof of the existence of any such contract, it would still not explain how it caused our present deprivation of grace to be an act of the free will.

Yet others come somewhat closer to the truth when they say that God had included the will of all men in the will of Adam who was also juridically the head of the human family, and that for this reason all men must be held to have consented to his sin. St Thomas (*De Malo*, q. 4, a. 1) says that man must not be treated as a single person but as a member of the human race (German: *der menschlichen Natur* = (literally) of human nature), which has its starting-point in Adam, as though all men were a single man (*ac si homines essent unus homo*).

This is as far as the theologians had got, but modern man is anxious to know how it is possible for all men to be one man. How can they *psychologically* represent one will in such a way that original sin would become a free act by every member of the race?

The only way of giving a certain answer to this question is to refer back to the pure spirituality of our first parents, a spirituality which would in part have been inherited by their descendants; to the latter there would also have passed that capacity for being influenced, that noopneustia, of which the writer spoke when he showed how angels partake of the knowledge of angels higher than themselves by illumination, and having partaken of that knowledge, obey them. They are influenced with a degree of power which we simply cannot imagine—a fact that has led Fr Gredt actually to deny that they

---

[10] *Lehrbuch der Dogmatik*, I, 297.
[11] ZKT, 1950, pp. 105 ff.

can be so influenced at all. This noopneustic power rested in Adam who would have been spiritually one with his son (who in his turn would have been similarly one with his own children) and would so have influenced that son that he would have been wholly obedient to his father's will. This will would have been passed on from generation to generation, and would have determined the wills of posterity precisely as the wills of the higher angels determine those of the lower ones—or as the will of the hypnotist influences the will of his subject. Thus we would have been born with the same disposition of will as Adam possessed. This does not mean that Adam influenced us before we ever existed, but that he would have influenced his son, and that son would then have influenced his own children, etc. There would have been unity and peaceful accord in every respect, an accord that would have grown stronger as Adam's posterity grew more numerous; strengthened in goodness, all men would have influenced each other for good and so men would have been happy and at unity with each other, "being of one mind one towards another" (Rom. 12. 16), "cleaving" ever more "to that which is good" (Rom. 12. 9). Any deviation from this, though physically possible, would have been impossible morally, or would at the most have only been possible in matters of little importance, in so far as this was necessary for the assertion of free will. This accord would have been firm, instantaneous and irrevocable, of the kind we have already noted in the case of pure spirits. Thus the will of posterity was actually contained within the will of Adam, so that his sin became our own, Adam's posterity was infected, "being prone to evil from . . . youth" (Gen. 8. 21) and "sold under sin" (Rom. 7. 14). Adam's sinful act thus became actually morally and psychologically our own. Dr J. Berrenberg[12] succinctly puts the matter thus: "Because our first parents could act through their children as today no hypnotist can act through his subject, thus conversely the children, so long as they had not entered existence out of their parents, were acting in those parents."

One cannot validly object to this that it causes our actions to be predetermined, for the mere physical possibility of acting in a manner different from that in which one ultimately acts is sufficient to make free will a reality, even though the moral possibility of thus acting differently is no

---

[12] *Das Leiden im Weltplan*, p. 364.

longer present—as is the case in the avoidance of venial sins. To gain heaven it was not necessary for every individual himself to decide in favour of the good; it was sufficient for our first parents to have done this for him and for his own nature to carry out that decision, as indeed in the case of original sin the decision of our first parents was the determining factor. If such a spiritual connection is not assumed, and one merely speaks of a condition which is displeasing to God,[13] it becomes necessary to impose excessive limitations on the freedom of the will. Thus we encounter the paradox of an involuntary state of sin, for it does not help us to fall back on the fact that the state of grace is also something that is not willed by us, since one may accept what is a gift, but the same does not apply to the acceptance of guilt. There only remains the punishment (without guilt), and as a Catholic one cannot reconcile oneself to that. That was the heresy of Abelard and certain others.

From the fact therefore that original sin partakes of the character of a free act, we deduce a relatively close connection between the will of Adam before the Fall and that of his posterity, we deduce a direct noopneustic connection of souls without any mediation of the senses, a connection of a kind that only subsists between pure spirits and one which came to an end after sin. Man lost his element of pure spirituality, because through that, by reason of his capacity for being influenced (see p. 37), the whole human race would have been miserably dragged into sin. The dividing wall of individualism was necessarily a consequence of sin. In this way the Catholic doctrine of original sin provides an indication that our first parents, in addition to their human nature, also possessed as the basis of their preternatural gifts that of pure spirits together with all the faculties appertaining to the latter which we have enumerated above. Let us now see what became of these gifts.

---

[13] König, ZKT, 1950, pp. 47 ff.

VII

THE FALL

[In the Fall man lost his preternatural gifts (as well as the supernatural) but not his natural powers. Something, however, must obviously remain when these natural powers are destroyed by death or dimmed by sleep, since the spiritual part of the soul still survives, and that something consists of the vestigial remains of the spiritual powers originally enjoyed.]

All too quickly everything was changed. We know of the tragic fall of our first parents, by reason of which we all suffer. According to the ethnologists, the sin of our first parents consisted in their refusal of the first-fruits, their refusal, that is to say, to offer the first, best, and most important fruits to God and thus to recognize him as the supreme Lord of Creation. God had necessarily to insist on such recognition.[1]

This seems to be the place to give some explanation of this conception of the testing command, which has furnished so many puzzles for us. Over the course of centuries theologians have taken great pains to study this question and have set up a number of theories to try and find an answer to it. The most plausible of these is that contained in Fr Wilhelm Schmidt's ethnological approach [*op. cit.*], for it is the most natural and rests upon an exact scientific foundation, which anyone is free to examine.

Fr Schmidt's starting-point is the fact that it is among the oldest peoples, among the most primitive cultures, that is to say, that one finds a world-wide extension of the so-called offering of the first fruits. This derives from the duty men feel, before they use or enjoy any of the gifts of nature, of giving the first portion to God. By doing this they express their recognition of him as their Lord and also express their thanks. They cut a piece off the quarry they have just killed and throw it into the forest "for the great spirit", or alternatively

---

[1] Cf. Fr W, Schmidt, "Die Uroffenbarung als Anfang der Offenbarungen Gottes", in Esser-Mausbach's *Religion, Christentum und Kirche*, Vol. I.

they refrain from eating the first-fruits of a tree, because—to quote one example—"Puluga, the God of the Andamanese, requires them for his nourishment". Fr Schmidt has proved that this practice of offering the first-fruits exists amongst nearly all primitive peoples in one form or another; he has done this in his great work *Ursprung der Gottesidee* (*Origin of the Idea of God*, of which ten volumes have so far been published, 1912-1952, Aschendorf, Münster).

This idea is also found in the Bible. We are expressly told: "Abel also offered of the firstlings of his flock and of their fat" (Gen. 4. 4), which means that he gave the best he had, "and the Lord had respect to Abel and his offerings". (When we are told of Cain that "he offered the fruits of the earth" (Gen. 4. 3), then we can read between the line that it was no longer the best (the first-fruits), but something that he did not happen to want for himself—which shows up his character and gives the reason for his rejection.)

Now Abel already belongs to the pastoral stage of civilization, in which men had to labour to look after their animals, when they did not find life as easy as in the hunting and foraging stage, in which the man simply went hunting, while the woman gathered fruits, and nobody was concerned with the cultivation of any kind of crops or trees. But from the ethnological point of view it is quite certain that the idea that everything comes from the great spirit who must have thanks rendered to him by sacrifice cannot have come into being during the time when man was already performing the labour of a herdsman and cattle breeder in order to supply himself with food. This idea clearly derives from an age when everything fell into his lap without effort on his part, that is to say from the hunting and foraging stage of civilization. Thus we must go farther back than Abel, to the most primitive stage of culture which was in point of fact that prevailing at the time of our first parents, the stage where the woman concerns herself with the fruits ("and the woman saw that the tree was good to eat . . . and she took of the fruit thereof"—Gen. 3. 6), while the man busies himself with the beasts (God brought "the beasts ... to Adam to see what he would call them"—Gen. 2. 19). It is at this stage that we would expect to find the genesis of the idea of the first-fruits and those scholars are probably right who give this interpretation to the testing command: "Of every tree of Paradise thou shalt eat . . . but of the tree in the midst of Paradise . . . thou shalt not eat" (Gen. 2:9, 16, 17) but shalt abstain from its fruits so that thou mayest know that "I am the Lord" (Leviticus).

Once we take this view of the testing command, it loses that arbitrary and even capricious character that seems to attach to it. God had necessarily to demand from rational beings that they should recognize the fact that he himself was the absolute being, and that man with all the rest of creation remains dependent on him. As evidence of this recognition, some symbolic act was required, and it is precisely this requirement that was met by the sacrifice here described, a sacrifice which was ultimately extended to the firstborn. This then had to be redeemed by other sacrifices, as we find still in the New Testament in the presentation of Jesus in the Temple.

This provides us with a simple explanation of the real gravity of the disobedience in question, namely of the eating of the forbidden fruit. We are here not concerned with the eating of a small piece of fruit, but with the refusal to recognize God as the supreme Lord of all.

The first member of the human race refuses this recognition by the act of appropriating to his own use the fruits of the tree in the middle of Paradise, and in doing so makes use of creation according to his own desires, as though he were himself the lord of all. This act of disobedience represented the complete reversal of order, an act of rebellion and revolt by which the Creator was rejected and condemned and the creature unlawfully assumed the mastery.

The consequences of such an act could only be terrible. Man lost the love and friendship of God, he lost sanctifying grace and the infused virtues, lost all the gifts that were designed to elevate, strengthen and perfect his nature. That nature therefore now remained dependent on itself and, being thus weakened, came under the domination of matter (Wisdom 9. 15) which made life more arduous by labour, sickness, suffering and death. Scholastic philosophy summed up these consequences in the following words: "Having been robbed by sin of the gifts which did not belong to his nature, man was wounded in the natural gifts themselves" and "In the pure gifts of nature man was not wounded". These two sentences seem at first to be contradictory and are evidence of a certain fumbling uncertainty on the part of the theologians; for these saw on the one hand that reason and will must have been weakened, despite the fact that these are part of our human nature. Yet if an actual weakening of the nature that is proper to man is (assumed, other problems arise which are difficult to resolve. It is thus worth while to examine the matter somewhat more closely.

One thing seems certain—that man lost all that pertained to the supernatural; sanctifying grace, that is to say, and every other quality that he could not claim in his own right. It is equally certain that all that truly pertained to his nature was retained by him, his body, his soul, his senses, the vegetative sensitive and intellectual life.

What happened now to his preternatural gifts? As has already been explained, these were the faculties and powers of a pure spirit; that is to say, they belonged to the nature of pure spirits. A pure spirit is immortal, is not subject to suffering, can influence matter, has an understanding that knows all things to which it directs its attention with absolute clarity, and possesses a will which holds fast to all that is presented to it by its understanding. It does not tire, forgets nothing, and so on. The preternatural character of these gifts did not consist in the gifts themselves, but in the circumstance that they were given to man although the latter was not himself a pure spirit at all; he consisted, it is true, of a spiritual soul but possessed a material body which had been "taken from the earth". This preternatural element also was lost by original sin—man, as such, that is to say, or his soul, in so far as the latter was bound up with his body, completely lost all preternatural gifts. This is the common opinion of theologians, which we have no desire to dispute.

If, however, it is true that the natural powers remained unimpaired (*naturalia integra manserunt*) and if the faculties alluded to above are proper only to pure spirits, the logical conclusion is inescapable that they are proper to the soul in so far as, and to the extent that, that soul has parted from the body or has even to a limited degree been separated from it. It is from this point of view that we must understand man after the Fall.

Psychologically what happened to him was this: his understanding was darkened, but this does not apply to his natural understanding which he could put to use by means of the senses and through which, by means of abstractions from his sense perceptions, he could know of the existence of God and of his law and also cognize the things of this world; what it means is that that extraordinary help from the spirit-soul disappeared which was designed to perfect his purely human understanding and by means of which he could directly apprehend the essence, the nature of things and become aware of dangers to his life; man's understanding now remained dependent on his body and on his senses (*non est in intellectu quod non fuit in sensu*) and, being thus very limited in its capacity, constituted a very imperfect instrument. Moreover even of that little knowledge that it was able to acquire, it forgot a large part owing to the weakness of the physical organ. Admittedly, of those things which it forgot, a certain memory remained in the subconscious, but this it is almost incapable of using. All that remains of the effects displayed by the powers of the spirit-soul are only fragments and rudiments of a once almost angelic faculty.

Sin also weakened man's will; not that his natural will was impaired and so ceased to be free—as Luther thought—but that preternatural help was no longer available for it from the spirit, so that the will lost its previous dominion over the body, its freedom from concupiscence, its power over matter, and ceased to be immune against diseases and death. It lost all such help from the spirit-soul and was thrown back upon itself. It also lost its direct influence on others, the noopneustic power of pure spirits, through which all men as a result of such influence (pp. 91-92) become as one man and are confirmed in goodness and happiness. Instead of all this, the will became subject to matter, while concupiscence drew it towards evil, and a great part of human action was wholly withdrawn from its influence—such for instance as the involuntary acts of the vegetative life. Its ability to exercise direct influence on other men also ceased. How difficult it is to influence another by advice, by commandments, laws or agreements! So poor a thing has the sometime paradisal will become, weakened, as it has been, by sin. Because man has upset the ordering of the world and sought to make himself the lord of all, refusing to recognize the over-lordship of God, God, as a punishment, has in his turn upset the true order and left man under the dominion of matter. All this provides an answer to the question as to how we are to understand the passage from the declaration of the Council of Orange (Denz, 174) and also that of the Council of Trent (Denz, 788), according to which man "deteriorated both in body and soul" as a result of original sin. Neither body nor soul themselves deteriorated in their natural faculties, but they were robbed of the aid of the preternatural gifts and could therefore no longer achieve what they had previously achieved.

Nevertheless certain roots of the paradisal gifts still remain, and of these God makes use to return a part of that which has been lost. Thus it became possible, on the strength of the *potentia obedientialis*, that man at a later stage should once more obtain supernatural divine sanctifying grace. As shown above, despite the loss of the preternatural gifts, there still remained the soul itself, which in so far as it loosened its connection with the body, re-attained that pure spirituality which enabled it to experience the revelations of God and in the exceptional conditions of the mystic state to speak directly with God, When in that state men perform their acts of knowledge after the manner of pure spirits and also perform miracles which serve to reveal the power of God. Admittedly on such occasions some kind of withdrawal of the senses can usually be observed, so that sense perceptions, and indeed the whole of our normal life, tend to recede; certain other consequences also ensue. This very withdrawal, however, is the bridge which we must cross if the spirit-soul is to be activated. This means that if the soul is to act more or less as it acted in Adam, it must be released from the body, either completely as in death, or at least partially, as in that state of removal from sense life which we call sleep. Being aware of these facts many seek to produce an artificial state of sleep through hypnosis or trance, in order thus to attain new forms of knowledge or perform unusual feats. In doing so they rely on the roots or rudiments of preternatural gifts. Yet these rudiments are not of much use—rudiments rarely are—and their use tends to damage the natural powers.

People have often asked why concerning ourselves with the occult should be dangerous or harmful. Here we find the answer; it is the fall of man that has turned everything upside down.

A theologian[2] has called these rudiments "residual powers" (*Restkräfte*) left over from Paradise. It is now our task to present their different forms. Philosophers of all ages from Plato to Hartmann have, as we saw above (p. 46), been vaguely aware of these extraordinary powers of the soul, without really knowing either their origin or extent—which last we must now discuss in detail.

Thus theology and profane science have worked together to produce a rounded picture of the spirit-soul. Basing itself on actual experience and

---

[2] Dr Berrenberg (Thomas Molina), *Das Leiden im Weltplan*, p. 356.

experiment, science has attained to an admittedly somewhat vague conception of a "subconscious", an "ego", a "psychic power", a "soul" that is more or less independent of the body, though that soul is still almost always vaguely interpreted in material terms. Theology, however, by delving into revelation and drawing its theological-philosophical conclusions therefrom, is able to tell us much more precisely that this something of which men have become aware is a spirit which has certain quite distinctive attributes. Admittedly this spirit no longer exists in its original freedom, but has become hampered as the result of an infinitely tragic breakdown, and can only occasionally peer forth at us when it contrives to free itself in some measure from that which holds it prisoner and push the bonds which contain it aside—unless, that is to say, it attains through the riches of redeeming grace to the freedom of the children of God.

Let us make a brief exploration of this twilit territory, so that, as by a glimmering light, we may at least guess at the greatness of this fallen cherub, and so take one little step forward in our knowledge of the nature of the spirit.

PART II

OCCULT PHENOMENA EXAMINED IN DETAIL IN THE LIGHT OF THE AUTHOR'S THEORY

I

NATURAL SLEEP

[We have now completed the deductive approach to the problem and can examine in greater detail the various types of occult phenomena and see how they fit the general theory outlined above. We have seen that the vestigial remnants of our lost powers tend to revive when the life of the body and the senses is slowed down. This occurs in the various forms of sleep, each of which produces slightly different types of phenomena which we shall proceed to examine in turn.

The activity of the spirit-soul manifests itself in ordinary sleep in our dream-life (Chap. I, A). Much of this dream-life is little more than a kind of froth and its significance is negligible, but in the deeper stages of sleep dreams can represent a genuine functioning of the powers of the purely spiritual element within us and are based on real spiritual powers of cognition. There are numerous examples of this on record, several of which are quoted by the author, and one of the most interesting among them is the dream of Bishop Lanyi on the morning of the Sarajevo assassinations, which were the origin of the First World War. Such dreams often seem to have a prophetic character, but this semblance of prophecy is usually an illusion. Where they appear to forecast the future as they sometimes do, it will generally be found that the dreamer is merely making inferences from some fact which his latent, purely spiritual powers enable him to apprehend, or that, by virtue of those powers, he has become aware of the inferences or anticipations of another. This last point is of great importance for the Catholic, in so far as the Church has consistently taught that not even angels can foresee the future, which can only be revealed by a special divine grace.

The spirit-soul also asserts itself in the phenomena of natural somnambulism (B)—the author designates it as "natural" because it arises out of the normal activities of our dream-life. In such a state, however, the subject develops powers of perception otherwise than through the senses, e.g. the ability of the sleep-walker to know his way in the dark. In addition to natural somnambulism, there is also artificial and pathological somnambulism, which is dealt with later.]

We have now examined the faculties of a pure spirit and of the body-free and partly body-free soul; we have also become acquainted with the preternatural gifts of our first parents, gifts whose remnants today lie buried in the subconscious and are nothing other than the faculties of the spirit-soul, which was before sin still able fully to perform its functions. We must now examine the rudiments of the above-mentioned powers as they are observable in fallen man, for these rudiments come to view, though only to a limited extent, in certain conditions where the senses have withdrawn, and they do this to a degree that enables the soul to free sufficient of its powers for it to occupy action stations that have been lost.

In sleep, whether it be natural or artificial, pathological or mystical, the senses are dimmed, either partially or completely; (even when the individual concerned seems to be awake, a certain numbness is unmistakable), and the soul then, being partly body-free, attains extraordinary powers. The first effect of this is that certain senses attain an unusual sharpness (hyperaesthesia—when certain senses are put out of action, others become sharper; blind people for instance acquire a very delicate sense of touch and hearing). After this, however, the effect of this reawakening of the powers is to enable the soul to use its purely spiritual faculties to absorb mental suggestion, to direct the vegetative life, to heal disease and to engage in all those other activities which were mentioned above. These phenomena for a long time seemed so astonishing that men ascribed them to the direct intervention of God, or alternatively to the demons, or left them without any explanation at all. Yet the concept of the spirit-soul is by itself sufficient—except in cases of possession or of the genuinely mystical state—to explain all these things.

Sleep is a state in which all our vital functions are by stages inhibited. Our awareness of the outside world is the first to disappear; this occurs through the gradual repression of our sense of sight, touch and hearing; after this there disappears the consciousness of our acts and of the ability of our will to direct them. The causes of such putting out of action of the waking personality are partly physiological and partly psychological. The first consists in the withdrawal of the blood from the surface of the brain into its interior and in the accumulation of the products of fatigue which are got rid of through the blood by an exceedingly complicated set of chemical processes. These substances are the products of the disintegration of muscular albumen, of kenotoxin, which for over a century has been used in medicine in the inducement of artificial sleep (narcosis). It is known today that the state of sleep can also be induced purely psychologically through rousing the mental image of sleep, which then produces actual sleep by the ideodynamic law.

Sleep is known as the brother of death. The latter is the separation of the soul from the body, and in sleep something similar occurs; the soul is not wholly separated from the body, but its activity is repressed. Bodily movements cease, then sense perceptions, sight and hearing are the first to disappear, after which there follows the sense of touch; the vegetative life becomes slower, only the life of the spirit remains, of which we are normally not conscious and which can concentrate itself on certain specific conditions of the body, so that we may become aware of an approaching disease. As a result of this diminished organic activity the cells of the brain can rest.

Actually our mental life is a dual one; there is the life of the corporal soul, which still has to make use of the organs of the body, and there is that of the spirit-soul in which the soul reaches out beyond the body and consequently makes less demand on the nerves of the brain; the activity of the corporal soul fatigues the body to a greater extent than does that of the spirit-soul. Sleep brings rest by stages. Medicine speaks of sopor, somnolence and coma, numbness, sleepiness and complete loss of consciousness. In numbness one can already perceive a raising of the threshold over which all impressions must pass (*eine Erhöhung der Reizschwelle für alle Empfindungen*), an increasing difficulty of apprehension, a change in the processes of thought, which now become disconnected, and a disturbance of the perceptive faculties. These groups of symptoms are also observable in other disturbances of consciousness though not in so complete a form. When sleep is induced by suggestion, it passes gradually from the artificial to the natural.

It is because the life of the spirit-soul (when it is really the spirit-soul that is at work) makes less claim on the nerves of the brain, that one can observe a diminished need for sleep in persons of genius and even in lunatics. Mystics can pray through an entire night without neglecting their duties during the day. Scholars will also study through an entire night without noticing it. The astronomer Andreas Gerafa, S.J., had always to be reminded by his servant that it was time for sleep, because otherwise he would not have gone to bed. One day the serving brother came to remind him to retire. In the morning he came again to wake him. "Yes, yes," said the good Father, "I'll go to bed at once." He had worked through the whole night without noticing the passage of time. Myers tells the story of a chronic maniac who, after a hard day's work as a sailor, would sit chatting all night long on his bed. During the day he showed no signs of sleepiness and after six weeks of this life had lost no weight. As against this, mental activity, in so far as it makes demands on the body at all, can tire it very considerably.

(A) THE NATURAL DREAM

Since the soul itself does not tire, it need not rest, but is continually active even during sleep; this activity shows itself in the dream life in which the soul often unfolds a very considerable power. The process is a perfectly natural one. The waking state is characterized by the fact that some external object corresponds to our perception thereof, and this is what contrasts it with pure imagination. In sleep our attention is no longer paid to external objects but is withdrawn therefrom, as was explained above, and the pictures of the imagination gam the upper hand. We call this state dreaming and it often occurs in our waking state, when we no longer pay attention to external reality and deliver ourselves over to our ideas and the pictures of our fancy, when we build castles in the air—which means that we give free rein to our imagination, so that our sense perceptions and our rational will are put out of action. As far back as the thirteenth century St Thomas summarized the whole matter as follows: *Cum offeruntur imaginariae similitudines, inhaeretur eis quasi ipsis rebus, nisi contradicat sensus aut ratio.*[1]

In actual sleep dreaming becomes the dream proper, in which the senses are almost completely put out of action, and the images and ideas do not pursue any rational purpose at all, but appear arbitrarily without direction by the will. Immediately after going to sleep and before waking up dreams are caused by falsely interpreted sense perceptions. These are called dreams of half sleep or "dreams of them that awake".[2] They mean very little. In them the soul experiences sense perceptions, but since it has been deprived of the possibility of judging them, it interprets them wrongly. These dreams are therefore for the most part folly, even though they sometimes represent symbols of fact.

---

[1] *De malo*, III, a. 3, ad 9.
[2] Psalm 72, 20.

Thus for instance we have the case of a person who dreamed she was undergoing an operation on the foot. After a few days a wound actually appeared on the foot which necessitated an operation. In this case the existence of the malady had made itself known in sleep. Since the soul has been removed from the senses, it is able to experience certain feelings with greater ease (hyperaesthesia), but gives them a faulty interpretation. Most dreams are dreams of half-sleep, "froth", as the proverb says. It is true of them that "dreams are a brief madness and madness is a long dream".

In deep sleep things are different, when all sense perceptions have been withdrawn and the soul approaches the partly body-free state, in which it receives back a part of its purely spiritual faculties. This is when true dreams occur, the dreams that were called ὄνειρος by the Greeks—the word is reputed to mean "saying the facts", if one may believe this etymology. This does not mean that the dreams are always "pure thinking"—that is to say, that they lie outside the sound and images of words (though dreams of that kind exist); they are imaginative callings to mind of things that are sensually perceptible—that is pieced together from optical, acoustic and sensitive impressions. The Romans were themselves acquainted with the nature of the true dream, as we can see from Horace's line: *Post mediam noctem, quando somnia vera*. In this condition the soul apprehends without the instrumentality of the senses, remembers things of which it has been previously aware and draws them out of the subconscious and often shows a surprisingly accurate grasp of the truth. Examples are on record of scientific problems being solved (by Professor Lamberton, by the zoologist Agassiz, and the Assyriologist Hilprecht), of secrets being revealed and warnings given; all of these things tend to strike us as extraordinary, but are not difficult to explain by the concept of the spirit-soul. It is worth observing that dreams often come to us with a wealth of creative imagery and compelling detail which must derive from an unlimited memory and great suggestive power—a memory and a power to which we cannot attain in our waking state. It is because people do not distinguish between deep sleep and half sleep that their views on dreams often diverge so widely.

Let us look at a few examples of the suggestive power of dreams. Malfatti tells in his book on *The Human Soul and Occultism* of a Tirolese who reported himself to the police and confessed to having set fire to the house of his neighbour; the police found that there had been no fire and that the man had only dreamed it. Taine tells of a gendarme who dreamed after an execution that he had himself been executed and ultimately, as a result, tried to take his own life. Professor Perty tells the story of a Mohammedan doctor who recovered his health after taking some medicine that had been handed to him in a dream. Such dreams can be transmitted from one person to another. Thus Podmore tells of a student who in a dream saw his bride with a swollen face. It subsequently transpired that the lady had suffered from toothache on the night in question and had been in bed with a swollen face. Father Lacroix relates the following experience on the part of his friend Magid Baruch in San Gonzalo (Brazil) in 1923. This man was the owner of a draper's shop, and lived with his family in a house in the next street. One night he dreamed that two persons had robbed this shop. He saw the robbers quite clearly and could note their size and other distinguishing marks and also their clothes. One of them was white and the other black. He woke up in a state of great excitement and said to his wife: "We have been robbed. I saw the robbers in my dream."

Early in the morning his brother came and knocked at his door. Mr Magid said: "You have come to tell me that we have been robbed." "Quite true," said the brother.

The police were informed and immediately communicated with the surrounding districts, and after one or two unsuccessful attempts the robbers were discovered and arrested, the stolen goods being recovered. Since the arrest had taken place in a neighbouring community, eight or ten people who were, of course, in ordinary civilian clothes were impressed to escort the prisoners. Magid went to meet them out of curiosity and was able from quite a distance to identify the two culprits, for they were the same men whom he had seen in his dream.

In the year 1914, in Wels, in Upper Austria, the monstrance with the Host inside it was stolen from the parish church. In the night a girl who was working as a servant with the local nuns had a dream and saw the sacred Host in a refuse heap. She directed the digging and the Host was found and solemnly taken back to the church.

In the year 1910, nineteen-year-old Mrs Lopanson of Chicago saw in a dream that her brother Oscar had been murdered by a neighbouring farmer. At her insistent request investigations were begun, and everything turned out as she had said. A rather similar story concerns the writer Beuer, who perished in the Messina earthquake; his body was found as the result of a dream.

People often talk of so-called warning or prospective dreams. Myers gives us an example of one relating to Colonel Reynolds, who saw in a dream that a nearby bridge was defective. After close examination it was found that the foundations had been almost completely undermined and that parts had been washed away. Moser tells of a gardener who wanted to offer a high price for a piece of land but learned in a dream that the owner, who was a neighbour of his, was going to offer it for half the sum, and a few days later she actually did so.

Sometimes coming events are actually foreseen in dreams. Thus early in the morning of 18th December, 1897, the actor Lanes dreamed of the murder of another actor Terriss, and the murder actually took place on the evening of the same day. Most people have heard of the dream of Bishop Dr Joseph Lanyi, who dreamed at 3.15 a.m. on the morning of the 28th June, 1914, that he had received a letter from the Archduke Franz Ferdinand in which the latter notified him of his own murder. At half-past three in the afternoon he received news of the assassination at Sarajevo. Since 1938 the following account by the Bishop has been circulated in the press:

> At a quarter past three on the morning of the 28th June, 1914, I awoke from a terrible dream. I dreamed that I had gone to my desk early in the morning to look through the post that had come in. On top of all the other letters there lay one with a black border, a black seal and the arms of the Archduke. I immediately recognized the latter's writing, and saw at the head of the notepaper in blue colouring a picture like those on picture postcards which showed me a street and a narrow side-street. Their Highnesses sat in a car, opposite them sat a general, and an officer next to the chauffeur. On both sides of the street there was a large crowd. Two young lads sprang forward and shot at their Highnesses. The text of the letter was as follows: "Dear Dr Lanyi, Your Excellency, I wish to inform you that my wife and I were the victims of a political assassination. We recommend ourselves to your prayers. Cordial greetings from your Archduke Franz, Sarajevo, 28th June, 3.15 a.m." Trembling and in tears I sprang out of bed and I looked at the clock, which showed 3.15. I immediately hurried to my desk and wrote down what I had read and seen in my dream. In doing so I even retained the form of certain letters just as the Archduke had written them. My servant entered my study at

a quarter to six that morning and saw me sitting there pale and saying my rosary. He asked whether I was ill. I said: "Call my mother and the guest at once. I will say Mass immediately for their Highnesses, for I have had a terrible dream." My mother and the guest came at a quarter to seven. I told my mother the dream in the presence of the guest and of my servant. Then I went into the house chapel. The day passed in fear and apprehension. At half-past three a telegram brought us the news of the murder.[3]

There may be a certain temptation to see in this dream a case of genuine prophecy, made possible by the intervention of a higher power, but closer examination of the facts suggests that there is no necessity to see in it anything of the kind, for the dream, though surprisingly accurate in some respects, is nevertheless inaccurate in others, and it is precisely these inaccuracies that are illuminating.

First, as to the points on which the dream is accurate. The most important of these is the fact that the bishop saw the exact spot where the assassination took place. This was at the corner of the Appel Quai and the narrow street leading to the (as it was then) Franz Josef's Strasse. This, however, was the obvious place for an attempt on the Archduke's life. According to the original plan the Archduke was to travel along the Appel Quai to the town hall, and on his return journey was to travel back along the Appel Quai, turn into the narrow street referred to, and then pass along the Franz Josef's Strasse. This would mean that his car would have to slow down at the corner of this same narrow street and so he would become an easier target for an assassin.

In point of fact, after the bomb had been thrown earlier in the day on his journey to the town hall—he escaped on this occasion without injury—it was decided to change the plan and cut out the journey along the Franz Josef's Strasse, which shows clearly that the authorities were alive to the fact that the corner of the narrow street was a particularly dangerous point. The Archduke and his wife were actually killed there because the chauffeur of the Burgomaster's car, which was preceding that of the Archduke, misunderstood his instructions and started to turn into the narrow street. When his error was pointed out to him, he stopped and so brought the Archduke's car to a halt at

---

[3] Moser, *Okkultismus*, p. 467, My own explanation is of course different from that of Moser, who is not influenced by any dogmatic considerations.

this critical place, and the Archduke was immediately shot, together with his wife.

The second point on which the dream is so surprisingly accurate is that it showed a general sitting opposite the archducal pair. The general in question was General Potiorek, the regional commanding officer. It is, however, quite probable that this fact, being part of the official programme, would have been known in advance to quite a number of people, including some of the conspirators.

There are, however, two serious inaccuracies in the dream. The first is that it shows two assassins shooting at the archduke, whereas only a single one shot at him on this occasion. The second serious inaccuracy is the fact that an officer was seen sitting next to the chauffeur. Now according to the programme, Count Harrach of the Motor Corps, the owner of the car, should have been sitting in that position. In actual fact, however, he was standing on the left-hand running-board of the car, a position which he had taken up in order to protect the Archduke, this decision resulting from the incident earlier in the day. Unfortunately he was on the wrong side.

We thus see that the facts in regard to which the dream was so accurate (the position of General Potiorek and the dangerous character of the point where the assassination was carried out) were things of which a number of people, including the conspirators, might have been aware before the assassination, whereas the points on which the dream was erroneous all related to matters which would not have been foreseen in advance, for the fact that only a single assassin fired a pistol was something that may well have been out of keeping with the general picture of coming events which the conspirators had formed in their minds.

Actually no less than six men had been posted to make an attempt on the Archduke's life, of whom some lost their nerve, a possibility upon which the conspirators might have reckoned. One, of course, used a bomb, but the decision to use a bomb may not have been taken at the time of the dream (3.15 a.m.). We know that the distribution of weapons did not take place till the morning of the assassination and that the assassins were allowed to choose their own weapons. It may well be that the leaders of the conspiracy, though they were ready to supply bombs if required, nevertheless did not particularly want them used. Bombs are dangerous and uncertain things and are liable to kill innocent bystanders—in this case possibly sympathizers with the Greater Serbia movement—and may thus antagonize potential friends. That being so, it is quite likely that at the time of the dream the attack was visualized by its organizers as one to be made by two or three men using pistols. It was no doubt this general picture that the Bishop's dream reflected. It was in fact a very remarkable case of telepathy, but nothing more than that. It was not prophecy in the true sense of the term.

A word may well be in place here on the subject of the real and supposed foreknowledge of coming events. Theology, of course, teaches us, as we have seen, that such coming events cannot be foreseen in advance even by spirits, but since dreams do often appear to foreshadow the future, or at any rate since it often happens that things dreamed about actually take place, there is a tendency to regard such happenings as instances of prophecy. Yet the truth is quite different. What really happens is that when we come across a case where events turn out in such a manner as to appear to confirm a supposedly prophetic dream, we pick on such cases and conveniently forget about the others, where our dreams have proved to be quite erroneous. We thus get the illusion of a genuine prediction, although actually we are dealing with no more than coincidence; at any rate the number of bull's eyes is not large enough to justify the belief that anything beyond the law of averages has been at work.

There are, however, cases where this explanation is insufficient. Certain details are often foreseen in a manner that cannot be accounted for by the operation of mere chance, and such phenomena may be explained as follows. When considering spirits, our ideas of time and space must be applied quite differently than to a bodily being, a truth which seems to find confirmation in the fact that dreams often proceed at a tremendous speed and even with disregard of the actual sequence of time. Thus, for instance, we may dream of a whole sequence of events that are causally connected with one another and end with a whistle or a shot, and this sequence has obviously been set going by the ringing of an alarm clock. The dream in such a case could only have begun at the first ringing of the alarm, yet this is also the final effect in the dream of a whole sequence of causally connected events. Thus Weygandt dreamed of taking a walk on a Sunday morning, of visiting a churchyard near a church, of meditatively contemplating this church and of hearing the church bell suddenly begin to sound. The dreamer then awoke to hear his alarm clock ringing. The circumstances seem to indicate that the dream was only set going by that sound.[4] In view of these things it has been asked whether we do not perhaps experience as a sequence of consecutive events what in reality is an ocean of simultaneous things, and thus cut our subjective years and centuries out of the timeless absolute. The kind of foretelling that we are here dealing with scarcely reaches beyond the life of the individual concerned. Let us then keep to this short span of time, and assume that our whole earthly life is really an instantaneous but very complicated phenomenon. Let us assume that my transcendental ego sees all the elements in this phenomenon directly and immediately, but that my empirical ego only sees them indirectly by means of mediating agents which in varying degrees produce a time lag, so that my experience is like that of hearing the thunder after I have seen the lightning. Einstein, when dealing with the fourth dimension, time, says that our judgment and comparison of periods of time is wholly relative. Moreover the present is not just a point but a continuum stretched out over some six to twelve seconds, which is gathered together by us into a unity; this last is done by our soul which acts through the body.[5] In this connection we may usefully draw attention to the Scholastics who also speak de instantibus of the angels and say that with these there is no such thing as time in our sense of the word, despite the fact that there is a consecutive sequence of acts of thought and will and that an instans or moment lasts a longer time with them and is not, as with ourselves, over in a flash. We should also at this stage mention Jung's[6] idea that the co-ordination of the various dream-images, as distinct from their content, occurs outside the categories of space and time and does so without being subject to the law of causality.

The soul that has been separated from the body, and also that which has only partly loosened its connection therewith, might well have to deal with such a duration, and so be able at a glance to see things which to us in our normal life are looked upon as belonging to the distant past or the equally

---

[4] Lindworsky, S. J., *Experimentelle Psychologie*, p. 286.
[5] Fröbes, *Experimentelle Psychologie*.
[6] Cf. Jacoby, *Die Psychologie Karl Gustav Jungs*.

distant future. If we take this view, warning and prospective dreams would appear to be more natural and even more intelligible.[7]

The dreams of deep sleep are thus functions of the contemplating spirit-soul that has almost entirely freed itself from its body. They may often give us knowledge of facts to which we cannot attain through the normal activities of the corporal soul. We shall see presently how this became a ground of suspicion against witches.[8] The activities of the soul in this connection are, however, not confined to such supranormal apprehensions but extend to sleep-walking.

(B) Natural Somnambulism

Sometimes dreams can be so vivid that the dreamer begins to speak or sits up in bed. It may even happen that, following the ideomotor law, he begins to enact what he has dreamed. We must note, however, that this is not to be interpreted in a crude anatomical sense, but as a mere impulse toward movement within a cellular or even an atomic structure. The result of this is somnambulism, which is designated as "an enacted dream". This last can be artificially produced by suggestion, so that the passive dream passes into the active one and increasingly resembles the manifestations of hypnosis, which is a kind of artificial somnambulism.[9]

There are various stages and kinds of natural somnambulism. What seems to be constant throughout them all is that sense activities are diminished, or put out of action altogether; the hyperaesthesia of which some people speak on these occasions is in actual fact only apparently present; it has in reality been replaced by the supra-sensual faculties of the spirit-soul. Thanks to this, the somnambulist moves with the greatest assurance in the darkness, carries out real acrobatic feats by walking about on roofs, feats which in his waking state he would never be able to perform. He writes in the dark and carries out manual work, talks with those present, finds the answers to problems that he is set, finds mistakes in a monthly account, distinguishes between colours with

---

[7] More will be said of this when we deal with the subject of prophecies, pp. 159 ff.

[8] P. 124.

[9] More of this later, p. 226.

great exactitude, sees objects of microscopic size which in his waking state he would have been unable to distinguish. All talk about hyperaesthesia, cryptoscopy and the like, and all efforts to explain these things in such terms is vain. One always ends, with such hypotheses, in having to admit that an unexplained residuum remains. It is only the concept of the spirit-soul that gives us anything that is at all satisfactory by way of elucidating them.

Father Lacroix tells us a story of his friend Magid in which we have a perfectly natural act of apprehension performed in a dream, the dream being followed by sleep-walking.[10] One day Magid entered his shop and noticed that a number of expensive ties were missing. Since there was a circus on in the market place, the idea came to him that one of its employees had stolen the goods. It was six o'clock in the evening. Without a hat and looking like a somnambulist, without saying a word to anyone and appearing almost demented, Magid rushed off to the circus, ran to the artists' living-quarters, took a ladder, climbed up and stretched out his arm and found behind a number of packages the box containing the ties. It was only when he was descending the ladder with the box of ties in his hand that he observed that other people were present. He then said: "Somebody has brought these ties here by mistake; they belong to me."

All this is natural enough and is a consequence of the spiritual character of the soul, which enters upon its rights as soon as it has become at least half-free of the senses. These manifestations have nothing to do with the devil. God, who sometimes joins his graces to the gifts of nature (*gratia supponit naturam*), sometimes makes use of this state of the soul in order to dispense his gifts of grace. "An angel of the Lord appeared in sleep to Joseph, saying 'Arise and take the child and his mother and fly into Egypt'."[11] Yes, God even promised such states of soul to his people as a great grace: "Your old men shall dream dreams and your young men shall see visions."[12]

Nevertheless it is not contended that the knowledge we gain in dreams is a more perfect thing than that acquired by us in the normal way. It has already been made sufficiently clear that the faculties alluded to above are nothing more than pitiful remnants of a perfection that belonged to men before the

---

[10] Der Spiritismus, p. 140.
[11] Luke 2. 13, 19.
[12] Joel 2. 28; cf. Acts 2. 17.

coming of sin; moreover a man very rarely remembers all that has appeared to him in a dream, and if he does so remember, it is often difficult for him to express in words the purely spiritual and what he has seen in images, for words are abstract concepts derived from sense perceptions and such concepts never fully adapt themselves to spiritual realities. Other states of sleep also occasionally pass over into somnambulism, and that is why we can distinguish, apart from natural somnambulism, an artificial somnambulism (especially in post-hypnotic manifestations) and a pathological or hysterical somnambulism. People even speak of the ecstatic or mystical state as a fifth form of somnambulism,[13] "in which the upsurge of the soul and its sovereign power over the body attain their most sublime expression".

It is even said that drops in temperature have been observed in the proximity of such somnambulists, and that there have often been streams of cool air. If such statements should be substantiated, the effect can only derive from some "reordering of physical energy".

---

[13] Moser, *Okkultismus*, p. 872.

II

PATHOLOGICAL SLEEP AND SOMNAMBULISM

[Among the phenomena of pathological sleep and somnambulism we must class certain states of day-dreaming, in which the senses are chronically dimmed, and the subject, who tends to go about in a kind of waking trance, enjoys powers of what is sometimes quite valid extra-sensory perception. The Spökenkiekers of Westphalia (A) are a case in point.

The author also reckons the phenomena of hysteria (B) as falling under those of pathological sleep, in so far as the perceptions of reality are distorted, while the subconscious influences the physical, making to some extent use of the mechanism of the spirit-soul.

The phenomenon of witches' dreams (C), so widespread throughout the Middle Ages, is even more aptly ranged under this head. Here the sensory mechanism was deliberately distorted and in part narcotized by drugs, which in their turn played havoc with the mental life. This dimming of the senses did, however, sometimes genuinely have the effect of releasing the dormant powers of the soul, and witches often saw things by clairvoyance which were actual facts, though they tended to misinterpret what they saw.

The medium (D) is another allied type, usually a person of hysterical disposition whose subconscious is unduly active, while his sense perceptions tend to be distorted. The relevant phenomena are dealt with later.

The activity of the residual spiritual elements of the soul, coupled, as such activity usually is, with an imperfect apprehension of objective reality, often is the essential stuff of madness (E). That madness and genius are allied is a commonplace. The author's theory helps to furnish an explanation for this fact.]

It is possible that the section on natural sleep and dreams and particularly the passages on natural somnambulism may have raised the question in the reader's mind whether these phenomena can still be regarded as normal and healthy, or whether we have not actually passed over into the abnormal and pathological. Actually the transition is gradual and proceeds by stages. Numbness (of the senses) does sometimes very gradually become chronic and the person concerned begins to dream with open eyes. People pass slowly through this development in cases of second sight, in the various states of hysteria and in actual madness.

It was mentioned above that the soul, as a spirit, forgets nothing that it has once learned. During life, however, it makes use of the body and of the convolutions of the brain in order to retain its experiences; but because bodily organs are very limited, much is necessarily forgotten, much, that is to say, must sink below the threshold of consciousness and remain stored up in the cells of the brain, one experience being packed above the other, so that these memories only exist on the spiritual side of the soul.

Although, however, these impressions do not remain in the consciousness, they nevertheless exercise their often devastating effect on the entire man according to the ideomotor law. Thus the suffering of an insult at some time in the past will, even when the insult has been forgotten, cause the personality of the individual who inflicted it to appear unsympathetic, and a single experience will influence us in all our actions, in our character and our behaviour (Cumberlandism); it will influence our voice, our physiognomy, the lines on our hand (chiromancy), the iris of our eye (eye diagnosis), it will influence the health of our body and of our soul. (Chiromancy and eye diagnosis are today treated as branches of genuine science.)

(A) SECOND SIGHT

A special form of these pathological dreams is to be found in the waking dreams which intermittently occur in the so-called second sight of the Spökenkieker in Westphalia and among similarly endowed persons in Scotland, the Tyrol, and other places where the inhabitants live far away from the noise and bustle of ordinary life and consequently lead a relatively monotonous life conducive to day-dreaming. In such people there is a natural tendency for sense perceptions to be dulled—as it is with the Indians or the Taoists of the Gobi deserts and the Druids or magicians in the woods. Such, by prophecy and healing, continually gain great influence over people. These visions are usually an intimation that takes the form of an image,[1] or the subconscious is in a special way activated by particular surroundings. The gift

---

[1] Bessmer, *Stimmen der Zeit*, 76, 1909.

vanishes when such people leave that territory, and returns to them when they themselves return. Such people are convinced that they will lose the gift if they reveal what they have foreseen, and they often do so for that very reason—in order to heal themselves, for they feel the gift to be a burden: *O sprich ein Gebet inbrünstig und echt, für den Seher der Nacht, das gequälte Geschlecht*[2] (Oh, say a prayer, fervent and true, for the seer of the night, the tortured race), and Karl Spitta's mother speaks of the "sorrowful gift" with which her son was cursed.

> In the Ötztal second sight is peculiarly endemic: In a village in winter [Malfatti tells us] all the members of a household sit round a fire, the men smoking, the women spinning. Suddenly two of the latter cry out aloud, "Did you see it too?"—"Yes." And now they declare, confirming each other, that at such and such a place an avalanche has overwhelmed such and such persons together with their wagon. And the men immediately stand up, fetch their gear, go off on the rough, dangerous road to save what still can be saved. They are as certain that the subject of the vision is true as if they had been present at the actual event and had seen the whole thing with their own eyes.[3]

Dr Zur Bonsen, who wrote a book[4] on this subject and followed it with a sequel (1920), criticizes Myers, who has also published on this theme,[5] and says: "They (the Spökenkieker) completely dispelled any doubts I may have had about the genuineness of this phenomenon, the existence of which was confirmed both by tradition and reports of actual experience, and filled me with the same certitude that animated the late Provost of Cologne Cathedral, Dr Berlage, who wrote in 1908: 'Those who foresee coming events are in my view transported into that condition which affects the soul, when it divests itself of the element of time and rises far above both time and space. The seer and his gifts are for me a proof of the existence and of the spiritual character of the soul, Josef von Görres took a similar view of the gift of second sight.'"[6]

Sound theology teaches that man can never know what is really future. He can only draw conclusions which are more or less certain and which postulate

---

[2] Droste-Hülshoff.
[3] Malfatti, *Menschenseele und Okkultismus*, p. 116.
[4] *Das zweite Gesicht*, Cologne, 1910-1914.
[5] *The Subliminal Self*.
[6] Cf. Feldmann, *Okkulte Philosophie*, p. 153.

the operation of natural causes. Where, however, the future remains to be determined by free decision, he cannot know it, not even through the subconscious, the sphere of the partly body-free soul, for not even the spirits, the angels have such knowledge, but only God, and since one cannot always assume that God is himself miraculously acting in such visions, we must always in such cases endeavour to find another solution.

Concerning second sight we may say this: where we are concerned with the knowing of the past, or the present, i.e. with something that is already an actual fact, this can be achieved by those people who live in a more or less perpetual state of trance. The case is different when they allegedly foresee the future. Since their visions almost always involve tragic happenings of some kind—fires, burials, serious mishaps and the like—it may well happen that a part of what they profess to foresee really comes to pass. The other happenings which they professed to foresee in their visions are forgotten, so that the impression ultimately remains that all that was foreseen actually happened, though in reality this was only true of a small percentage, when mere chance caused the thing foretold to occur. In any case people do not usually know what their visions mean. They see a fire, for instance, but it is only later, when something actually happens, that they relate it to the thing they have seen (see Staudenmaier; Bessmer, S.J.).

The visions of the Spökenkiekers are therefore not true predictions but pathological dreams, mixed with clairvoyance, of a kind that occurs under exceptional conditions. This does not imply that God does not ever grant men genuine prophecy, for many instances are on record. We have already spoken of the Sibyls. In recent times people always refer to Lenin's prophecy concerning the end of the Hohenzollerns and that of Malachi concerning the Popes. The most striking of all, however, is perhaps that of the Curé d'Ars, who said, "People will want to canonize me but they will have no time to do so because of the war that will have broken out," and indeed all was ready for his canonization in 1914, but because of the troubles of the war, this was delayed till 1925. That we should treat the utterances of saintly persons in a manner different from that in which we treat the phenomena of second sight is a matter which is explained elsewhere.[7]

---

[7] P. 117

(B) Hysteria

Naturally enough we cannot here decide the purely medical question as to the actual nature of hysteria; we are here discussing it from the psychological point of view, from that of the action of the spirit-soul and of the subconscious. We have already discussed the suggestive power exercised by dreams, that is, of the purely spiritual activities of the soul over the body. In hysteria this power attains pathological dimensions. It can begin almost imperceptibly, so that one doubts whether the symptoms are actually abnormal at all, and may then progress to full hysterical mania. One could therefore well speak of hysteria as hysterical somnambulism, even though the sufferer seems to be fully awake. The patient's corporal soul is partly asleep and is therefore impervious to rational processes of thought, while the subconscious exercises its devastating influences on the body. Hysterical sleep falls into the category of half-sleep dreams and must be due to some psychic or physical cause.

Medical science defines hysteria as a disturbed condition of the nerves whose anatomical nature and seat it does not yet know. It has thus become the "lumber room for the medically inexplicable", and the tendency is to enumerate under this head the most varied and even mutually contradictory symptoms. The name is usually derived from the Greek ὑστέρα (womb) and this brings it into connection with certain sexual states of the female body.

Dealing with the matter from the point of view of psychology, which is concerned with the spirit-soul, we must necessarily locate the seat of hysteria in the subconscious, which in this case acts upon the human body in the incalculable manner of a dream.

The name is also derived from the Greek word ὕστερον ("later", or "behind") and also from ὑστερέω (to remain over) and thus clearly expresses the idea that the source of the malady lies behind consciousness, in the subconscious, where experiences that lie buried there exert their baneful influence on the person concerned, producing disease, mania, compulsive actions and eccentricities. It is certain that thoughts and emotions can produce organic changes such as blushing, loss of colour and sensual excitement. The word "emotion", with its notion of movement, is here peculiarly apt, for according to the psychiatrist Ebbinghaus, our thought and will can only have power over our motor apparatus as the result of kinaesthetic imagery.[8] In hysteria such imagery is present in the subconscious and exerts its influence on the patient's motor nerves.

Hysteria and a hysterical character are therefore two different things. Hysteria is an abnormal psychical condition which occurs when psychical experiences bring correlated physical phenomena in their train, which then, either through interest or habit, become permanent and fixed. What we have to deal with are psychogenic functional disturbances of the body, based on the instinct for self-preservation or preservation of the race and usually brought into being by a "flight into disease". Niedermeyer defines hysteria as the faculty of producing psychogenic somatic disease symptoms, which he alleges originate in the subconscious.[9]

Since moreover these subconscious faculties are closely related to the purely spiritual powers of the soul, they are able to exert the same influence upon the body and on matter as is exerted by a pure spirit. As once the preternatural powers of man in Paradise influenced the body, so today the powers of the subconscious can do harm to a degree that resists every medical skill, and only disappear when the cause is removed from the spirit itself This is today attempted in psychoanalysis, in which Professor Sigmund Freud did such remarkable pioneer work, although this scientist almost entirely nullified what he had gained by asserting, in accordance with the pansexual ideas of his time, that only repressed sexual desires were hidden in the subconscious, and that these need only be awakened and satisfied for the patient to be healed.

Scientists like Alfred Adler,[10] Maurice Rappaport,[11] Alexis Carrel,[12] Fr Josef Donat, S.J.,[13] reject the Freudian conception, partly because of its forced interpretation of the facts, and also because of its disproportionate emphasis on the sexual element, particularly in the case of children. "In regard to this last," writes the liberal Alfred Lehmann,[14] "Freud may have had a more ample

---

[8] *Grundzüge der Psychologie*, I, 719 ff.

[9] *Handbuch der speziellen Pastoralmedizin*, V, B., pp. 87 ff.

[10] *Individualpsychologie*.

[11] *Sozialismus, Religion und Judenfrage*, Vienna-Leipzig, 1919.

[12] Der *Mensch*, Stuttgart, 1937, p. 282: "Freud has done more harm even than those scientists whose outlook is completely mechanistic."

[13] *Über Psychoanalyse und Individualpsychologie*, Innsbruck, 1932.

[14] *Aberglaube und Zauberei* 3, Stuttgart, 1925, p. 553.

field of observation in Vienna than is normally available to those engaged on research, and thus have become somewhat one-sided in his outlook. He certainly cannot be considered very greatly to have increased our understanding of the psychological relevance of our dreams or our proficiency in applying to their analysis the many latent elements in our psychic life, elements which in many instances reach far back into the past". Freud's thought therefore seems on the whole too narrow. For all that, however, he has pointed the way toward an understanding of the power and dangers in the subconscious and has thus helped us towards the possibility of curing these diseases. Frankl in his "Logotherapy" correctly carries on the line of reasoning. The attempt is being made to reawaken the impressions that lie in the subconscious, to analyse them, and so to get the whole process of thought to run correctly, and in this fashion to effect a cure. A few examples may serve to elucidate what has been said:

A girl who was very fond of reading was suddenly seized with a completely inexplicable loathing for this pursuit. Psychoanalysis disclosed that once while she was reading a book, she suddenly saw the house in which her sick father was living in flames. She ran to the place in terror and could only save her father with great difficulty. The experience remained in her subconscious and was the cause of the feeling of loathing in question. Psychoanalysis corrected her judgment, and the morbid idea disappeared.

A young man of blameless life suffered under the handicap that he blushed whenever there was mention of a theft in his presence, or of any circumstance that might suggest the suspicion of such a thing. As a result his friends began to think that he had something on his conscience. Once when he was a boy he came under suspicion of having stolen a sum of money, and although the true facts of the matter were soon discovered and his innocence established, nevertheless the suspicion of his honesty caused so profound a spiritual disturbance that he could never banish the fear that he might again be accused of such a crime. He therefore blushed on every occasion. It needed the whole of the psychoanalyst's skill to talk him out of his fear.

A well-bred woman was in the habit of continually washing the water-taps in the house. Sometimes she got up at night to repeat this washing, although she had already done it just before. While she was a child she had seen a sick dog lick a tap and .had felt such repulsion that she had acquired the habit in question. Medical skill opened up her subconscious mind, partly with the aid of hypnosis and partly without it, and thus administered the necessary corrective action.

The uncanny characteristic of the subconscious is that it acts "nonsensically", since, like the dream, it lacks the leadership of reasons. The latter draws its experience from sense perceptions, and to these it must again submit its judgments. The same process is artificially repeated in psychoanalysis, and thus inferences which were originally erroneous are corrected.

We can draw an inference from the nature of the cure as to the character of the actual disease. In so far as action on the subconscious contrives to remove the disturbances, it follows that it is in the subconscious that these are to be found, and our general suspicion—down to the very derivation of this word—seems to be confirmed. Therefore, however many symptoms one enumerates, and however much doctors may feel under an obligation to direct their attention to the individual bodily disabilities and to distinguish between different types of hysteria in their diagnoses, there can be no more doubt as to the basic nature of the disease. The essence of hysteria is that certain ideas which have taken crude symbolic shape have become fixed in the unconscious part of the (spirit)-soul, and that these act upon the body and influence its health. A true therapy must therefore not confine itself to bodily symptoms but must seek the seat of the disease in the unconscious, and must seek to discover the concrete idea that is the cause of the disturbance.[15]

We might usefully make an addition to this general conclusion by discussing another matter which has become topical through the large number of appearances of the Blessed Virgin which have recently taken place. This is the so-called *Eidetik*, which frequently occurs among children at the age of puberty. It consists of the circumstance that impressions that have been previously received affect the imagination so vividly and are so translated by that same imagination and endowed to such an extent with verisimilitude and movement that the persons concerned genuinely believe that they are having a vision. The psychophysical causes are the same as those of hysteria, i.e. impressions which have become fixed in the subconscious affect the body as

---

[15] See below pp. 196-197.

in hysteria and produce functional disturbance of the optic nerves so that a psychogenic image results before the individual's vision. In the much discussed Heroldsbach case, for instance, it has been proved that the children saw pictures of biblical history, or other pictures that existed in the neighbourhood, in the form of a vision which was so vivid that they were convinced of its objective reality, and remained so convinced.

Much experience and a very subtle discernment are necessary to distinguish such eidetic images[16] from genuine visions. Thus, for instance, when the children in Heroldsbach saw the Holy Trinity, they reproduced a picture that hung in the local presbytery showing the Trinity with Our Lady in front of it. The children represented their vision as consisting of three persons, but their confused memory caused them to see Our Lady as one of the persons of the Trinity. They also saw the figure of the dove above it. When cross-questioned, they became uncertain and declared that the Holy Ghost, "the dove", could be left out—otherwise there would have been four persons.

When one compares the certitude of St Bernadette or of the children of Fatima with this kind of thing, the difference is clear enough, though ordinary folk are not always very ready to recognize it.

Admittedly the matter becomes more complicated when these eidetic pictures are mingled with genuine visions. In such cases distinction becomes for all practical purposes impossible. The Church therefore explicitly states that the canonization of a saint does not mean that she recognizes all his visions as genuine. Very few visions are admitted by her.

(C) Witches and their Delusions

We have all heard of the epidemic of witches' dreams in the Middle Ages, dreams which the dreamers mistook for reality, and which, of course, sometimes actually contained an admixture of truth. Thus a certain witch dreamed that she had murdered a child of a family that lived some hundred miles away, and accused herself of this crime before the judges. These in their turn started enquiries, and found that the child had actually died that night. What really happened was that the witch had seen the child's death in a true

---

[16] εἴδωλον=a thing seen, a picture: εἴδομαι=to see (*video*).

dream, and had quite erroneously ascribed it to her own sorceries. The judges, who were of course completely ignorant of any scientific explanation of the phenomenon and who agreed that the witch could not have known of all the circumstances by lawful means, condemned the woman to be burnt. The case can be looked on as typical, and we shudder when we reflect how many innocent people must have been condemned in this fashion. Most witches' dreams can be similarly interpreted—those for instance which led the dreamers to declare that they had attended a witches' Sabbath and presumably experienced all the sensual delights that this implied. Such dreams were the remnants and the results of vivid day-time fancies, reinforced by the witches' salve. This last was composed of belladonna and opium and was well calculated to produce hallucinations. Today things are rather different; today our anxious Christendom dreams up visions of the mother of God. Since 1931 no fewer than thirty-one cases involving some three hundred alleged appearances of Mary have been the subject of ecclesiastical examination and the great majority have been completely rejected. From the eastern states there have come since 1945 some two thousand reports of miraculous happenings, prophecies and other forms of solace for displaced persons who have been driven from their homes. People find comfort in these things as they do in the eidetic phenomena described above. It would therefore appear that Christian morality is today on a somewhat higher level,[17] although the belief in witches is still said to persist in such places as the Lüneburger Heide.[18]

Schneider[19] writes in this connection:

If we seek for a cause of these sad and ugly hallucinations, we can discover both a physical and a psychic one. In the days of the witches the craze for sorcery, which till then had hidden itself in darkness, had seized on the masses like a plague. The physical means which helped this ruinous mania to spread were the narcotic potions and salves. The salves are described in considerable detail by Johannes Wierus (Weier), the personal physician of the Duke of Cleves, in his book *De praestigiis daemonum et incantationibus ac veneficiis, libri IV* (Bâle, 1563). Weier was a Calvinist and one of the first opponents with any influence of the witch trials. The salves were chiefly made up of wild celery

---

[17] *Orbis catholicus*, 1952, p. 497.
[18] See *Süddeutsche Zeitung*, 30.8.1952.
[19] *Der neuere Geisterglaube*, pp. 74 ff.

(*Apium palustre*), wolf's bane (*Aconitum lycoctonum*), poplar, birch and other ingredients; often the juice of deadly nightshade and henbane were added. The salve induced sleep and numbness, and was also reckoned as a safeguard against witchcraft. The magical character of what were accounted the most important herbs in witchcraft appears to some extent in their names—wolf's milk (*Euphorbium*) (also known as devil's milk), devil's claw (*lycopodium clavatum*), etc. For the conjuring of the weather, witches used traveller's joy (*Clematis vitalba*) and cornbind (*Convolvulus arvensis*)—the German names are devil's thread and devil's gut—and besides this there were ramping fumitory, horse elder, wormwood, red spur-valerian and others.

In the old pharmacopeias and medical books,[20] there is a whole host of prescriptions against witchcraft and diabolical assault. Among these antimagical preparations there is frequent mention of a magic balsam and of a smoke powder. Particularly famous among magical herbs were St John's wort, the juice of which was administered to witches to make them confess under torture. The use of this herb was already known to the pagans and was in the nineteenth century employed by the seer of Prevorst in the preparation of amulets. Devil's bit scabious (*Morsus diabolic* or *scabiosa succisa*) was also among the herbs used for anti-magical purposes. For the use of aphrodisiacs, see Freimarck (*Hexensalben*), also Schrenck-Notzing, who has dealt with the important rôle played by narcotic drugs in hypnotism, with especial regard to Indian hemp (Leipzig, 1891); see also *Anthropos*, 1935, 276, on *Die Peijotewurzel*. These salves engendered feelings of lust, hallucinations, visions of spirits, and opened the door of the soul to magic, as it was at that time understood. Aconite, according to Cardanus, produces the sensation of flying, while atropin causes horrific spectres to appear, and thorn-apple, used in the preparation of philtres, incites to voluptuousness.

These allegedly magic preparations, derived as they were from ingredients that were particularly harmful to man, easily threw out of control the female organism and brought it to that loathsome form of ecstasy known as the witches' sabbath, which culminates in a kind of devilish antithesis to that tender and ideal bridal relation, itself a product of special grace, that subsists between Christ and the soul that truly loves God. The use of these physical stimulants soon became so widespread that the witch and her pot of salves became indissolubly associated with one another in the popular mind. A number of judicial enquiries have established the fact that there were substantial grounds for this widespread feeling.

---

[20] Cf. Horst, *Dämonomagie*, Vol. II, pp. 305 ff.

Moreover since these hideous fantasies of the witches' ride and the witches' dance actually became the subjects of plastic and pictorial representation, nothing could dispel the conviction of these duped and unfortunate women that they had truly wantoned with the devil, kissed the goat, and assisted at all the other orgies of the witches' sabbath. Even after the original witch mania had died down, a kind of shadow cult of the witches' sabbath seems to have occurred in the form of the so-called Black Mass, though Freimarck tells us that there is very little record of any actual celebration of Black Masses except in the luxuriant imagination of litérateurs. The remarkable thing in these cases is the persistence of the illusion. We get the same phenomena in hysterical people and in sufferers from typhus. Often such persons remain incapable long after the time of the attack of distinguishing between their hallucinations and the real world.

This is really what happened in the matter of these witches' dreams. They were often so vivid that the witches themselves persisted in believing in their reality. It was this that made them confess to their wholly imaginary misdeeds. It is of course quite true that had they not in their waking state had some desire for intercourse with the devil, and had they not when in that state made use of these disgusting drugs, their dreams would not have had this quality of intense vividness which we find in them over a period of some five hundred year. It is this unlawful desire and the acts for which it provided the motive that constitutes the tragic guilt of these poor women and also lends some slight justification to their persecution. Nevertheless all the tests applied during this time in the supposed discovery of witches—such tests usually depended in one way or another on the insensibility to physical pain—merely illustrate that withdrawal of the senses which we have now come to recognize as one of the conditions for the functioning of the partly body-free soul and is the necessary means for this form of knowledge and dreams.

(D) THE MEDIUM

Another form in which the subconscious manifests itself is in the activities of mediums which today have attained such a sorry notoriety. More will be said on this subject when we deal with artificial sleep; it is mentioned here because these phenomena are often of a pathological kind. People are surprised when they hear of a medium disclosing things that till then had been hidden, or when they hear of them speaking in foreign tongues, though actually they obtain all this either out of their own subconscious or out of that of other people. That is why they have never really revealed anything new that could be of service to science.

Professor Th. Flournoy in his book *Des Indes à la Planete Mars* gives a very instructive example of this truth; he cites the case of the medium Helen Smith, who passed through four different phases. In the first of these her guide was a certain Leopold who had protected her when she was ten years old and was attacked by a large dog, and who now also took her part when in her mediumistic phases she was pestered by irresponsible boys.

Later she represented herself to be the Indian princess Simondini who lived in the sixteenth century as the wife of an Indian rajah. Helen spoke Sanscrit and Arabic. Actually, however, she had found the information about India in her father's library, where she had also read sentences in Sanscrit and Arabic, which, when in a trance, she brought forth from her subconscious.

On another occasion she invented a story about Marie Antoinette, in which she represented herself as the incarnation of the latter. She had in point of fact dreamed the whole thing; ever since childhood she had imagined herself to be the child of highly placed persons and believed that she had merely been handed over to another family for her upbringing. She found a symbol of her imaginative yearnings in the unhappy queen. Finally she believed herself to be in communication with an inhabitant of Mars and also spoke the Martian language, which turned out to be a debased form of French. All we heard from the said Martian was a selection of what was at the time already being written concerning the putative inhabitants of that planet. Thus it was in every case the subconscious and nothing else that came to the surface in her somnambulistic states. The woman herself died in a madhouse.

The example of this woman not only shows the extent of the influence of the subconscious but also the danger involved when it is permitted to usurp the place of the waking consciousness; indeed this usually leads to complete madness. It has been the practice to intensify this putting out of action of the waking mind by various artificial means, such as suggestion and hypnosis. This has often been done, despite the existence of pathological hysterical proclivities, such as are in point of fact usually present in most mediums.

Let us here confine ourselves to some of the more famous mediums, to those in fact who in their day, and particularly in the nineteenth century, attracted considerable attention. Since the first world war such people have tended more and more to diminish in number, for the phenomenon is bound up with the character of the time; the witches had their day, as did the magicians before them. After the witches came the mediums. Today the typical figures are probably the eidetics, who certainly are much more harmless than the rest.

Eusapia Paladino is generally referred to as the most famous of all mediums. She was born in Naples and was examined by Lombroso (1836-1909) and by other scientists in Milan, Paris and America, and produced all the usual phenomena that mediums at one time or another produce—luminosities, movement of objects, levitations, changes of weight, hallucinations, spirit messages, materializations, cold winds—and finally fraud.

Another medium was Home, who was examined by Crookes (1832-1919). He was the only medium who was never caught in any kind of fraud. He was himself a writer and did much to help expose frauds by other mediums.[21] Slade, who had good abilities, was repeatedly exposed as a fraud.

We Austrians are particularly interested in the Schneider family in Braunau. Two of its sons, Willy and Rudy, showed mediumistic powers. They were examined by Schrenck-Notzing and were finally exposed by him. Today Rudy owns an automobile driving school in Weyer and has lost all his old faculties. Frau Silbert in Graz attracted much notice among her friends. Unlike other mediums, who like to work in the dark, she displayed her arts in the light. However, she descended to many theatrical tricks, so that in the end she was no longer taken seriously. For a time, however, she was studied by serious researchers and held in considerable esteem.

The Hungarian Laszlo and the Dane Eynar Nielsen were caught in frauds. Eva C., who took a number of other names, Angelique Cottin, Gottliebin Dittius, the Polish woman Tomczyk, Kluski and Guzik, for some time attracted the attention of men of science; so did Erto, Kraus, Zugun, Vollhart, Margery, Millesimo and finally Mirabelli.

---

[21] *Lights and Shadows of Spiritualism*, Virtue & Co., London, 1877.

If we speak of fraud here, we must distinguish between deliberate fraud such as was practised by Schneider père in Braunau and the so-called mediumistic deceit which mediums practise quite unknowingly. These may know that some particular phenomenon is to occur, but they cannot bring it off. It is then that the subconscious starts to take a hand and, as in hysteria, sets the motor centres of the body going, so that these simulate the desired effect. This is why the activities of mediums and occultism in general are today in bad odour, and why so many serious men of science have quite made up their minds that they will have nothing to do with it. There is, of course, also the effect of the prevalent materialist philosophy, which may well fear for its survival once it starts busying itself objectively with the miraculous or the diabolical.

The activity of mediums is therefore most certainly a pathological thing, though it can serve as a basis for a number of purely spiritual phenomena.

(E) ACTUAL MADNESS

To show that this kind of dreaming can lead to the complete derangement of the mind, and that even in that state traces of the original paradisal powers would still be present, it would be necessary to write an entire book on psychiatry and this is not the writer's intention. A few illustrations may, however, be given. People say, "Children and fools speak the truth", which means that though the last-named are for all practical purposes incapable, they nevertheless sometimes, by means of a marvellous intuition, grasp truths that escape other people. In the medieval courts of the nobility the court fool often played a very important part; he was allowed great freedom and often displayed a degree of intuition which others did not possess and so was often able to declare truths by which the rulers were quite ready to profit.

Such people are often actually invalids. Schneider[22] tells the story of the servant of a Spanish diplomat who was often present during important interviews on which his master was engaged, despite the fact that he was a man of very limited education. "Then one day he was attacked by a disease of the brain and now in his delirium developed the most brilliant ideas on the

---

[22] *Der neuere Geisterglaube*, p. 490.

political interests of the various powers, so much so that his master began to believe that a hidden genius was here coming to light and decided in future to employ him as a secretary, but to his great regret the gift disappeared as soon as the brain malady was cured."

A similar story, dating back to imperial times, is told in Brazil. Pedro II once was visiting a hospital and was accompanied by a gentleman who gave him the most excellent explanations of the medical arrangements, the nature of the various ailments that were being treated, the probability of cures, etc., so much so that the Emperor marvelled and was actually considering him for a post of great responsibility. As he left he said a few words of appreciation, whereupon his learned guide remarked, "I can do more than that, I can crow like a cock", and the man immediately gave some powerful examples of this accomplishment. The Emperor now realized that the man who had displayed such intuitive versatility was actually a madman.

Even the ancients knew how closely related were genius and madness. Thus Plato speaks in the *Phaedrus* of a "divine madness" that was superior to all sober reflection. Cicero speaks of a *furor poeticus* and Horace of *amabilis insania*, Shakespeare of the poet's eye "in a fine frenzy rolling", Lamartine of "*cette maladie mentale qu'on appelle genie*"; Pascal says "*L'extrême esprit est voisin de l'extreme folie*", while Schiller, in a letter to Körner of 1st December, 1788, makes this observation his own, and is glad of the "madness that is to be found in all creative spirits".[23]

Another thing that we can observe and that helps to illuminate the truth about this matter is the fact that eccentricities and even manias are often the accompaniment of inventive genius. We are here concerned with persons who intuitively grasp a truth, but are unable to interpret it correctly and yet cannot shake themselves free from it; since they cannot translate it into practical terms they twist it into a mania, from which they cannot escape back into the world of practical reality.

Fixed ideas and compulsive obsessions often have this origin. One could define these and indeed all manias as the results of acts of knowledge on the part of the purely spiritual soul which could not translate them into terms of ordinary life, and consequently failed to give them a correct interpretation.

---

[23] Schneider, *op. cit.*, p. 492.

Demonomania arises from the fact that some persons become aware of the influence of the subconscious. Since they conceive of this as something essentially different from themselves, and even as something hostile to themselves, they believe that they are the victims of diabolical possession. That there actually is such a thing as diabolical possession is a matter which we shall discuss at a later stage.

In all these conditions of madness, that condition of detachment from sense, of numbness, sets in which we shall also find in the various states of artificial sleep. It is indeed liable to become chronic, so that such persons are useless for the purposes of ordinary life. All this merely provides further proof of the danger involved in all the games played with and by mediums under hypnosis and in spiritualism generally and shows that they are quite liable to end in actual madness.

The statement that madmen may possess the faculty of intuitive knowledge need not puzzle the reader, for the soul itself is never sick. Indeed, as a spirit, it is immune against sickness; only the body and senses can be thus afflicted. Madmen and mental defectives are either persons who have suffered some impairment—blind persons and deaf-mutes usually do not attain a mentality exceeding that of a fourteen-year-old—or they are "deranged" so that they cannot carry over the acts of the reason and the will into actual life, as they ought, but must twist them and correlate them incorrectly and so make them appear meaningless.

Actually we distinguish between anaesthesia, hyperaesthesia, and paraesthesia, according to whether the sensibilities of the patient are too slight, too strong or erroneous—that is to say, if he has sense perceptions which correspond to no objective reality but are imposed on him by the subconscious, as is the case with people under hypnotic influence. The imagination in such cases is tortured by hallucinations and illusions of the kind which Staudenmaier evoked artificially, there then ensue loss of memory, aphasia, perversions, distracted behaviour and the kind of irritability that afflicts the hysterical, also compulsive and maniacal ideas, phobias, various compulsive actions, cleptomania, pyromania, dipsomania (alcoholism), all of which according to the latest medical opinion owe their origin to invasions of the subconscious mind and can only be treated on that basis—assuming of course that there has been no actual physical damage. The patients are really in a state similar to that of sleep; the actions of the soul are uncontrolled and uncontrollable.

> Madness [writes Mercier] has been called "the dream of the waking man" and it is a very long dream. In his normal state man has the power of directing the attention of his faculty of knowledge towards the cognition of things and of subordinating his acts to a willed and rational purpose, in a word, he is master of his will and understanding; that man is mad who has lost possession of the conscious and free ego.[24]

Obviously these states of partial sleep which dull the sensorium can also be due to bodily injury; in such cases they can only be successfully dealt with by psychic treatment when the bodily defect has been removed. This last is admittedly more difficult in the case of such notorious forms of neurosis as neurasthenia, psychasthenia, in which the actual nerves are in a diseased condition. A strong resemblance to dreamers is borne by schizophrenics and by many victims of mania. In such cases the influences of the subconscious can best be dealt with by one of the Freudian methods—at least in the initial stages of the malady:

> Freud's method [writes Donat] demonstrates the correctness of the theory that half-conscious psychic processes and those that have stuck in the unconscious memory and are reproduced from there, have a great influence on our inner life, and also on disease . . . it regards the whole man, his development, and in particular his childhood, and seeks to form a correct estimate of the aptitudes, difficulties and maladies from the whole picture thus obtained, and to treat them; it strives diligently to penetrate to the hidden recesses of the inner life. It lays particular stress on the subconscious . . . and has made a considerable contribution to psychotherapy.[25]

Nevertheless the defects mentioned above still affect the method, and it will only be after it has purified itself from these that it will be able to lead us to our goal.

The further madness progresses towards amentia and paranoia, to feebleness of mind and idiocy, the less chance there is of eliminating the bodily

---

[24] Mercier, *Psychologie*, II, p. 206.
[25] Donat, *Psychologie*, pp. 381 ff.

impairments and so of creating the necessary conditions for psychological influence; the rarer then also become the so-called lucid intervals, which constitute a kind of awakening; still less then can we speak of intuitive perceptions in certain matters, a thing which in milder cases is sometimes to be observed and which thus lays bare the whole psychic mechanism in a manner which confirms the theory here set forth. We noted above that in the hour of death such lucid moments often occur when the perception is very profound indeed. This derives from the fact that the diseased parts of the body die first. The soul thus becomes free for the aforementioned perceptions—though unfortunately this is then too late. But this explains why even mad persons have often quite remarkably wise insight into things in the hour of death.

At the conclusion of this chapter we might add that at the moment research is being undertaken into the connections between mental derangement and extra-sensory perception.[26] This is being done at Durham University, U.S.A., under Rhine[27] and at Innsbruck by Köck, Caruso and Urban.[28] No agreed results have as yet been obtained. Rhine cannot show a number of positive results in excess of what might be expected from the general law of chance, but Urban has been able to show a much larger number, when the patients could be subjected to influences which dispelled their inhibitions, i.e. when they were put into a semi-soporific state, as was the case with schizophrenics after narco-analysis and electro-shock.

These results entirely agree with the assumptions here set forth, since people, in so far as they are able still to have perceptions at all, are better able to perform intuitive acts of knowledge when their senses are dimmed than in a state of normal waking consciousness.

---

[26] ESP, see pp. 73 and 151.

[27] J. B. Rhine, "Psi Phenomena and Psychiatry", in *Proceedings of the Royal Society of Medicine*, Vol. 43, 1950.

[28] *Parapsychologie und Psychiatry*, by H. J. Urban, in *Pöltzl Festschrift*, Innsbruck, Deutsche medizinische Rundschau, 1949.

III

THE PHENOMENA OF ARTIFICIAL SLEEP

[Artificial sleep by means of hypnosis, or self-induced trance, is one of the most important and one of the most successful means of calling occult phenomena into being. These are usually classified under the heads of telepathy (A), clairvoyance (B) and the physical phenomena (C). Telepathy and clairvoyance are, in the author's view, the same, but contemporary opinion has tended to concentrate on the phenomena that can be more appropriately classified under the first of these heads, because they appear to it, quite erroneously, to be explicable by the analogy of radio waves. The physical phenomena, telacoustic phenomena, usually known as raps (i), telekinesis, i.e. levitation of objects (ii), and the teleplastic phenomena (iii), materializations, apports, etc., seem only explicable, where they are not the result of fraud, if we accept the author's contention that the human soul possesses vestigially the powers of a pure spirit and so can act directly on matter.]

I have tried to establish the general principle that the soul, if it is to function as a pure spirit, must withdraw itself from the life of the senses. Such a withdrawal takes place chiefly in sleep. Even in their waking state, many people can lapse into a dream state that is more or less morbid and may find its expression in actual words and deeds. This occurs to an even greater degree in sleep, in which this day-dreaming becomes a dream in the ordinary sense of that term. Such a dream may become an acted dream, i.e. it may develop into somnambulism, which may gradually become morbid and chronic and may actually turn into madness. Since, however, certain phenomena occur in this state which give grounds for assuming a heightened spiritual life, people have hit on the idea of producing it artificially, as in trance and hypnosis.

The techniques of producing such a state are various, and trance is to be distinguished from hypnosis by the fact that in the latter a person other than the subject has a part to play, and puts the hypnotized person under his influence and guidance; trance is a form of self-hypnotism, and is regularly practised by those persons who produce occult phenomena. Such persons are called mediums, because they are supposed to act as intermediaries between this and "the other world"; for the most part they are already sick people, and tend, as we have already seen, to be nervous, distracted or at any rate erratic and unsteady in their psychological make-up. Their peculiarities are intensified in trance.

Though in the case of more highly developed mediums appearances would seem to indicate that there was no trance at all, nevertheless such a state actually obtains in greater or lesser degree, so that in their case also one can speak of an artificial sleep, and all of them confirm the curious fact, for which modern science can offer no explanation, that the experiments are the more successful, the more the waking consciousness is put out of action—which our theory would automatically lead us to expect. It is most rare (indeed, it only happens in the case of highly developed subjects) for a state of at least partial somnolence not to be required, if phenomena are to result. Three groups of extrasensory happenings are usually referred to, namely: telepathy, clairvoyance and physical manifestations; and with these we now propose to deal.

(A) Telepathy

Telepathy, that is to say, "feeling at a distance" τέλος = far, πάσχειν, to suffer or feel), is defined as the influencing of one mind by another otherwise than through the organs of sense ("mind acts on mind otherwise than through the recognized organs of sense", Myers and Gurney); many parapsychologists treat it as the only occult manifestation with a claim to serious recognition, while clairvoyance and physical manifestations are either ascribed to telepathy or written down as illusion and fraud. Telepathy is more favourably regarded because it is believed by some people to admit in the last resort of a physical explanation, for they imagine that the communication between the two souls takes place by means of invisible waves, analogous to radio waves, which emanate from the "transmitting soul" and are duly "received" by the other. We do not actually know anything of these waves, they say, but they must exist; they are a postulate which must be accepted, if the laws of nature are not to be violated, for when the least example of telepathy is established as a spiritual phenomenon, "the reality of the world of the spirit has been scientifically established" (W. Rathenau) and, to quote Jodl, "such transference of thought from one brain to another, without any perceptible physical agency being there to receive it, would imply the making of a rent through the entire structure of the sciences and, if compelling proof were to be established, would lead to a revision of our most fundamental conceptions".[1] In telepathy two souls are assumed, of which one can be regarded as the transmitter and the other as the receiver, but in clairvoyance only one soul is concerned, the receiving soul, which apprehends a lifeless object, though this last, according to the theory, can also transmit because the rays adhere to it like an infection, because it has been "bethought". Since this appears somewhat too far-fetched, clairvoyance is rejected out of hand—by such men as Baerwald, for instance. Baerwald's theory is thus shown to be wholly uncritical and one-sided. It is obviously, and in the deepest sense of the words, one which is not based on sound objective grounds at all, but merely on the arbitrary assumption that such a thing as clairvoyance must not be admitted to exist. Indeed so mild a writer as Driesch remarks that such a view seems so forced, and so governed by a preconceived opinion, that it does not deserve serious consideration at all.[2] Admittedly Driesch himself goes too far, for, to explain the fact of clairvoyance, he postulates the spiritualist hypothesis.[3]

However, not everything that calls itself telepathy is necessarily such. It would therefore be well to start by eliminating the various phenomena which can be explained by fraud, conscious and unconscious, by illusion, faulty interpretation of fact, jugglery, Cumberlandism (muscle-reading), or in some similar manner.

Among the actual instances of a genuine influencing of soul by soul we must first of all take account of the phenomena of mental suggestion. That people could be influenced by being spoken to has always been known; what has been in doubt is whether one person could be influenced by the thoughts of another when there has been no sense-perceptible sign by which the thought was communicated. Yet today it has been proved beyond any shadow of a doubt that this actually occurs. Mental suggestion is, as has already been indicated, a faint reflection of that intercourse of pure spirits which we called noopneustia.

---

[1] Jodl, *Lehrbuch der Psychologie*, Vienna, I, 166.
[2] Tischner, *Ergebnisse okkulter Forschung*, Stuttgart, 1950, p. 63.
[3] See *Hochland*, 1925-6, p. 93, in article "Parapsychologie und anerkannte Wissenschaft".

We have for instance this astonishing story: A medium by means of knocks elicits a communication. The supposed spirit says to a young man: "I am your aunt. When you were eight years old you sprained your ankle by falling off a tree, up which you had climbed to get a bird's nest. I was the only one who knew about this incident, since you mentioned it to nobody, not even to your mother." Does this really mean that the deceased aunt was manifesting herself? Certainly not! How else then can the thing be explained? Fr Heredia succinctly writes: "It is the human spirit which is able to read what is in the spirit of another." The communicating agent is simply the subconscious spirit of the person taking part in the seance. Memories of that day, the day on which he fell from a tree and told his aunt, were buried in that subconscious. Through his abnormal sensitivity the medium becomes aware of this influence on the young man's mind, and tells those present about it. This, or something very like it, is certainly my own explanation. The subconscious of the medium, while the latter is in a deep sleep, communicates directly with the spirit of the other person present, and so gains knowledge of the latter's thoughts, experiences, and even gets to know something about a place with which that other is familiar.

Mediums have the art of drawing knowledge out of the subconscious of the persons concerned, even when the latter are not themselves conscious of possessing that knowledge at all. A priest who was present at a seance was told by the medium that the soul of a friend was standing by him, and the medium then proceeded to spell the alleged friend's name out in detail. The good father then said that the name was unknown to him, and that he knew nothing of the dead person concerned. It was only on the way home that he doubted the accuracy of his own statement, and began to wonder whether the man in question had not been a colleague of his at the seminary. Finally he looked at the annual list, and found the name of a student who had died some fifteen years previously.

When confronted by such facts, uninstructed people believe that the medium is actually in communication with the dead, and that the dead person has really manifested himself. Actually the truth is very different. What happens is that the medium reads something in the subconscious of a person, who may be close at hand or far off, and influences those at the seance, who must remain as passive as possible, so that they assist in getting the table to rap out the desired message.

Bishop Schneider writes[4]: "It is stated that a purely mental suggestion is possible without any kind of sensory perception, so that all that is necessary on the part of the hypnotist is a simple act of the will, and he can thus send a person to sleep." So critical a scientist as Löwenfeld, the Munich neurologist, mentions various cases of so-called telepathy or suprasensory transmission of thought,[5] while Dr Dufoy relates a most interesting case of influence exerted from a distance. This doctor contrived to send an actress to sleep in her dressing-room in the theatre; the doctor himself was in a box unseen by anybody and the actress did not know of his presence. While exerting his influence upon her, he suggested to her that she should take over the part of a colleague who was ill—a part which she had seen acted, but not actually studied. The suggestion took effect at 10.30 p.m. According to Dr Dufoy's subsequent information, the actress, who was at this moment dressing, sank on to a couch and asked her dresser to let her rest a little. After a few minutes she got up, finished her dressing and went on to the stage, where, no doubt in a somnambulist state, she played the part with consummate skill. After the performance Dr Dufoy was compelled to awaken the actress, so that she could be present at a supper given by the manager.

Fr Castelein quotes the example of a woman who vomited gall on certain days and was healed by Dr Dufoy by means of hypnotism. When later the disease recurred, he was again called in; the woman recognized him when he rang the doorbell, and even when he turned into the street, so that later on he did not trouble to visit her at all, but treated her from a distance. He could even hypnotize and awaken her from a distance, a procedure which he followed with equally unvarying success with other patients. Fr Janet made the same experiments and was, as he tells us, able to hypnotize simply by the power of thought.[6] Another doctor named Lelut relates the following: he ordered a certain patient to wake up, and at the same moment concentrated on the thought that he did not want her to awake. The subject seemed

---

[4] *Der neuere Geisterglaube*, p. 117.

[5] Löwenfeld, *Somnambulismus und Spiritismus*, Wiesbaden, 1900, I. Heft, Von Grenzfragen des Nerven- und Seelenlebens, pp. 37 ff.

[6] In *Revue scientifique*, 1866.

confused and said, "Why do you order me to awake, when you don't want me to awake?"

Tischner[7] quotes the example of Dr Dusart, who, from a distance often kilometres, forbade a girl whom he had previously treated himself, and who was now being magnetized by her father, to fall asleep. Half an hour later, however, it struck him that this prohibition, if it actually became effective, might do the girl harm. He therefore cancelled it. Early next day he received an express letter from the father who informed him that on the previous day he had only succeeded in putting his daughter to sleep with great difficulty. She had declared that she had resisted him by special instruction from Dr Dusart and that she had only gone to sleep after receiving his permission. Moser (p. 283 ff.) records a whole list of such experiments where sleep was induced from a distance; the actual distance between the controlling individual and his subject is immaterial.

It is moreover possible not only to put a person to sleep by purely spiritual influence; movements and acts can also be suggested by this means. Thus the Frenchman Giberts gives a mental command to his somnambulist Léonie to go next day to the drawing-room and look at an album of photographs, despite the fact that at this hour she is usually in the kitchen. The command is meticulously carried out. Such orders tend to be carried out with a precision that increases with the degree to which the persons concerned are attuned to one another, and also with the degree to which the waking consciousness is put out of action.

Feelings and sensations can also be transmitted in this manner. A well-known trick is to give a person a glass of water and to suggest to them that it contains cod-liver oil. The person then rejects the drink with horror, but will quietly drink cod-liver oil when it is suggested to them that it is water. Such persons will also experience the taste of salt, cinnamon, sugar or ginger when ordered to do so, and can be made drunk with well water when the suggestion is made that it is alcohol. Pains can also be transmitted, so much so that dressings have to be put on burns; next day there is still "a pronounced swelling and redness" on a supposedly burnt arm.[8] It is said that drawings can be transmitted with marked success, though here clairvoyance appears to be

---

[7] *Ergebnisse*, p. 66.
[8] Moser, p. 302.

at work, for the drawing is not only a subject of thought, but is actually reproduced, even though the transmitting person only sees it for a moment. This is apparent from the gradual, piece by piece production of the drawings, as though the experimental subject could not see properly, and also from the confusion between right and left and between top and bottom.

That we are here chiefly concerned with the subconscious is apparent from the nature of the experience gained; the experiments are most successful when there is neither intensive attention nor complete distraction, for both these are functions of the waking consciousness. Intensive efforts of the will are also a disturbing factor, and can produce a lag in the effectiveness of the stimuli. The hypnosis must neither be too deep nor too slight; wholly deranged persons fail completely to yield results, but good results can be obtained from invalids with slightly manic tendencies.

An interesting subject is the transmission of dreams, both those that are deliberately induced and those of a spontaneous nature. Certain people wish to appear to others in the night, and actually do appear to them; that is to say, those others have a hallucination based on telepathy. There is, for instance, the case of a man who shares in all the dreams of his wife; even three persons can share a dream.[9] Flammarion records a whole number of dreams[10] which nearly all seem attributable to telepathy or clairvoyance, since in such cases the soul acts like that of a somnambulist or of a hypnotized person, and thus shows that it is equipped with faculties of which science knows nothing.

One of the most enigmatic phenomena is that which is known to parapsychology as rapport; it consists in an exceptional relationship or connection between the hypnotist and his subject, so that the latter thinks, feels and acts as the hypnotist desires. A distinction is often made between magnetic and hypnotic rapport, the latter being looked upon as much the weaker, indeed as a mere shadow of the former. The difference, however, is only one of degree, the magnetic rapport being the stronger because under the passes a greater part of the nervous system, which still remains wakeful under hypnosis, is sent to sleep, and the sleep of the whole subject thus becomes more profound than is the case when the hypnotist merely acts on the mind—

---

[9] Cf. Moser, pp. 340 ff.

[10] *Riddles of the Life of the Soul*, Flammarion (pp. 274-328 of German translation, Stuttgart, 1908).

though here too there are marked differences between one individual and another.

The reader will remember what was said above about a pure spirit's power of being influenced by suggestion on the part of another. Fr Gredt was so much impressed by the strength of this suggestive power that he rejected it *a priori* on the grounds that a spirit that was subject to it would no longer be free. Actually it is on the basis of this suggestibility that I have attempted to explain more closely one of the great mysteries of the Catholic faith. Now in hypnosis one of the persons concerned is in a state where the senses have withdrawn their functions, and is therefore more receptive to the influence of another intelligence, thus establishing a contact with that intelligence such as is not established with others. Thus in the case of this phenomenon also our hypothesis brings us closer to an explanation.

We have, however, also to reckon with yet another phenomenon of a purely physical nature, that of so-called animal magnetism. Certain students have suffered some confusion in this matter and have shown a tendency to reject certain truths about the soul which had already been established in favour of this theory of magnetism. We stand, they think, quite at a "turning-point".[11] Certainly there are phenomena such as luminosity, wind, the billowing of curtains which may be due to some kind of magnetic radiation and pathological emanations from the skin; it is just in the case of these physical phenomena that one has to be particularly careful. Even so, these influences cannot explain the raising of heavy tables and purely spiritual phenomena. Such physical powers, even if they are of a nuclear kind (positrons and electrons), still belong to the world of matter and cannot explain processes that are wholly within the soul.

J. Wüst and W. Wimmer have caused an even greater stir in the world of science by the discovery of magnetoid polarities in water diviners,[12] which can be transmitted like electric currents, and diverted and screened, and which are connected both with the magnetism of the earth and with animal magnetism. People even think that the magnetism of the earth is the ultimate source of life

---

[11] E.g. Moser, *Okkultismus*, pp. 851 ff.
[12] "Über neuartige Schwingungen der Wellenlänge 1-70 cm. in der Umgebung anorganischer und organischer Substanzen sowie biologischer Objekte", 1934, in Roux, *Archiv für Entwicklungsmechanik der Organismen*, 131, 389.

because the air that is breathed out is north-polar magnetoid, after the south-polar magnetism has been consumed in the lungs. The Indian breathing exercises are connected with this fact, exercises that have the power of endowing the person concerned with mediumistic faculties. The fact that in certain cases objects have to be touched if mediumistic powers are to be obtained (and indeed the phenomena of hylomancy as a whole) are believed by some to be explicable along these lines.

Yet these avenues of research have really yielded nothing new, valuable as their exploration has undoubtedly proved; for it was already known that magnetoid cosmic radiation could be perceived by sensitive nerves, and could to some extent be used to neutralize nervous energy, which in its turn tends to result in the powers of the spirit-soul becoming effective—as in hylomancy (psychometry). So far, at any rate, we know of no physical or physiological power which could be capable of transmitting telepsychic perceptions. This applies, amongst other things, to the cosmic and vital waves of which Lakhovsky speaks and the existence of which he is at such pains to prove.[13] Yet from all that has so far become known, the limits within which animal magnetism can be said to operate are very restricted. Many scientists have busied themselves with this subject and seem to think that they have discovered a new universal law, and with it answered all the riddles of the occult ("the spiritualist sphinx"), if they succeed in detecting some minute variation in the readings of their instruments. Thus in 1903 Blondlot discovered the so-called N-rays which were subsequently also observed by Bequerel and Charpentier.[14] Reichenbach[15] called them Od; Rochas[16] saw blue and red radiations from magnets, crystals, flowers, etc., which could at times become dangerous. Professor Haschek[17] established that the luminosity of the human body was due to the gradual oxidization of matter excreted from the skin, which was especially noticeable in the cases of certain nervous persons where emanations from the body were very marked.

---

[13] Das *Geheimnis des Lebens*, Munich, 1932.
[14] Cf. Moser, *Okkultismus*, p. 860.
[15] *Odisch-magnetische Briefe*, Stuttgart, 1852.
[16] *Die Ausscheidung des Empfindungsvermögens*, Leipzig, 1909.
[17] Über *Leuchterscheinungen des Menschlichen Körpers*, Hölder, Vienna, 1914.

A great stir was created when in 1923 E. K. Müller succeeded in electrically tracing an emanation from the body which came especially from the fingertips, the toes, the armpits and the breath. There have been similar experiments, dating back as much as half a century, which showed that the hand left traces like that of breath on a mirror, and that these could be intensified by concentration of the will. In one such experiment, an emanation in the form of a "pale shortened finger" passed over the surface of a small bottle and left "particles of teleplasma" ("Teleplasmabrocken") behind. The experiment could not, however, be repeated, because the medium became ill.[18]

The Frankfurt neurologist Dr G. Oppenheimer can move matches without touching them, and cause electric lamps to glow. This may perhaps become possible through frictional electricity generated between the clothes and the skin. It is stated that anybody can do this, if he carries out the experiments after having made some kind of effort, although thorough insulation must be provided lest the electricity escape into the ground. All this seems to fit in with Müller's emanation and Blondlot's N-rays.

These various chemical and physical discoveries may help to provide an explanation for such phenomena as luminosity and other minor physical experiments, and they may help to put the life of the human senses more completely out of action, and thus make the soul's freedom from the body more complete, but they have no direct influence on telepathic manifestations, nor on those of clairvoyance.

It seems possible to include under the manifestations of telepathy the so-called "cross-correspondence"—*Querentsprechungen* (Mattiesen); *wechselseitige Entsprechungen*, or *verteilte Botschaften* (Baerwald). That is to say, it is possible to regard them as the phenomena of genuine telepathy, which means that we need not interpret them according to Baerwald's theory as caused by "radiations". It is said that the actual facts of the phenomenon were discovered by the secretaries of the Society for Psychical Research, which is a clearing house for the declarations of mediums in all parts of the world. In the most widely separated places, it sometimes happens that mediums make fragmentary utterances which, when each is taken in isolation, are in themselves meaningless but make sense when combined. It is assumed that

---

[18] E. K. Müller, *Objektiver elektrischer Nachweis der Existenz einer Emanation des lebenden menschlichen Körpers und ihre sichtbaren Wirkungen*, Bâle, 1932.

this would be impossible without the directing intelligence of a dead person and that the proof of the spiritualist thesis is thus complete.[19]

Yet if we examine it more closely, the case is really much more simple. The first thing to note is that nothing really rational is said at all. Thus somewhere in India a medium mentioned yellow ivory, while in Cambridge other mediums used the word yellow.

The foreseeing of certain things in dreams is well within the bounds of the possible. It is, for instance, sometimes foreseen that houses and landed properties will one day have a different price from that which is set on them at the moment, and in certain cases no other explanation is possible than that the thoughts and intentions of the owners become known telepathically. Even crimes are sometimes prophetically foreseen in advance. The murder of the actor Terriss of the Adelphi Theatre in London is an example of this, as is also that of the Archduke Franz Ferdinand in Sarajevo to which we have already referred. There is here, however, no genuine precognition in the strict sense of the term. What happens is that the thoughts of the murderers, who are naturally intensely preoccupied with their sinister intentions, become known to other persons whose subconscious is particularly wakeful. In such cases the soul is very far from leaving the body, nor does it "go upon a journey", nor is there any question of an "ethereal body" or a "perispirit". All we are concerned with here is the partly body-free soul which has knowledge by purely spiritual means.

Let us, however, here note the fact that the cases of which we hear so often, where a person is made aware of the death of another, are not to be accounted as telepathy, but as clairvoyance. We may say the same thing of the utterances of fortune-tellers and of persons who predict the future from cards. Such people have much experience in putting themselves into a trance.

The famous phenomenon known as "speaking with tongues" should be viewed in a similar light. Carlyle tells us of a Whitsun conference of the Irvingites in Colorado, at which a woman suddenly began to speak. Nobody could understand what she said, but some Japanese who were sitting right at the back began to weep. When someone turned to them, they said, "Tell us again in our own tongue how he died for the Japanese." The woman had

---

[19] Cf. Alfred Winterstein, *Telepathie und Hellsehen*, Wiener Phönix-Verlag, 1948, pp. 144 ff.

spoken in Japanese of the death of Christ. There are records of many cases whose authenticity need not be impugned but which give no grounds for assuming divine intervention, since many of the actual observations made in foreign languages are quite stupid. Telepathy is quite a possible explanation, since the persons concerned tend to fall into a trance during the session.

It is just these cases of speaking with tongues, however, that show clearly that we are for the most part concerned with a transference of thought, and not with an actual knowledge of languages. Charles Lafontaine[20] relates the following:

> In Tours I magnetized a woman who was a somnambulist. People spoke to her in Spanish, Latin, English, Portuguese, German and Greek; she answered all questions in French. When, however, someone put a question to her in Hebrew she did not reply, I urged her to say why she did not answer, whereupon she said quite simply: "This gentleman is saying words which he does not understand himself; he does not know what they mean. That is why I can't answer. He does not think. I take no notice of words. I do not understand them. I can only answer the thought that I see."

In passing we must note that in the miracle of Pentecost, and in the similar happenings connected with St Francis Xavier and St Anthony—in the last-named events the hearers each heard the saint's sermon in his own tongue—there was no question of the people being in a state of trance. Thus their understanding was in a much sharper state than in the cases related above. Even so those cases help us to see the Bible narratives, about which people are sometimes inclined to smile, in a somewhat different light, for they show us that here too grace builds on nature.

The feats of Indian jugglers have always aroused much attention; these can only be explained in terms of telepathy and on the assumption that these men have the faculty of putting their audiences into some sort of trance; a few persons who refuse to submit to this influence see nothing at all, and photographs similarly show us nothing. The persons, however, who have been put into a trance see everything that the conjuror thinks, or whatever he wants them to see.

---

[20] *L'art de magnétiser...*, Brussels, 1851, p. 189.

There is first of all the celebrated basket-stabbing trick. A child is placed in a basket which is closed and then pierced with a sword, so that blood flows through the apertures, and it is impossible to believe that the child is not dead. Yet suddenly the child jumps out alive and well.

There are also Indians who walk through a fire without taking harm. In such cases the crowed has itself brought the wood for the fire and actually experienced the intolerable heat of the flames. Moser describes such an event. "When all was ablaze," she writes, "the priest walked slowly through the sea of fire before the eyes of the believing crowd and of the sceptical American who witnessed the scene, and came out unharmed at the other end. Overcome by the apparently undeniable fact, the American returned home with his photographs which would presumably record what he had seen; but what did he find when they were developed? The bonfire, the blazing flames, the crowd—but no priest." The priest only existed in the telepathically-induced hallucination of the crowd.

Bishop Valoucek von Kremsier met an Indian in the house of a friend in Vienna who, as a favour, displayed his arts before about a dozen friends. The Indian put some powder into a bowl of coals, thus generating a powerful smoke. All those present were now told to think of some departed person, and that person would appear. All saw in the smoke the person of whom they had thought. It is obvious that the senses had become confused as a result of the smoke, and that the hallucination had thus been made possible.

One often hears of the mango-tree trick. A Yogi brings a seed which he places in the ground and covers with a cloth. This last is then lifted up by the growing tree, from which everyone can then pick a leaf Unless the seed has in such a case been specially prepared, and enabled to achieve exceptionally rapid growth by means of a liquid placed in the sand—and it is hardly likely that such rapid growth could thus be achieved—then we are here again clearly concerned with telepathy.

Even more astonishing is the rope trick, of which Marco Polo already gives an account and which keeps recurring in accounts of India since the fourteenth century. Amongst others, Munchausen seems to have heard of it. An Indian throws a rope into the air and lets a boy climb up it. Then he orders him to come down. When the boy refuses to obey, the Indian climbs up the rope himself, hacks the boy to pieces and lets the bleeding parts of his body, the arms, the legs and finally the head, fall to the ground, so that a terrible panic occurs among the onlookers. In a moment, however, the boy leaps up, apparently none the worse for his treatment. There are various versions of this story. In some cases it is animals—lions, for instance—which do the climbing, and after having climbed the rope they vanish. Here too the Indian uses smoke, stares at those present and sings a monotonous song, thus creating the spiritual disposition that renders the onlookers amenable to be influenced by his thought. It is obvious that mass suggestion on such a scale as this is only possible to a master of the craft, though the tropical climate and the rich imagination of the Orient may help. Even so Dr Schönbrunn, together with the hypnotist Paulsen, reproduced all this publicly in Vienna in 1919 by means of waking suggestion.[21]

The effect of such induced acts of the imagination is shown by a story in the *Reader's Digest*: About twenty persons are sleeping in the sleeping quarters of a ship. It is very close, and somebody asks to have the window opened that gives on to the upper deck. When this has been done, everybody is aware of the fresh air that flows in and sleeps wonderfully till the morning. It is afterwards discovered that the shaft on to which the window gave had another window at the end of it, and that this window was shut, so that no fresh air had flowed in at all through the opening of the lower window. It was imagination that had brought the relief. It is in the same category that we should place the feats of the Brazilian medium Mirabelli. Mirabelli caused a skull to move of its own accord out of a cupboard; the skull floated about the room, then developed a body, "which gave out an almost unbearable odour of putrefaction", and afterwards dissolved into smoke; the skull finally fell on to the table.[22]

Here then we have the first group of artificially produced phenomena which can be explained by telepathy, that is to say, by the influence and suggestion exerted by one spirit upon another.

---

[21] Cf. Moser, *Okkultismus*, pp. 392 ff.
[22] Sünner, *Carlos Mirabelli, das neue brasilianische Medium*, Mutze, Leipzig, 1927.

(B) Clairvoyance

The second group of suprasensory phenomena consists of those of so-called clairvoyance, and the discussion of them may be accounted as the second step on the road leading away from the world of sense into the realm of the occult. The names used in this connection vary. People speak of clairvoyance, of *lucidité*, of telaesthesia and cryptaesthesia. We use the word clairvoyance to denote the direct suprasensory perception of things or conditions, of which at the time nobody has any knowledge. It is the last characteristic which in particular distinguishes second sight from telepathy, for in the latter the thoughts of one person are transmitted to another. In clairvoyance it is not thoughts but things that are apprehended, and they are things which nobody yet knows, and concerning which no one, therefore, can influence another. For instance we are concerned with clairvoyance when a person takes cards at random from a pack and the medium names the cards thus chosen.

It is a faculty which normally a man does not possess, though in so far as he is able to repress the senses and thus free the soul from the body, he will, after the manner of pure spirits, perceive all things towards which he directs his attention. According to our view, therefore, clairvoyance is something that follows directly from the very nature of the spirit. Our ordinary science, with its materialistic orientation, which cannot recognize such powers of the soul, in this matter, is less fortunately placed than we are. It will still graciously recognize the existence of telepathy, because it believes that it can assume some kind of waves analogous to radio waves, but with clairvoyance no such assumption is possible, since there is no person to "transmit". That is why clairvoyance is rejected, or treated as an illusion, or at best explained as telepathy (Baerwald, Dessoir).

Actually, though a distinction has been drawn between the two phenomena, they are essentially the same. In both cases the intelligence at work is that of the spirit-soul which can be directed towards the thoughts of others or towards any other thing, whether or not that thing be possessed of life. In the case of such intelligence being directed toward the thoughts of another, we speak of telepathy; where it is directed towards some other thing we speak of clairvoyance. Even in telepathy, however, we are not concerned with anything in the nature of actual transmission on the part of the person whose thoughts are being read by another; all that is necessary is that the latter should have the desire to communicate his thoughts; that desire can, however, have varying degrees of intensity—that is to say, it can be anything between mere consent and a conscious and deliberate exerting of influence. The role of the recipient intelligence is simply to give its attention; it must therefore be guided, and this too takes place with varying degrees of intensity. In telepathy it takes place through mental suggestion, in clairvoyance by direction of the hypnotist or through the influence of some directing object, as, for instance, in psychometry (hylomancy), or in cases of possession through the foreign intelligence concerned.

When people like Dr Lakhovsky[23] and Bishop Waldmann[24] point to the existence of an ability to perceive certain electric radiations by means of special faculties which have this capacity, they give an explanation that could only apply to short-distance influence. Where greater distances are concerned, people will really have to find some other explanation. The soul may indeed have the support of something of this kind, but as Driesch points out, it can at best be only a bridge to real knowledge.

Clairvoyance is of two kinds, clairvoyance in space and clairvoyance in time; the former gives knowledge of things that are distant or hidden, while the latter is concerned with things that lie in the future or in the past.

Let us deal first with the knowledge of things hidden, with so-called cryptoscopy, Over and above sheer illusion and fraud, there remains a considerable residuum of well-attested fact, which cannot be explained by hyperaesthesia, nor by "sense-transposition", nor by the touching of the forehead and similar practices. Dr Chowrin, in his book *Experimentelle Untersuchungen auf dem Gebiete des Räumlichen Hellsehens* (Munich, 1919) (Experimental Research in Spatial Clairvoyance), recounts the following experiment with a thirty-two-year-old medium, a schoolteacher of noble birth. He wrote five different problems on five separate sheets of paper, put them into envelopes of identical kind, and sealed the envelopes. Then he took one such envelope at random and destroyed the others, so that nobody knew what the remaining envelope contained. The medium was able to say exactly what it contained (cf. Moser, *Okkultismus*, P. 416).

---

[23] *Geheimnis des Lebens*, Munich, 1932.
[24] *Parapsychologie, Lexicon für Theol. und Kirche*, VI I, 960 ff.

Similar experiments were made by J. B. Rhine,[25] in which the subject was to perceive by extrasensory perception the devices on five cards. The devices were a square, a star, a triple-wave line, a circle and a cross. There were twenty-five cards in the pack, each sign appearing once in five different cards. The pack was played through four times; there were thus one hundred questions and answers, of which of course a percentage was likely to be correct. This ESP (extra-sensory perception) test, however, showed a higher percentage of correct answers than could be ascribed to chance. The fact that the success of the experiment was not greater than it actually was, is due to the circumstance that the subjects in question were not sufficiently in a state of trance. In much the same way colours are perceived, books are opened at random and, though what is on the page is quite unknown to anybody, it is correctly "read". Further, people see through objects which for us are not optically transparent; the subjects can indeed perceive everything to which their attention is directed; they see in the dark, see through walls, and can, among other things, declare the whereabouts of the body of a missing person.

Many of the remarkable achievements of Swedenborg, which aroused so much attention in his day, fall into this category. Jung Stilling tells us of an Elberfeld merchant who came to Swedenborg and asked him if he knew what he, the merchant, had been discussing some time previously in Duisburg with a friend of his, a consumptive student of theology. Swedenborg told him to come back a few days later. When the merchant returned, he said to him with a smile: "I have met your friend. The subject of your talk was the ultimate return of all things"—and this was actually true. The attention Swedenborg attracted extended far beyond his home, and this not so much because of his religious revelations as on account of certain revelations of a purely secular character. One of these concerned the widow of the Dutch ambassador in Stockholm, a certain Countess Martefeld. This lady was handed a bill by a goldsmith named Cron for a service of silver that he had delivered. The Countess, who knew how prompt her husband had been in all money matters, was firmly convinced that the goldsmith's account had long ago been settled. Nevertheless she was unable to find the receipt. In her embarrassment, for the sum involved was considerable, she approached Swedenborg with the request

---

[25] J. B. Rhine, *The Reach of the Mind* (cf. Introduction, n. 4).

that he should make enquiry among his spirits about the matter. Only a few days later Swedenborg informed her that he had consulted her husband's spirit, and that the latter had indicated a wardrobe in a room in the upper storey as the place where the receipt was to be found. The lady replied that this wardrobe had been completely cleared and that the receipt had not been discovered among any of the papers. Swedenborg rejoined that her husband had written to him that if a drawer was pulled out on the left-hand side, a board would be discovered, and if this were pushed aside, a secret drawer would be found in which his secret Dutch correspondence had been kept and that the receipt was in this drawer. Everything turned out as Swedenborg had said. The account had been settled seven months ago and the cheat was sent about his business. (The conjecture that Swedenborg had perhaps been lent some of the Count's secret correspondence and had seen the receipt, which had been used as a marker therein, is the kind of thing by which only sceptics could be satisfied.)

In 1759 Swedenborg saw, while in Göteborg, the fire that was raging in Stockholm five hundred kilometres away. He made a report to the municipal authorities, naming the victims of the disaster, and stated the hour when the fire was put out. Some days later a royal messenger arrived who confirmed the accuracy of this vision (Rhine, *The Reach of the Mind*).

Here is another remarkable case which has been the subject of some controversy. In San Francisco a medium at a spiritualist seance wrote that in Melbourne, Australia, a strong, bearded man, wearing metal-rimmed glasses and aged sixty, had lost his life in a car crash. His name was stated to be Thomas L. Queen and he was said once to have lived in Los Angeles. He was also said to wish to have his son John, who lived in San Francisco, notified of his death. Everything proved to be correct. They found the son, and it was established that the father had lost his life in a car accident on the very day that the medium had seen it all. In Fr Lacroix's opinion, there could not possibly be a purely natural explanation of this case. Fr Heredia believes the explanation to lie

> in telepathy, by virtue of which the spirit of one person can communicate with that of another, the two persons being like the sending and receiving stations in radiotelegraphy. In the case in question the spirit of the dying man thought of the son at home and the transmission is received by the medium who acts

after the manner of an aerial. The thoughts of the dying man are naturally more intense, because of the very circumstances in which he finds himself. The transmission is thus more powerful, and is thus easier to receive. Admittedly telepathy in this hypothetical case cannot explain how the medium can perceive the features of the dying man, but some kind of clairvoyance on the part of the medium surely functioned together with the dying man's thoughts.[26]

Thus far progressed Fr Heredia, and one must be grateful for this step forward, which at least excludes the devil. And yet one feels how uncertain everything still is, and how this explanation merely serves to increase our difficulties. Had there really been brain waves at the bottom of it, they would have had to be very strong indeed if they were to be received at a distance of eight thousand miles, for their effectiveness decreases with the square of the distance. We also have no real explanation of how the medium could tell what the old man looked like, that he was "strong, bearded and wore metal-rimmed glasses", since that appearance could not be "transmitted". To talk of clairvoyance in these circumstances does not help us at all, for as it is here conceived, it is only a word and explains nothing of this manner of seeing and its possibility. Bessmer[27] too is of the opinion that the factor of distance invalidates this explanation.

How simple is the explanation that our own theory provides for all this. The medium was in a profound sleep, and during such a sleep the soul, being partly body-free, can, after the manner of pure spirits, perceive anything to which for any reason it directs its attention; distance is in such a matter quite irrelevant. The condition is the same as that described by the lady who said to Raupert[28] "that for her there were no secrets in the world. There is a sphere in which all happenings are known, a sphere that might be compared to a book in which all the secrets of all men—yes, even the most secret of them—are inscribed, and in which a few persons with exceptional psychic development can read". This woman described his past life to Raupert in the greatest detail. "Whence did the medium receive this exact knowledge about the inner life of

---

[26] Heredia, *Der Spiritismus*, p. 160.

[27] *Stimmen der Zeit*, vol. 76, p. 281.

[28] *Spiritismus*, p. 96.

a man who was completely unknown to her?" Our own answer to that question is quite clear.

The apparent knowledge of languages possessed by mediums often occasions considerable surprise, since the latter are often quite uneducated, but nevertheless dictate sentences in foreign tongues, sentences that can frequently be found after a long search in some book or other, which the subject has read by clairvoyance.

D. Felicios dos Santos[29] relates that when he requested a medium to recite a Latin couplet, he was given the following:

> *Commovit Petrum Gallus, ploravit et ille;*
> *Nunc Petrus Galium corrigit, ille negat.*

This was a couplet that referred to the Encyclical of Leo XIII to the bishops of France, in which he advised the people to accept the Republic; the majority refused to obey, and the couplet relates to this resistance.

The play on the word "Gallus", which can mean both cock and Frenchman, had, however, been known since the Council of Trent. It is said that at this council a French bishop criticized conditions in Rome. Another bishop then called out, "*Nimis ille Gallus cantat*", whereupon with great presence of mind the Frenchman replied, "*Utinam Petrus ad cantum galli resipiscat*". The medium could, of course, have read this couplet in some book or have received it out of the subconscious of some other person.

The same researcher obtained another verse, concerning his relations with his wife, "*Heus, viator, hic vir et uxor non litigant*", which was taken from a gravestone, as the medium actually admitted. There was also a third verse given which the researcher asked to be in English: "He was a sword whose blade has never been wet but in Liberty's foe"—a sentence sufficiently well known to those who have studied the literature of North America and the works of Washington.

Raupert[30] tells how he himself heard a quite ignorant medium conversing with another person in fluent Hindustani; that other person had lived long in India and therefore spoke the language idiomatically. In this case it is again possible that the medium read a few sentences from the mind of that other

---

[29] *Casos reais* . . . , 1937.
[30] *Spiritismtis*, p. 15.

person, although it is always difficult for another person who does not actually know the language to tell whether a language is being spoken fluently or not. For such a person, any spoken sentence seems "fluent".

Even when mediums write a foreign language in foreign characters, they do so like people copying a drawing, not like someone writing fluently, that is to say, they see the picture of the written word in their subconscious and copy it. We therefore deplore the remark of Fr Heredia, who writes[31]: "In such cases the medium writes or speaks (or does both) automatically and, in doing so, displays a knowledge which in his normal state he does not possess. According to trustworthy accounts, this knowledge is of such an extraordinary character that it permits of no satisfactory explanation save that of the presence of an alien intelligence." The writer has come across the kind of accounts of which Fr Heredia speaks, and would be grateful to any reader who would bring to his notice any cases which his own theory seems incapable of explaining, for anything which these alleged third intelligences can do can also be done by the human soul itself in the various states of sleep.

Often the whole thing degenerates into mere virtuosity in which the subjects write with reversed characters, or in such a manner that one letter has always to be omitted for the words to make any sense. Alternatively the sense must be derived by reading the letters that form vertical lines running across the lines of writing. This last may have been suggested by wartime cypher methods, though such a cypher would have been easier to break than any actually used for military purposes.

Somnambulists are often able to diagnose disease and its causes by a kind of clairvoyance; they can discover the seat of a malady although the sufferers themselves may not experience any pain in that particular part, and can do so with the greatest exactitude. Over a century ago Haddock expressed the view that knowledge obtained by clairvoyance could be of value to a doctor. "I must own," he writes, "that I have derived information from this source which I should not have obtained from other methods of study; and at the same time more confidence in certain remedial applications. Clairvoyance and mesmerism are not to supersede the physician and medical agents; but the *former* is to be used by the physician as he uses a stethoscope—that is, as an

---

[31] *Spiritismus*, p. 109.

instrument of investigation; in fact a true lucid clairvoyant may be styled a *living stethoscope*; and the latter is but one among many remedial agents."[32] It is true that they do not describe the nature of a malady in erudite technical terms, but do so in simple language like popular healers; they have an intuitive understanding and intuitive skills of healing which the physician often does not possess. Doctors Comar and Sollier report cases in which persons subjected to magnetic treatment became conscious of alien substances within their own bodies, such, for instance, as a pin or a piece of bone, which could be removed by suitable peristaltic movement of the bowel.

A somnambulist can also "feel" the physical condition of another, though the descriptions given on these occasions tend to be an inextricable mixture of truth and error; the depth of the trance and the extent to which rapport has been established with the patient seems here to be the determining factor. In view of this it is, as Moser says, desirable to "keep to the rational considerations of science rather than to the incalculable uncertainties of so fallible an instrument".

. A certain fame attaches to the so-called criminal mediums whose powers of clairvoyance have often served to discover those guilty of crimes, to throw light on thefts and find missing persons, though naturally enough these potentialities have been exploited, as is so often the case in these matters, for purposes of fraudulent gain. Nevertheless these "medium-detectives" have been increasingly used, so much so that serious consideration has been given to the idea of attaching them to the security services, where they would play something in the nature of the part of human police dogs. However, when for some time these mediums had been active in this particular field, certain suspicious circumstances in their conduct attracted attention, and a number of them were arrested and put on trial. Some notoriety attaches to the case of Christian Droste, who was tried in Bernburg. He was not himself a medium, but "worked" with about twenty such mediums, his method being to put some object connected with the crime in question into their hand. He would then hypnotize the medium and elucidate the facts by a series of questions which he put to the latter. Droste was acquitted.

---

[32] *Somnolence and Psychism*, London, 1851.

In Insterburg a certain Else Günther-Geffers was put on trial; she was a medium herself and had the habit of putting herself into a trance by means of a crystal, and of making the relevant statements while in that trance. She too was acquitted both in the lower and the superior court, since she had successfully thrown light on several crimes, and had been consulted by the authorities in several difficult cases. A third case was rather more unsavoury; this was the case of a certain Hermann Steinschneider, who called himself Erik Jan Hanussen and was very active in this particular trade. The trial took place in Leitmeritz, but ended with an acquittal. Naturally enough the court did not in any of these cases pronounce any opinion as to whether the defendants possessed genuine occult powers or no, though experiments were in several cases actually conducted in the courtroom in what would appear to have been a somewhat amateurish fashion. The experts were divided in their opinions, but witnesses spoke up for the accused with great enthusiasm.

All this raises a question of principle, namely whether there is really room for the employment of such mediums in a court of law at all. Certainly the same thing holds good here as in the matter of their employment in medical cases; the greatest caution must be exercised, for there is always the danger that owing to the very great suggestibility which is present in a condition of trance, they will be telepathically influenced by the opinion that the crowd is bound to form. Even so, they can render valuable service, as was recently shown by the mediums M. Schmidt and R. Scherman, of whom the former disclosed the identity of the murderer Siefert, while the latter reconstructed with complete accuracy the murder of a girl by Franz and Rosalie Schneider, a murder which had taken place twenty-six years previously. It would seem therefore that with certain safeguards there is the possibility of useful employment for mediums both in the legal and the medical field.

In many cases there is a doubt as to whether it is really a case of telepathy or clairvoyance, though in our view there is no essential difference between the two. In some instances, however, telepathy would hardly seem the appropriate category. To quote an example: "A certain Dr Ferrand sent to Paris from Antibes a Roman coin which he had found on a property of his; the coin was shown to Alexis Didier, a medium who had attained considerable fame under the Second Empire. Didier stated that there was an urn on Dr Ferrand's ground which was full of such coins, and gave an exact description of the place where it was to be found. Digging was begun at the place indicated, and an urn was found containing some seven pounds of such coins."[33] This can only be classified as clairvoyance, since no living being possessed this knowledge.

Such clairvoyance can also occur in dreams and can sometimes throw light on problems of scientific research. The following story, the truth of which there is no reason to doubt, is told by Professor Hilprecht, the Assyriologist. While engaged on the study of Babylonian inscriptions he had experienced some difficulty in deciphering what had been engraved on some fragments of agate found in the Temple of Baal at Nippur. The results of his study were already in print, but he was not satisfied with them. Then in March 1893 he dreamed this dream: A priest, some forty years of age, thin, tall and dressed in a simple alb, led him to the treasury of the temple, a small room without windows in which there was a wooden chest. On the bottom of it were fragments of agate and lapis lazuli. The priest then said: "The two fragments of which you spoke on pages 22 and 26 belong together, but they are not finger rings. Their history is as follows. King Kurigalzu (*c.* 1300 B.C.) once sent an inscribed votive cylinder of agate to the Temple of Baal. Then we priests were ordered to make ear-rings of agate for the statue of the god Ninib. Since we had no material, we had to cut the cylinder into three. This produced three rings, each with a part of the inscription. The first two served as ear-rings. The fragments which are causing you so much trouble are fragments of these. If you will put them together, you will find that this is true." The priest then vanished. Hilprecht woke up and immediately told his wife of the dream, so that it should not be forgotten. In the morning he placed the two pieces together and found that what he had been told was absolutely correct. The problem was solved and the necessary corrections were made in the preface to his work.

It is under this group that we should really include all cases concerned with the finding of lost objects—those of Helen Smith for instance, the seer of Prevorst, in the matter of Mayor Bournier and Fr Chessenazi as well as that of Anne Catherine Emmerich and the finding of Mary's grave at Ephesus.

---

[33] Winterstein, *Telepathie und Hellsehen*, p. 90.

Such feats present no difficulty to the body-free soul when it is concerned with matters that are contemporary or lie in the past, since it need only direct its attention to the thoughts of some fellow creature or to the object itself. The matter is, however, very different when dealing with the precognition of future events and since the days of Pythagoras, Plato and Cicero the most varied accounts and explanations have been given of these phenomena.

Reference was made some way back to an explanation by Myers, but this needs some amplification. Many authors write such happenings down to pure chance—Lehmann for instance[34]—but well-attested concrete cases are very numerous, and this interpretation cannot be considered satisfactory. Baerwald again takes refuge in telepathy and assumes so-called "telepathic talents" which unite all men in a universal telepathy and which act suggestively on certain persons; the result is that those who are called upon to make a prophecy come true, do this by virtue of the suggestive power of the prophet and of the thing prophesied. Thus cause and effect are made to change places—a very bold hypothesis indeed. Winterstein adduces a number of other theories, all of which profess to establish the fact of prophecy.[35]

Tischner does not help us much when in his latest book, *Ergebnisse Okkulter Forschung*, he passes into a world which is no longer that of space as we know it. Tischner bases his view on Kant, "who looks upon space and time as the inescapable forms under which we make our acts of knowledge. They are valid for the world of phenomena but not for the thing in itself." He also refers to Driesch, who speaks of the "extra-spatial field of the soul" which could also be spoken of as extra-temporal, for we are here concerned with things which do not yet exist, but are nevertheless supposedly objects of knowledge.

Mesmer's pupil, the Marquis de Puységur, assumed the existence of a sixth sense. Richet takes the view that "certain qualities of matter, both dead and living, thinking and unthinking (!) to which our normal senses are closed, can nevertheless be apprehended by certain persons at certain moments of time".[36] Moser[37] despairs of finding an explanation at all, but comes fairly close to the

---

[34] *Aberglaube und Zauberei*, p. 596.
[35] *Telepathie und Hellsehen*, pp. 115 ff.
[36] Lehmann, *Aberglaube und Zauberei*, p. 599
[37] *Okkultismus*, p. 473.

truth when she says that the fulfilment of prophecy is a consequence of circumstances that can be foreseen.

And indeed, if we are to attain clarity, we must distinguish between a future that is already unequivocally determined by its causes and a future that is free. The former can be calculated after the manner in which an eclipse of the sun is foretold by an astronomer, while the latter depends on the free human will, whose decisions human knowledge can only ascertain in so far as a motive has already become apparent. For when we say that the will is free, we do not mean by this that it is completely uninfluenced by any motive; we merely have the fact in mind that these motives do not absolutely constrain the will and determine it. Actually we know that in most cases motives do guide the will, although it can if necessary withstand them; motives therefore to a very marked degree determine the issue of action, indeed there can be such a combination of them—modern novelists are notoriously fond of creating this impression—that people may think any decision to be impossible other than the one actually made.

In precognition therefore we are concerned chiefly with a knowledge of actual physical circumstances and of motives acting on the will. What remains over for the free will is accessible to no created intelligence, but in any case it is very small.

Further it is plain that the extent to which actual causes of coming events are apprehended depends on the gifts of the persons concerned, on their experiences of life and on the breadth of vision with which they can co-ordinate their data. These of course vary with different people. Thus in May, 1942, at Casablanca the four statesmen were able to forecast the future course of the war and to demand the unconditional surrender of Germany, an act that seemed premature to the rest of the world and was designated by the head of the German state as an impertinence, but events proved the statesmen to have been right.

There now only remains to be considered the special case where the spirit-soul's special powers of knowledge come into play, for the faculties of clairvoyance which the latter possesses give a far more accurate insight into the character and abilities, not only of individuals but of entire peoples (as also into the nature of political tensions and the inter-relationship of political events) than that enjoyed by men in their normal state. Moreover the spirit-soul can read the motives, temptations, weaknesses and inclinations of such individuals much more accurately than the person in question can read them himself. It is scarcely, therefore, to be wondered at if a person in a dream or a trance or under hypnosis should be able to foresee and foretell future events much more accurately than he would be capable of doing in his normal state. We are continually told that the upper consciousness is a positive hindrance to such cognition. All this makes many cases of prophecy, which till now have puzzled us and defied all explanation, much easier to understand, and if it is now objected that there still is a small group of cases where the will has been entirely free in determining events, our answer must be that either it was never prophesied correctly or it was so only by chance. We may therefore draw the general conclusion that prophecies of future events are only possible in so far as those events depend on their determining causes, but that in so far as they result from the action of a will that is entirely free, prophecy is impossible.

Let us look at the matter more closely. People are very fond of citing the following well-attested case of alleged prophecy: A young Frenchman, a nervous type, was told by M. Lenormand on the 26th December, 1879: "You will lose your father on this day a year from now. You will soon be a soldier"—the lad was nineteen—"but not for long. You will marry young, have two children and die when you are twenty-six." All this came true. His father died on the 26th of December, 1880; he became a soldier, was soon discharged and then married. Then came the fear that the last part of the prophecy would also be fulfilled and that he should die at the age of twenty-six. Liébault, who recounts this case, and who was consulted by the young man in question, endeavoured to hypnotize, but was unsuccessful, and so sent him to one of his somnambulists, who suggested to him under hypnosis that he would die forty-one years from that date—but he died at the age of twenty-six, as M. Lenormand had prophesied.

The exact fulfilment of prophecy is in this case admittedly astonishing—all the more so since, in part at least, events appear to be wholly determined by a free will. Yet much of the story is by no means inexplicable. There is nothing very remarkable in the fact that a young man of nineteen should in this military state have become a soldier, nor is it particularly odd that his bad nerves should have resulted in his discharge, that shortly after this he should have married, and that in this country of the "progressive two-children system" he should have had two children. We are not told of the extent to which a spirit could have been aware of the first signs of death within the father, nor whether the latter gained knowledge of the prophecy either directly or telepathically, and literally worried himself to death over it. Actually the young man's own death may well have been hastened by this very cause, for the memory of the prophecy may have continued in his subconscious despite the contrary suggestion given under hypnosis, and may have had a deleterious effect on his physical health.

In this case, therefore, of apparent foreknowledge we can admittedly observe the heightened faculties of cognition that exist in a state of trance, but we cannot speak of the matter as an instance of genuine prophecy, a thing impossible according to the theologians, even to the angelic intelligence. Other accounts of supposed prophecy must be similarly interpreted—in so far as they are true at all; a good test here is whether the prophecy was actually recorded before the event. Where the record has been made afterwards there has usually been some doctoring.

Schopenhauer relates in his *Versuche über das Geistersehen* (p. 282) that he had written a letter one morning and instead of sprinkling sand over it had picked up the ink-pot by mistake, the ink going not only over the letter but also on to the floor. A maid, whom he called to wipe up the mess, remarked that she had dreamed that night of cleaning up ink stains at that place. Schopenhauer made careful enquiries and found the girl's story was confirmed by the second maid, to whom the other had told her dream immediately on awakening.

As in so many other cases, there is no need in this one to discern a genuine foreknowledge of the future. The fact is that many dreams are not fulfilled at all, while the dream of Schopenhauer's maid had to do with the ordinary processes of her occupation and no doubt she had been of service to her master in many similar situations. When one of the many dreams we have happens to be fulfilled, we forget all about the others which were not fulfilled and start talking about foreknowledge. This is all wrong. The most we could say in the present instance is that the maid had by clairvoyance become aware of the tiredness of her learned master under the symbol of the confusion of the two containers (of ink and sand) and had then drawn conclusions from this.

People are sometimes puzzled by things like the vision of Major von Gillhausen (which is well attested), at the outbreak of the first world war. Major von Gillhausen recorded his vision on 3rd August, 1914, and sent the account to Prince Friedrich Wilhelm of Prussia. The latter delayed reading it till the autumn of 1915 and then returned it to its author. When Major von Gillhausen died on 2nd May, 1918, the document, which had been sealed, was found by his brother. Like all German officers. Major von Gillhausen, so far as his waking consciousness was concerned, was a conscientious, level-headed sort of man, but there were times when he lapsed into a dreamy state. Such a state occurred on 3rd August, 1914, and during it he had a vision, the general nature of which can be gathered from the following account:

> How will the war end? Not within a short period of time, nor will it be carried on against only a single powerful enemy. I see many enemies and clearly recognize Belgium as one that will inflict terrible wounds upon us. In the West by the side of France, which I see trodden on, buffeted and violated by England, there appears that same England as our most formidable foe. In Africa we are compelled to engage in heavy fighting. Italy hastens to make common cause against us with England and Russia. In the Balkans there is Serbia and Roumania. I resist the idea of Roumania; I cannot understand it, but the conviction remains. Russia gives us a lot of trouble but we shall succeed there, despite the fact that Japan helps her, as America helps England. I see Roosevelt handing bread and wine to the King of England, patting him on the shoulder, giving him money, a powder-horn, a dagger and leaden bullets—and Roosevelt seemed to be our friend!
>
> The war is terrible and will last many years. Always there are new enemies. I see them hurry to England, our opponent, from all countries of the world. Many places where we fight are far, far away and nearly all peoples of the world are drawn in—from North America to Australia, Serbia, Japan right up to Cape Horn. England appears everywhere. Is it possible? Germany's situation becomes terrible and things are worst in 1918. It is not till 1920 that the war seems to be at an end or even to have reached the stage of an armistice. That is how things appear to go. Will the Kaiser survive 1921? ... It seems to me as though England receives the death blow in India and Egypt. Germany emerges from the war in a fearful state. It will take her thirty years to recover. Russia awakes and struggles with America for the possession of the future—God be with us!

> I see the Kaiser, wearing his crown and an ermine mantle, sawing off the legs of his overturned throne. While he was thus engaged his ermine mantle became more and more grey and dusty and gradually fell away from him, while his crown grew smaller and smaller, and the Kaiser himself dissolved into nothing.... Germany's situation will be terrible.

Here all was seen beforehand: it was written down, sent to the Crown Prince, who read it a year later and returned it to Gillhausen. After the latter's death it was found sealed.

Another instance of apparent prophecy is the holy Curé Vianney's description in 1862 of the first world war:

> Our enemies [he declared] will not completely withdraw [Battle of the Marne], they will return and destroy all that stands in their way. We shall not resist but shall allow them to advance and afterwards cut off their food supply and cause them heavy losses; they will withdraw towards their own country and we shall keep up with them, and none of them will return home. Then everything will be taken from them that they have taken from others and a great deal more besides... They will want to canonize me but will have no time for it. [This was said in 1862, and published in 1872.]

These two supposed prophecies are worth a few moments' attention. In the case of Major von Gillhausen the main prediction, namely that Germany would be defeated, tells us nothing more than would have been said by the majority of trained military observers, by the kind of people, that is to say, who would not have been hypnotized by the mystique of an unconquerable German army. Such people would in all probability have estimated the chances of a German victory at 70 to 30 "against", and no doubt this was the opinion, though they may not have uttered it aloud, of many officers of the German general staff. Once the probability of an ultimate German defeat has been accepted, the other conclusions, namely the long duration of the war and even the fall of the Hohenzollerns, etc., follow pretty naturally.

As to the Hohenzollerns it is worth noting that the decisive factor in the jettisoning of the dynasty was the action of the General Staff under Hindenburg, and it is not too fanciful to suppose that a German officer might have been dimly aware of this potentiality in the mental make-up of the German officer corps. That Russia would one day "awaken" was a truism repeated by almost every schoolboy at the time, and it was not too difficult to foresee that a protracted war would bring about changes in the relationship between Britain and her subject peoples.

The one really interesting thing in this so-called "vision" is the reference to Roosevelt, and one is at first tempted to infer that the major foresaw the advent of Franklin D. Roosevelt, the second world war, and lend-lease. This would indeed be a sensational conclusion. There is, however, no need to draw it, since a far more plausible explanation lies ready to hand. It seems on the whole likely that the Roosevelt referred to is not Franklin but Theodore, who, during his presidency, which terminated in 1908, had been largely responsible for the calling of the Algeciras conference after the Morocco crisis of 1905.

Roosevelt was thus the American President who had dealings with Germany during a particularly aggressive phase of her diplomacy. Is it unreasonable to suppose that a secret fear was at this time born in the major's mind, as it was doubtless born in the minds of many other Germans, that their country was making more enemies than the amenities of diplomatic intercourse might lead her to believe, and that Roosevelt, in the case of Major von Gillhausen, became the symbol of that fear? There must after all be some explanation for the name of Roosevelt occurring at all, since he was not President at the outbreak of the war, and this seems as good a one as any.

If this explanation is accepted, it furnishes an illuminating illustration of the kind of mental process in which the "vision" originated. The vision is in fact nothing more than a series of deductions from the facts of an existing situation, nor is there the least ground for assuming the intervention of a higher power.

The so-called prophecy of the Curé d'Ars is of a very similar character. The most significant thing about it is the date when it was first made: 1862. This was the year in which Bismarck became Prime Minister of Prussia and forced the army bill through the Diet for the King of Prussia under what was really an implicit threat of force. It was a highly significant moment in the history of Europe, and one the importance of which would not be lost on a Frenchman with a strongly developed intuition. Nor is it surprising that the Curé should have foreseen the weapon of blockade. This was an even more obvious method of warfare in 1862, when Prussia had virtually no navy, than it was in 1914.

What, however, really excludes the possibility of this being a case of genuine prophecy is the fact that it is wrong on a most important point. It declares that none of the Germans would return home, whereas in point of actual fact they did go home, marching back, according to a plan that had long been prepared by the General Staff, under their own officers, and carrying their weapons. Detachments even made a triumphal entry into Berlin through the Brandenburg Gate, which was decorated with the inscription "Unconquered in the Field". The psychological consequences of this were enormous and affected the whole subsequent history of Europe. To have been wrong on this particular point renders the whole utterance worthless as prophecy—all of which merely shows that even great sanctity does not confer the gift of foreknowledge. The point on which the Curé's prophecy is accurate, namely the delay, due to the war, in his own canonization, may safely be regarded as nothing more than a lucky shot.

The question of the possibility of foreseeing the future played an important part in the First International Congress on Parapsychology in Utrecht, 1953, where Professor Tenhaeff (Utrecht) and Professor Bender (Freiburg, Germany) undertook with the medium Croiset experiments which became known as "The Chair Experiments". At meetings held over a period of five days, where those present were free to choose their places, the medium foretold who would sit in a certain specified chair. Many attempts were made, with a startling number of correct predictions. The predictions were taken on a tape recorder, as also their actual fulfilment, representing "an anticipation of the future which is an invasion of our thoughts and the moral postulate of free will" (Hartlaub).

We suggest that it is quite unnecessary to take refuge here in non-Euclidean mathematics, in the fourth dimension, or in "spirits" in order to explain this foreseeing of the future. The solution is to be found in the explanation given on pages 159-160, namely that it is a question of calculating the effect of certain known causes, and this is easier for the soul in a state of trance than for the normal consciousness. This can be gathered from the wrong conclusions and the near guesses that constantly occur (the prediction fits the person who sits *next to* the place decided upon, who may also be a relative); moreover only a narrow circle is involved. Croiset has specialized in this chair experiment, for which only a small circle of voluntary and "chance" subjects is in question, not the combined working of the free will of large numbers of people in the most diverse circumstances, with its effects on the lives of men over a period of years.

Considerable fame attached at one time to the prophecies of Madame de Thebes (her actual name was Anne Victorine Savary, d. 1915), who edited an almanac every year (Jouen, Paris) in which she published her prophecies. Schrenck-Notzing[38] has given us a compilation of these prophecies which plainly shows how much error they contained, so that certain words regarding Austria (*"He who has been designated to reign will not reign, the throne will go to a young man who was not intended to reign"*) appear like a chance oasis in the desert. One has a similar feeling when one reads the prophecies concerning the first world war in Bächtold-Stäublis' *Handwörterbuch des deutschen Aberglaubens* (IX, B, Berlin, 1927-41). Not a single one of these prophecies proved correct. Naturally there is some difference of opinion among those who seek to make the dark sayings of Nostradamus (Michel de Notredame, d. 1566) refer to actual historical events. He is alleged deliberately to have used false names and to have distorted words (*noyon*, for instance, for *royon* = "kinglet") so that it should be impossible to foretell the future from his verses, "since this was not fitting for piman".[39] Perty[40] also enumerates a number of prophecies which, scientifically speaking, are quite useless, in so far as they are not recorded in writing before the event. Anyone who really believes in foreknowledge of the future can make a very simple test; let him get a medium to foretell the winning number in the next state lottery. His success will not only convince us of the reality of prophecy but will bring about the disappearance of this drawing-room gangsterism of lotteries that exploits man's love of gain.

(C) Physical Manifestations

Since we have already dealt with the power of pure spirits to influence the physical world, we shall not be astonished if we encounter occult phenomena

---

[38] *Gesammelte Aufsätze zur Parapsychologie*, 1929, pp. 47 ff.
[39] See above, pp. 117 ff.
[40] *Die sichtbare und unsichtbare Welt*, Winterscher Verlag, Leipzig, 1881, pp. 125 ff.

in which this power is manifested by the human soul. Admittedly the occurrence of such manifestations is very rare, for the element of illusion and fraud is here very considerable. Moreover there is rarely any useful purpose behind them, except possibly in medicine. Nevertheless it seems to be clear that man can act on his surroundings in two ways, first indirectly by means of his muscles, and secondly, immediately through his spirit-soul. When acting in this last way he can produce sounds (telacoustic phenomena), movements (telekinesis) and materializations (teleplastic phenomena).

(i) Telacoustic phenomena (raps)

One of the first occult phenomena in the case of the notorious Fox family of Hydesville, U.S.A., was the occurrence in the year 1847 of a number of raps, which gradually became the means of getting questions answered. Raps, of course, are not the only kind of sounds that are heard in this connection. Indeed we have records of all kinds of knocking and banging sounds. Some such sounds resemble the pecking of hens, others again are like heavy hammer blows. One hears of gratings and scratchings, of sounds like the rattle of a machine-gun, a sound like that of a brush, and of yet others, like the sawing and planing of wood. There are sounds like music and like the whistling of wind, very loud sounds like the dropping of a cannon ball or a bomb, sounds that make the whole house shake. These sounds are produced by the light touching of an object, and sometimes by mere thought; the presence of a medium increases their volume. Often, however, the sounds occur quite unprovoked in any way, and even against the will of the person in question, at least as far as the waking consciousness of that person is concerned. They occur, in a word, in a fashion that is as arbitrary and incalculable as a dream. Often there is a reciprocal action with the movements of the medium (sympathetic movement and mimicry); or again there occurs a connection between the sounds and the medium's muscular contractions and the stimuli acting on the medium's nerves, so that a kind of conversation is made possible and questions can be answered. Moreover these sounds can only be controlled through the subconscious, as is clearly shown by the case of the medium Karin. This person lived in a villa, and in this villa heavy footsteps were heard in the evening on the steps leading to the veranda. Doctors then hit on the idea of hypnotizing the medium and ordering her to make the footsteps cease. They were only heard twice after that, and even then were very subdued. Then they were never heard again at all.

A case very similar to that of Karin is related by Malfatti.[41]

Most telacoustic phenomena raise a twofold problem. There is first of all the question of the origin of the message or meaning they are intended to convey, and normally this reflects some piece of knowledge or some thought in the subconscious of some individual. There is also, however, the much more thorny problem of how that individual, or the medium who reads his mind, causes the telacoustic phenomena to take place.

A case is related by Grabinski[42] in which the law played a certain part; indeed the law did this while the actual "spook" phenomena were taking place. The whole matter took place, so to speak, under police control. The following is a summary:

Old Frau Minna Sauerbrey was lying gravely ill with an incurable abdominal disease. Her twenty-one-year-old stepson Otto had had a certain amount to do with hypnotism and spiritualism. He now hypnotized the old lady, and then went away without releasing her from the hypnotic state. This was on the 13th February, 1921. The patient's condition grew worse; she became unclear in her speech and started addressing remarks to her stepson. In these she defended herself against imaginary imputations—that she had stolen chickens from her neighbour, for instance. Shortly thereafter, on the 15th February, raps, becoming ever louder, began to be heard in the kitchen where the old woman was lying, and bowls, buckets, chairs and tables began to move about. This took place chiefly at night, but under the full glare of the electric light. Since the stepson had meanwhile been charged with criminal negligence on account of having failed to awaken his patient from her trance, police were now present during these manifestations—no fewer than twelve police officers being present, including a superintendent. Those poor wretches had then actually to put up with being made fools of by the "spirits" and in the end were compelled to certify that the sick woman, who could not move from her bed, and who died on 27th March, could not possibly have caused these things to happen with her hands or her feet.

---

[41] *Menschenseele und Okkultismus*, p. 179.

[42] *Spuk und Geistererscheinungen oder was sonst?*, 1922, pp. 266-275.

The police being helpless, the doctor was called. It was assumed that the twilight state induced by hypnosis was at the bottom of the whole thing, and for this reason the nerve specialist, Dr Kahle, of Weimar, endeavoured to apply counter-hypnosis. The belief in the exceptional power and strength of will supposedly possessed by the stepson was thus destroyed and the patient ultimately returned to reality, uttering the words "Now I am released." From that moment all the "spooking" stopped and was not repeated.

Here we see clearly how such spook manifestations are brought about experimentally at a spiritualist seance. The medium—in this case a dying woman—is put into a hypnotic twilight state and the telekinetic phenomena begin; when the medium awakes, they vanish.

People often ask who or what it is that directs these raps. Most certainly the answer is that it is those present at a seance together with the medium— even though they may not know it and actually think the opposite with the waking part of their consciousness. Sometimes a medium is not required at all for these manifestations to occur, as is shown us by Fr Castelein, S, J.,[43] whose experiments have demonstrated just how people who take part at a seance are influenced.

At the time when the spiritualist question was greatly exercising people's minds, members of the University of Louvain asked him to lecture on the subject, and he relates the following:

> In order to be able to come forward with well-attested facts, I chose four talented students who were of a sufficiently nervous disposition to suit the purpose I had in mind, one, a medical student, being particularly marked by these characteristics. I asked them whether they were prepared to take part in a scientific and religious experiment, and added, in order to quiet their conscience, that we would break off immediately, if there were any indication of diabolical intervention. In order to prepare them, however, for the autosuggestion which I intended to induce, I added that if the soul of an unbaptized child should appear, we would continue to speak with it, since such intercourse in itself involved nothing that was contrary to faith or reason. This, too, I said so that this my intention to induce autosuggestion should be more easily realized.

---

[43] *L'Hypnotisme*, p. 251.

My four students then closed the chain by lightly touching the table. Would it move? "Listen, friends, spirits, particularly spirits of the kind we want to summon; do not come so quickly." I tried to make them patient, and got them to wait about ten minutes, which was sufficient to tire their fingers and to get them into a condition in which nervous disturbances would be transmitted. I myself stood about three yards away from the table and supervised the experiment. At a given moment I called out "Stop, the base of the table is moving", and suddenly the table did start to move and to turn with slight tremors. I gave a description of the movement and asked all to direct their wills that it should continue. Great consternation and joy! I had been able to influence the subconscious of my assistants in the manner I desired. "And now," I said, "we will ask the table to answer 'yes' and 'no'. One knock will mean yes, and two, no. "Spirit, are you there?" A sufficiently loud rap opposite the very nervous boy was heard. "So it's here! Let us first put decisive preliminary question. Are you a devil or one of the damned?" One rap. Fortunately at this point the table again began to move and we heard two raps. We could now proceed in safety.

Second question: "Are you baptized?" "No." "How old are you?" Three firm raps, then another—weak, and yet another, still weaker; another after that, scarcely audible at all; my "spirits" were apparently agreed on this much—that this was an unbaptized child which had died before attaining the use of reason. They differed, however, in their estimate of its age. The most nervous of these "spirits" no doubt thought that the child had been three, the other believed it to have been a year or two older. I noted that I myself had the age of three firmly fixed in my mind and was no doubt able to communicate this suggestion to my young friends.

There then followed a series of about fifty questions which I had answered by "yes" and "no" in such a manner that they confirmed the full teaching of the Catholic Church concerning the state of children who died unbaptized. Thanks to autosuggestion, we were told that such children enjoy a natural happiness, but cannot be raised up to enjoy the supernatural vision to which indeed they have no right by nature.

My four students went away utterly astonished, and quite sure that they had been instructed by a spirit from the next world. In reality, it was I myself who had ensured the orthodoxy of the "spirit's" answers.

How great was the surprise of my four students when in my lecture on the following day I explained the phenomena of the talking table by the psychological theory of autosuggestion and unconscious nervous movements.

We need not here concern ourselves with the actual manner in which the raps were produced—whether, that is to say, they were caused by the unconscious muscular action of the students, as the author seems to think, or by the souls of the students (or of some of them) acting after the manner of pure spirits. The importance of the story resides in the fact that it identifies the directing intelligence, in this particular case, that of the priest himself. In other cases it is the medium's intelligence which produces the messages by influencing those present at the seance. The medium does this in a state of trance, in which it remembers the knowledge stored in its own subconscious and, like pure spirits, can read what is taking place in that of others. All this explains why the messages can never go beyond the medium's own intellectual horizon and that of the others present—which has led one commentator to remark that: "If these messages really come from the other world, then that world is not worth much."[44]

For the most part mediums and the others present at seances do not know the teaching of the Church and are even hostile to it. This is apparent when they jeer at the "heavenly porter", or say that Cardinal Vaughan had taught error during his lifetime,[45] or utter other follies of the kind recorded by Fr Lacroix in no fewer than fifty pages, and also by Bishop Schneider.[46] The deliria of dreamers are really not worth refuting.

There are people who think that this table-turning, which is in such ill odour, may become "the means of solving the most profound problems of human nature, and of abolishing all superstition. At the same time, much that is derided today as superstition may be recognized as belonging to the natural processes of a magnetically creative or psychodynamic activity on the part of the human spirit. This may help to provide an answer to the deepest questions of psychology and philosophy."[47]

It is said that cases are not unknown where actual human voices have been heard at seances, though here we are on very uncertain ground, for in the darkness observation is rarely exact. The case of a certain Margery, the wife of a Boston surgeon, Dr Graham, has been much disputed. This lady causes the

---

[44] Dr Lucio dos Santos, *Diario*, Bello Horizonte, 1923.
[45] Raupert-Lucio dos Santos, *Espiritismo*, p. 82.
[46] Pp. 220-261.
[47] H. Schindler, *Das magische Geistesleben*, Breslau, 1857.

voice of her brother "Walter" to be heard. George Valiantine brought about similar manifestations, using a trumpet for the purpose, while Bradley has made hundreds of recordings on which voices speak in English, Italian, Hindustani and Chinese, although the medium concerned had no knowledge of any of these languages.

But a medium who is able completely to enter into the personality of a dead person subconsciously may really develop the ability to portray the man's whole character and to imitate his bearing and even his voice. A case is reported of a young man who had considerable skill in imitating other people's signatures. It was his practice to try and put himself completely into the position of the person concerned, and to try and adopt his voice and gestures. It was only then that he signed that person's name, achieving on these occasions an astonishing resemblance to the authentic signature. When one personality moves in complete harmony with another, down to the subconscious itself, it is not really surprising that a good imitation of voice and bearing should become possible, though when this occurs at a spiritualist seance, the medium gets knowledge of the character concerned by drawing it out of the consciousness or the subconscious of those taking part or putting the questions.

(ii) Telekinesis

There is much more reliable evidence for the phenomena of telekinesis, the movement of objects without the application of physical power, movements to which no recognizable cause can be assigned. Thus in broad daylight at a seance with Frau Silbert in Graz a table weighing sixty pounds was moved up and down and tipped up. Frau Moser[48] describes the levitation of a table at which she was present. The table was moved up and down and tipped up at an angle.

> There was a soft but clearly audible cracking sound, then suddenly it rose up with such power and speed that we all jumped up with fright and pushed back our chairs, my own being knocked right over. As though raised up by an enormous fist, or by a beam which had suddenly sprung out of the earth, the

---

[48] *Okkultismus*, pp. 40 ff.

table shot about three feet into the air, remained suspended there for a short time and then sank slowly back.... Suddenly it rose a second time, and to such a height that Herr Fischer, the medium's husband, cried out, "Stop it, or it will break the lamp." We started to press down with all the strength at our command; the table continued to float with its top at eye level, so that the hands that formed the chain had actually to be raised up above the shoulders. I pressed as hard as I could, and so apparently did the others. It was all in vain. The table did not rise any higher, but it did not move downwards either; it remained suspended under the hanging lamp as though it were held by iron chains. It remained thus for a long time, the pressure we put on it having no more effect than a fly. Then suddenly it crashed down with a tilt in my direction, so that the medium and I were forced to move back. It landed with such force that one of the feet broke off and flew with a crash against the door. The table now stood crooked; its position was near the wall, and only partly on the carpet.

We then had yet a third levitation, after which we picked up the chairs that had been knocked over and pushed the table back to its original position. At the medium's suggestion, we took our places around it yet once more, whereupon it rose into the air again. This time, however—and this was the extraordinary thing—it floated at a slant, so that the right end was about breast high, while the other end, which was towards the doctor, was about at eye level. Though I again pressed with all my might, I could not produce the slightest movement, or even the slightest vibration. It hung immovable, as though on a solid base. My impression that something must be carrying it, or that there must be some kind of machinery at work, was so strong that an irresistible urge compelled me to say: "May I examine this thing?" "Certainly," answered Herr Fischer. I broke the chain—and this had no influence on the table at all—knelt down on the carpet and felt with both hands under the feet of the table, searching in all directions. Nothing—absolutely nothing was to be found. Then the table sank back on to the floor—this time very slowly and gently.

Yet there are other phenomena than such moving tables. Bells, violins, water bottles, plants and skulls fly through the air. Mediums raise themselves by autolevitation, or become perceptibly lighter, as can be proved by the weighing scale, or fail to sink in water, much as witches used to fail to sink. One such medium "could not be brought into a bath at all, since she would bob up like a cork". The medium Home is stated to have flown out of one window and in at the other, afterwards expressing the hope that the police had not witnessed the incident, as they might have misinterpreted the significance of a figure moving along a house wall.

It is said that mediums can move objects by mere thought, without touching them at all. In this way they can also cause weighing scales to sink and instruments to play. Once when the highly nervous and weakly Stanislava Tomczyk was consulting a doctor, the ink-pot suddenly began to dance about, causing considerable alarm to all that witnessed the incident. Eusapia Paladino, who had a wound in the head and was an epileptic, caused heavy objects such as a typewriter to be lifted up at a distance. We also hear of materializations—that is, the appearance of hands, feet, heads and of persons that walk about and talk.

Fr Gatterer, S.J., writes in his book as follows[49]:

In the seances with Rudi Schneider and Maria Silbert, telekinetic movements took place before my eyes and quite close to me, for instance, the breaking of a violin next to Schrenck-Notzing. I was also able to witness in Braunau the materialization of a small hand, which seized a bell out of my own. It appeared with complete clarity in a number of diverse circumstances, and I can guarantee that it was not the hand of Rudi or of any other member of the seance.

The conditions of supervision and observation I can only describe as perfect. In the seances with Maria Silbert, the clearest phenomena were the messages communicated by means of raps, and this was observed innumerable times by bright lamplight and even by daylight, and I myself could observe this phenomenon at every seance. The circumstances in which the manifestation took place excluded in my opinion any possibility of fraud.

I do not hesitate to express my personal conviction on the subject of paraphysical phenomena ... that in our day, as in any other, we have witnessed genuine occult phenomena, both spontaneous and experimental.

So writes the learned Jesuit, and indeed, though excessive credulity would be a mistake, it would be equally foolish to deny plain facts which have been observed by serious men of science, especially when the theory of the special gifts of the spirit makes such facts appear possible. Serious authors recount facts such as the following:

---

[49] *Wissenschaftlicher Okkultismus*, (1927).

The Mexican Jesuit de Heredia reproduced a levitation under strict control, of which a newspaper reporter gives this account: The body of P. d. H., which was scarcely visible in the darkened cabinet, rose slowly upward, assumed a horizontal position, remained there for some time, and then sank down and resumed its natural position. The help of two doctors was required to bring H. round again. After this exhibition, the Jesuit asked those present to come on the stage and to search most carefully for any possible deception. Several persons accepted this invitation and reported that they could find nothing. This scientifically trained Jesuit looks upon levitation as a fact which will probably one day be explained in terms of magnetism.[50]

Of course, we deny that there is any need for dragging in magnetism; let us, however, proceed to yet other instances. Jacolliot[51] relates the following of the Fakirs Salvanidèn-Odèar and Covin-Dasomij: "They rise into the air and float out of the open window." "The most striking instances of levitation occurred in the case of Mr Home," says Grookes. "I have myself seen him rise right off the floor on three separate occasions." "That the raising of tables has actually occurred seems well established," writes Bishop Schneider.[52]

The multiplicity of such accounts causes Professor Malfatti to write[53]: "There is no reason to suppose that the soul loses its ability to put out power and act on matter once it has left the body; after all, it remains even after death—such is its nature—the vital spiritual force of man." We might add that it retains these powers when it is only in a state of semi-freedom from the body.

Much controverted are the so-called "apports". We use this term for occurrences such as those when fresh flowers or birds fall from the ceiling, when knots are untied after both ends have been sealed, when wooden rings are fastened one into the other, when objects or even persons are made to vanish and then to reappear, when letters are written on slates after normal human agency has done no more than put a piece of chalk in readiness. One cannot say how large a part is played by hallucination in these cases. "Even so," writes Moser, "we cannot wholly reject these cases of apport, however great

---

[50] Feldmann, *Okkulte Philosophie*, p. 116.
[51] *Le spiritisme dans le monde*, Paris, 1875.
[52] *Der neuere Geisterglaube*, p. 501.
[53] *Menschenseele und Okkultismus*, p. 148.

the temptation. My two experiences with Rudi Schneider must be classified under this head; in one of these a handkerchief suddenly and inexplicably disappeared out of my clenched fist; on another a violin disappeared while I had my arms actually around it."[54]

Zöllner, the physicist, working together with a friend, made elaborate studies of these cases of interlocking rings, knots, and the writing on locked-up slates—to the great scandal of the scientific world, since these effects were reproduced later by professional conjurors. It is difficult to tell whether Zöllner was right or his materialist critics.

There was also the case of a seance with Eusapia Paladino, attended by certain men of science. On this occasion "heavy curtains were lifted from the window and hurled on to the table, and the zither gave out the same note eleven times. Then it moved in leaps over the floor, and was finally hurled on to the table, where it remained with the strings downwards; in this position it continued to give out sounds under our eyes. . . . This time Myers and the whole company were absolutely convinced, and regarded the proof as complete."[55] Certainly many scientific minds have been so carried away that they already speak of the "unveiling of the spiritualist Sphinx".[56] Some hold that the medium accumulates electric charges, which under psychodynamic direction can produce astonishing releases of power. It was, it is said, the fact of being electrically charged that enabled thirteen-year-old Angelica Cottin of Bauvigny to cause furniture weighing three hundred pounds to be hurled about. Moser's comment seems to hit the nail on the head when she says[57]: "The human soul has the ability to act on the external world in two ways, through the muscles and directly through the will", although in the following chapter, that on animal magnetism, she feels impelled to treat the two things as one.

---

[54] Moser, *Okkultismus*, pp. 811 ff.
[55] Flournoy, *Des Indes à la planète Mars*, p. 126.
[56] *Linzer Quartalschrift*, 1937, p. 253.
[57] *Okkultismus*, p. 850.

(iii) Teleplastic phenomena

The most disputed phenomena of all, however, are so-called materializations. We hear of limbs of the human body appearing and even of complete phantoms, of imprints of hands and faces on paraffin wax. Crookes made a particular examination of changes of weight in objects, and employed the most delicate apparatus for this purpose, and the most ingenious methods to ensure the complete absence of fraud. His conclusion is that these phenomena undoubtedly occur—as do also the playing of tunes by musical instruments. He ascribed these things, however, not to spirits but to the psychic powers of the mediums, which he refrained from defining further. As against this, Myers believed that they confirmed the spiritualist hypothesis. Mattiesen spoke of an "excursive ego" which radiated from the body and thus set up an additional theory.

Tischner writes: "While Slade, a well-known medium, sat quietly on the left of Zöllner with his hands resting on the table, there suddenly appeared from under the edge of the table a large hand which seized Zöllner's left upper-arm. Zöllner was able to watch it closely for three or four minutes in the brightly-lit room. Shortly afterwards his right hand was painfully pinched."[58] Zöllner also put two slates together with a piece of chalk between and closed and sealed them. Suddenly something started to write between the two slates, and when they were opened up, the writing was there to see.

Materializations proper, when they are not mere frauds, must be better examined than they have been hitherto, the best technical means being employed that our time affords—the extraordinary nature of the claims demands nothing less—for such accounts as that of Flammarion[59] concerning the experiments of Sir William Crookes verge on the unbelievable. Crookes is said to have observed the phantom "Katy" walking up and down the room for two hours and witnessed her talking in a quite intimate way with all those present, while the medium Florence Cook lay in a trance behind a curtain. On several occasions, moreover, the phantom took Crookes's arm and all could see that this was a genuine living creature and not a shadow from the next

---

[58] Tischner, *Ergebnisse*, p. 157.
[59] *Unbekannte Naturkräfte*, p. 300.

world. To what extent fraud, or the hallucination of all those present, was at work here, it is as yet impossible to say.

A great part of these "physical" manifestations are most certainly hallucinations—and genuine phenomena are few and far between, but we must certainly take them into account, nor are they in theory impossible, since a spirit can act upon matter. Whether people have really succeeded in photographing such "spirits" is a moot point. Photographs are of course sometimes shown, but it is always an open question whether they are genuine. It is difficult to believe that real spirits show themselves to the experimenters clad in silken or cotton garments which are then duly dematerialized.

All that is reported in the way of such manifestations can be arranged under one of the three categories named above, even if they make their appearance in various disguises. Sometimes several of these different kinds of phenomena are combined—a circumstance that enhances the element of the wonderful and the inexplicable. We cannot therefore follow any more the same sequence, dealing first with the purely spiritual and then with the physical, but must now choose another arrangement and classify them according to the manner in which they appear to be guided by a conscious intelligence.

The phenomena in which such guidance is least clearly in evidence, which show the maximum of confusion and are most marked by their dreamlike quality, are those connected with magic, theosophy and astrology; in radiaesthesia the intellect has already a conscious aim before it, and this is even more true of Couéism and Christian Science, for in these the object is healing. In the case of crystal gazing, spiritualism and spook phenomena (at any rate the personal ones) the subject is exposed to the wildest suggestions. Hylomancy, or psychometry, where dreams are based on some directing object, forms the transition stage to those phenomena which are clearly dependent on another intelligence, namely hypnotism, possession and mystical experience. In these the soul which is hidden in our body is influenced respectively by the hypnotist, the devil and (in the last case) by God.

IV

CERTAIN SPECIAL ASPECTS OF THE PHENOMENA OF ARTIFICIAL SLEEP

[There seem good grounds for looking upon magic (A) as an attempt by man to regain some of the preternatural powers that he had lost by the Fall. Its most typical forms are usually associated with some dulling of the sense mechanism, and in this state the magician becomes endowed with clairvoyance. Radiaesthesia or divining (B) is partly susceptible of a physical explanation, but there is strong evidence that the soul's powers of purely spiritual cognition are involved. Couéism and Christian Science (C) may aptly be considered here, since the powers of the unconscious mind are involved, and Coué actually makes use of incipient sleep to get results. Crystal-gazing (D) is explained as a form of mild self-hypnosis, while all the phenomena of spiritualism (E) can be satisfactorily interpreted in terms of the author's thesis. The medium at a seance is in a self-induced trance and in that state can gain knowledge of events in the past or at a distance and can also read the thoughts of other people, whether conscious or unconscious. The manner in which the medium's knowledge is translated into messages has already been indicated. Most ghosts and spook phenomena (F) come, in the author's view, into the same class of phenomena as the physical manifestations at seances and the apports of spiritualism, i.e. they come under the head of teleplastic and telekinetic phenomena. A genuine reappearance of the dead is of course not to be wholly ruled out in certain special circumstances.

Hylomantic phenomena (G), in which the handling of some object induces clairvoyance, are best interpreted under the assumption that the object acts as a kind of organizer of the chaotic life of the subconscious, by turning its attention in a particular direction. This last is also the main characteristic of hypnotism (H) and probably why it gets such good results, the organizer being in this case the hypnotist.

From this organizing of the mental life of another by the hypnotist we pass logically to the phenomenon of possession (I), in which an alien intelligence takes complete control of the personality of a human being and acts and speaks through it.]

(A) Magic

Magic is one of the oldest ways by which men have sought—and still seek—to use the powers of the subconscious. The writer proposes to show that the manifestations of magic are all explicable in natural terms and are in the main of the same character as those normally associated with artificial sleep. This will enable us at a stroke to dispose of all the mysticizing manias which seem nowadays to bedevil people's minds.

The theologians define magic as the art of doing miraculous things either with the help of the devil (black magic) or without him (white magic). It is possible that there have been people who made compacts with the devil in order to perform their miraculous deeds, but the record that has remained of cases to which no natural explanation would appear to apply is negligible. At any rate the whole subject of so-called magic has today attained the status of an experimental science, and we can now turn the full light of day on to all the alleged mysteries of ancient times.

The Bavarian seminary professor Dr Staudenmaier tells us in his book[1] that by advice of his colleagues he attempted and achieved all the things that once caused consternation to Christian and heathen alike. Dr Staudenmaier began his studies by schooling himself to produce the manifestations of mediumistic writing. He took a pencil between his fingers and waited for them to produce the motion of writing of their own accord. The attempt had no results. Repeating the experiment next day, he was equally unsuccessful. Tired out and disappointed, he would have abandoned the whole thing, had not his friends urged him to continue. He yielded to them, and started afresh.

One day he observed, while concentrating his thoughts on the pencil, that there was a motion in his fingers, and the pencil began to draw circles, which however did not have the form of letters at all. Thoroughly worn out, he abandoned the experiment, only to resume it on the following day. This time he noticed that the motion was stronger than before, and the pencil ultimately wrote "Julie Nome is here", this being the name of a well-known medium. Shortly after this the pencil wrote a number of other names and recorded a number of communications.

---

[1] *Die Magie als Experimentelle Naturwissenschaft,* Leipzig, 1932.

It was not long before he did not require the pencil at all in order to become the recipient of messages. The various personalities themselves spoke, one after the other, whenever he wished them to do so. On these occasions he almost lost consciousness (he had passed into a condition of artificial sleep), but he was still able to observe that his throat become constricted when a child appeared and spoke to him (it was really he himself who was the speaker), while he felt his chest expand and was conscious of assuming a soldierly bearing when the Emperor appeared and spoke to him in his characteristic fashion. Again he was still aware of the fact that it was not the Emperor, but he himself who was doing the speaking.

As his proficiency increased, people began to appear to him and told him things which in his waking condition he had not known before, but now read in the souls of others, even when those others were not present at all; thus he was able by degrees to reproduce all the manifestations of spiritualism and occultism—a feat, incidentally, which was reproduced later by Meyer[2] and by Heredia—and was actually able to achieve the movement of objects by the power of his thought, to bring about the breaking of peas in a glass, the movement of food in the bowel, the stinking of the devil, and other allegedly magical phenomena.

His supposedly magical powers developed still further. He saw and heard quarrelling between the people with whom he conversed, and they came to him without his even wanting them to do so; they came by day and by night, leaving him no peace at all. He now realized how his nervous system had already suffered, that he was nearly going mad and could no longer protect himself against the spirits. It was only by a great effort, and by applying the whole power of his soul, that he was able to free himself from the grip of these "spirits". He has described his experiences in the above-mentioned book. If it were not for the fact that it was so dangerous to health, one would feel tempted to urge others to try these experiments, and that means not only the tricks of a Heredia and a Dunninger, which hurt nobody, but also the purely spiritual experiments. Thus all could convince themselves that there is no need for any devil in order to explain either mental suggestion or the reading of the thoughts of distant persons. In this way the proof would be established that

---

[2] Dessoir, *Okkultismus in Urkunden*, I-V, p. 454.

all that was previously, and still is, assumed to be the work of spirits derives from one's own soul, when, in an abnormal state, it produces hallucinations. We could then leave a Dr Faustus, a Paracelsus, a Nostradamus, a Cagliostro and such strange creatures as the fantastic Heinrich Cornelius Agrippa of Nettesheim, to have as many "conversations with the devil" as they desired.

We knew a certain countess who had communications with the souls of the dead, which actually appeared to her, and another lady who believed herself to be possessed, both of whom came near to going insane. They are the kind of people who, as Dr Hélot points out,[3] spend their whole lives in a state of hallucination, split personality and madness—a miserable state. The sorry story of the witches and their dreams, the "necromancy" and "crystallomancy" of the ancients, to which there are references in classical writers such as Horace,[4] Cicero,[5] Tacitus,[6] Suetonius and the elder Pliny, in Diocassius and Lucan—these things apparently were not enough, we still had to have the modern epidemic of spiritualism, of which mention is already made in Holy Scripture, and which is condemned there.[7]

Ethnology teaches us that in the earliest stage of civilization, namely in the hunting and foraging stage, where pure monotheism prevailed, there is no trace either of magic or witchcraft. It was only when man sank to the secondary stages that the belief in one God became more remote to him and that he surrendered himself to the devil, with whom he both played and fought. This is equivalent to saying that the further removed men became from the innocence of Paradise, the more they sought to make use of the rudiments of their sometimes preternatural gifts, and thus attempted to achieve by this round-about method what they were no longer capable of doing directly, namely to know and to be masters of nature after the manner of pure spirits. These magical practices were of course not indulged in in order to gain that better knowledge of the Creator which was sought by the mystics; the purpose was rather to get the better of him so that he might cease to be in a position of advantage; or it was to obtain sensual gratification or material

---

[3] *Les névrosés et les possessions diaboliques.*
[4] Sat., I, 8, 25.
[5] *Tuscul. Quaest.*, I, 16.
[6] *Annales*, II, 28.
[7] Deut. 18. 10; I Kings 28. 8, 7; Lev. 20. 27.

benefit, or to achieve revenge on an enemy by frightening him, harming him or destroying him.

That is why magic assumed world dimensions, so that in the course of centuries it has become a real disease of the spirit. It is therefore high time to lay bare its sources—and, with these, perhaps, its cure. An example related by Bishop Schneider[8] will serve this purpose very well.

> A certain explorer named Matzuschkin gave this description of a piece of magic, encountered while on an expedition to the North Pole, to a friend in St Petersburg: "In the middle of the Jurta a bright fire was flickering around which there was a circle of black sheep skins. On these last a Shaman was walking around with a measured rhythmical tread and repeating the magic formulae in a low voice. His long, black shaggy hair covered his swollen dark red face almost completely. From beneath this veil there flashed from under bushy eyebrows a pair of glowing bloodshot eyes. His clothing, a long robe made of animal skins, was covered from top to bottom with more animal skins, chains, bells, and pieces of copper and iron. In his right hand he had his magic drum, which was similarly decorated with bells and took the form of a tambourine, while in his left he held a bow with the string relaxed. His face was gruesome, wild and terrible. The company sat in silence, tensely attentive. Gradually the flame in the centre of the Jurta burned low, only the coals still glowed and radiated a dim light. The Shaman threw himself on to the ground, and when he had been lying there about five minutes, he broke into a kind of melancholy sighing, a dull suppressed kind of crying which sounded as though it was produced by a number of voices. After a time the fire became bright again, and the flames rose high. The Shaman leapt up, placed his bow upon the ground, then leaning his forehead on one end of it, be began to move around this bow in a circle, at first moving slowly and then accelerating the pace. After this circular motion had continued for so long that my head had begun to swim from merely watching him, the Shaman suddenly stopped and stood still, showing no sign whatever of giddiness, and began to trace all manner of figures in the air with his hands, then with a sort of enthusiasm he seized his drum, which he tapped, as it seemed to me, in a definite tune, shortly after which he began to leap about, now faster, now more slowly, jerking his whole body with astonishing rapidity. What particularly struck me was the movement of his head, which he continually turned with such rapidity that it

---

[8] *Der neuere Geisterglaube*, pp. 40 ff.

resembled a ball hurled around at the end of a piece of string. During all these activities the Shaman had smoked with a certain greed a number of pipes of the strongest Circassian tobacco, drinking a sip of brandy in between. Both articles were handed him at a sign which he made from time to time. The tobacco, the brandy and the continual turning must after all have induced giddiness at last, for he suddenly fell to the ground and remained there stark and motionless. Two of the onlookers now sprang up and began to sharpen a pair of large knives against each other immediately above his head. This seems to have recalled the Shaman to consciousness. He began his strange melancholy sighing anew, and commenced slowly and jerkily to move his body. The two men who had been whetting their knives raised him and stood him upright. His aspect was hideous. His eyes stood out staring from his head, his face was red all over; he seemed to be completely unconscious and apart from a slight trembling of his whole body, there was no movement or sign of life to be observed in him. Suddenly he seemed to awaken from this paralytic state. With his right hand resting upon the bow, he swung the magic drum rapidly round his head and then let it fall to earth, which showed, as the onlookers explained to me, that he was now fully inspired and could have questions addressed to him. I approached him; he stood there motionless, with completely lifeless face and eyes, and neither my questions nor the answers which he gave, without for a moment reflecting on them, brought any change in his dazed appearance. I asked him about the outcome and success of our expedition, of which most certainly no one in that whole gathering had the remotest conception, and he answered every question, doing so in a somewhat oracular style indeed, but nevertheless with a kind of certainty which suggested that he was familiar with the main purpose and also with the incidental circumstances of my journey. Here are some of his answers which I have reproduced as far as possible word for word. 'How long will our journey last?' 'Over three years.' 'Shall we achieve much?' 'More than your people expect at home.' 'Shall we all remain in good health?' 'All except yourself, but you will not be ill,' (All this was to prove more or less true, for Matzuschkin was to suffer for some time from a cut on his thumb, which owing to frequent frost-bite was to become very nasty.) I asked him among other things after one of our colleagues. Lieutenant Anjou, from whom I had been separated for some time. 'He is now three days' journey from Balna, where he had to endure a fearful storm on the Lena and only saved his life with difficulty.' (This too was later to be exactly confirmed.) He also spoke of my wife's large blue eyes. This caused the women and girls of the Jurta to ask what was meant by blue eyes, and the whole gathering' was astonished at hearing of blue eyes in a human face, for the only eyes of which they could form any conception were the small black eyes which are the only kind of eyes to be found in this region. Many of his answers, however, were so obscure—one might almost say, so poetic—that none of my interpreters were able to translate them for me. They declared these utterances to be "exalted or, as they call them here, 'fable language'. When all the curious in the company had been satisfied, the Shaman again fell down and remained lying on the ground for about a quarter of an hour, twitching all the time and being shaken by violent spasms. It was explained to me that during this time the devils were going out of him again, and for this reason, in addition to their ordinary passage of exit, which was the chimney, the door was also opened for them. Incidentally their departure seemed an easier matter than their entry, for which four hours had been required. At last all was over. The Shaman got up and on his face there was an expression of surprise and wonder, like that of a man who wakens from a deep sleep and finds himself in a large company. He looked at all those around him, one after the other, my own person in particular attracted his attention, and it seemed as though he saw me for the first time. I turned to him and requested elucidation of some of his darker sayings. He looked at me in astonishment and shook his head in token of negation, as though he had never heard the like."

"As often as I observed the Siberian Shamans performing their official functions," says another eye-witness,[9] "they made a most uncanny, an unforgettable impression upon me. The wild look, the bloodshot eyes, the labouring breast, the inarticulate cries, the seemingly involuntary distortions of the face and twistings of the body, the waving hair—yes, even the hollow sound of the drum, heightened the effect, and I fully understand that such a sight must, to an uneducated observer, appear to be the work of evil spirits"—which may well be exactly what it is.

Here we have a description of the various phases of magical procedure, the efforts to fall into a trance, the suppression of the senses, clairvoyance and all the other customary phenomena, and finally the awakening. Even if all this appears to be abnormal, it can almost all be explained by the powers of the spirit-soul.

---

[9] Cf. Castren, *Reiseberichte* . . . , 1845-1849, p. 173.

That this is the true explanation is proved by the ways in which the Shaman is chosen and prepared for his task. These are described for us by Pater Schmidt[10] (following Lankenau). "To become a Shaman," he writes, "it is essential that the candidates should be sickly, weak, and thin. A strong and vigorous man is not consecrated to this calling, but if, by favour of the 'tagei' or wood spirit, a man develops a meditative habit, becomes an epileptic or shows a disposition to fall into a violent rage, then it is considered that he will certainly be a good Shaman and the 'Ulu Kam' chooses him for initiation into his own secrets." If he is exhausted by disease, he is magnetized and left alone for a year, so that the spirits may appear to him. After undergoing this experience the usages and obligations of the Shaman's state become easy for him—all of which confirms the views here expressed. [A word of comment is in place here on one aspect of Matzuschkin's experience, for it might appear at first sight that the Shaman was actually endowed with prophetic powers. There is, however, no reason to suppose this. It is highly probable that Matzuschkin had himself already formed some estimate of the probable duration of his expedition and that this estimate was correct. In that case we can surely assume that the Shaman did no more than read what was in his mind. In the matter of the cut thumb, it is probable that a small cut had actually already been made, in which case the Shaman would know the probable consequences of such a cut in such a climate. A more likely explanation is that he became aware of some minor latent malady in Matzuschkin and that the superimposition of the trouble with the thumb was a coincidence.—*Translator's note.*]

> Wherever we encounter magic (or mediumistic powers), we find things very much as described above. Newspapers dated the 28th January, 1925, recount that at the "Jakobimarkt" in Mastholte large-scale thefts took place every year without anyone being able to trace the thief. The family that owned the inn always anticipated the Feast of St James with feelings of fear, and the emergency was so great that it was decided to have recourse to a man reputed to be clairvoyant, namely the "magnetopath" Petzold of Bielefeld. This man came and by means of autosuggestion put himself into a trance, then

---

[10] *Ursprung der Gottesidee*, Vol. IX, p. 687.

he began to dance ecstatically around the room, like a dervish, spreading out his fingers, and looking with his great sparkling eyes, which resembled those of an animal trainer, like a man utterly lost in a dream, as he stared into space. Then, as though speaking from another world, he said with a voice that resembled that of a ghost: "The thief will come again this year. I see a man with black hair, powerfully and stockily built, entering the inn at the stroke of eleven. He passes right through the crowd in the tap room, and goes immediately to the stairs, climbs them, and I lose sight of him; he disappears in a dark passage. This man is the thief you are looking for." After this Petzold awoke from his dream state, rubbed his eyes and came to himself sufficiently to collect his fee. The police were notified. On the day in question, at the stroke of eleven, the man arrived, pushed his way through the crowd and mounted the stairs. Such was the excitement of the police that they nearly sounded the alarm too soon. Five minutes later they did so. The thief had hidden himself in the curing room and had already stolen a number of things, which were now taken from him, and a search of his home brought to light everything that had been stolen in previous years.

When Petzold was asked how it was possible for him to have a detailed knowledge of things with which he was wholly unacquainted, he replied: "I cannot explain it. I see a thing, and I hear a thing, but I do not know how this comes about. Naturally these things are only possible when I can attain the maximum of concentration, and when I am completely undisturbed."[11]

It is impossible to say whether we are here dealing with the old-fashioned type of magician or with a modern medium in a trance; the phenomena connected with each really merge into one another. Incidentally it is worth noting that here also we might infer the possession of prophetic powers, but, as in other cases, there is really no need to do anything of the kind. Petzold, being gifted with clairvoyance, certainly saw what happened in the past, and also to some extent the reasons for it. Thus the articles taken were mostly cutlery, which would have been locked away had the thief come at a different hour, and there were doubtless other reasons connected with the routine of the inn which made him choose this particular time; and it was a reasonable inference to suppose that the same reasons would influence his actions in any future visit. That Petzold should have foretold that the thief would repeat his

---

[11] Feldmann, *Okkulte Philosophie*, pp. 122 ff.

visit that year may have been a lucky guess, or Petzold may have read the intention in the thief's mind.

We will refrain from adding to these examples, for examples can be found in sufficient quantity in the relevant books (which exist in almost every language) by anyone who cares to consult them. The explanation of the phenomena in question is a far more important matter, and there is at present no theory which explains them adequately; for it does not help matters simply to give these manifestations a name, and to call them telepathy or telaesthesia. This helps us as little as the denial of the actual facts themselves.

Our explanation must be based on the existence of powers whose reality is proved in some other fashion, or which can be deduced philosophically from other branches of knowledge. We have called these powers remnants of the exceptional gifts of the first men, which though atrophied by the Fall, are still present in us.

It is true that today these remnants show two forms of faultiness. First of all, they only represent a small residuum of the purely spiritual qualities of the soul, since this same soul is still bound to the body. It is for this reason that they can never attain the full scope of the achievements which we have above ascribed to pure spirits or to the human soul free from the body. The soul under hypnosis, as also in the other states of sleep, is only half free of the body; that is why in all these manifestations the element of rationality peculiar to the corporal soul, the element of "sense" is absent, as it is absent in the dreams that come during natural sleep. In hypnotism this gap in rationality is filled by the hypnotist who guides the powers of his subject. That is why better results are produced under hypnosis than in spiritualist seances. This element of guidance, which in normal circumstances pertains to the corporal soul and in hypnosis to the hypnotist, is supplied in psychometry by some object which acts as a reminder of the person concerning whom some information is desired; in spiritualism it is supplied by the wishes of those present, in the dreams of witches by the general mania of the time. These last, however, are not sufficiently clear for the guidance to be really sure.

So much for the first weakness, which is partially corrected in the various ways described. There remains, however, a second one. It is the general weakness and slightness of the power, which is after all only a rudiment or shadow of one that was originally angelic. The greatness of that original power can be guessed if one considers the extraordinary things which can still be achieved by its vestigial remnants as exemplified in the case of a person who was laid across two chairs with only the head resting on one and the heels on the other. Here is another which anybody can try out for themselves. Let them get a strong man to stretch out his hand and remain in that position for as long as he can. It may be that he will be able to do this for some minutes, but a person under hypnosis can remain in this position for any time that is desired.[12] How great then must have been the powers of the first man.

The use of these vestigial powers has in its time been exploited for the purposes of all kinds of magic; it has been used, for instance, both to harm others and to heal disease, it was used for purposes of prophecy, of conjuration, of cursing, and for all manner of astonishing arts. Immense injury has thus been done to our belief in God and to the welfare of souls.

(B) Radiaesthesia (Water-Divining and Metal-Divining)

The harm done in the aggregate to mental health by spiritualism and occultism is so great that it justifies the avoidance of certain practices which are innocent enough in themselves, but which tend to lead to an unhealthy mysticism. Among these last is what is called rabdomantia, or radiaesthesia, which is supposed to disclose the whereabouts of water or metal deposits. In these experiments, a rod of wood or metal is used, bent into the form of a Latin V, or alternatively a pendulum which oscillates above the object that is to be discovered.

To form a correct estimate of the value of the divining-rod, one must realize that nearly all elements radiate, that is to say give out certain rays; this is done by radium, uranium and thorium, substances whose radioactive properties are known. These heavy elements, with ninety or more negatively charged electrons circling around a positively charged nucleus like planets around the sun, are continually breaking up and dividing, and in doing so emit those rays which are called Alpha rays (positively charged), Beta rays (negatively charged) and Gamma rays (X-rays, or Röntgen rays). Scientists

---

[12] Cf. Schneider, *op. cit.*, p. 114, the accounts of Zöllner.

assert that all other elements also send out similar rays, even though this cannot as yet be definitely proved. Since the various elements are distributed in the earth, there is continual radiation passing from the earth to the air, a radiation which has so great an effect on Living things that the health of their bodies largely depends on it, and where such radiation does not exist, the vital processes of plants and animals are impaired.

People often talk of harmful earth radiations,[13, 14] though the expression is incorrect. What one should really say is that certain strata of the earth *screen* these radiations and that over them there are no radiations, a circumstance which has a deleterious effect on the growth of plants and animals and causes them to contract cancer. Radium rays heal cancer, but never or only very rarely cause it. Nevertheless it is clearly shown by the experiments of J, G. Wüst and J. Wimmer[15] that we are concerned here with certain types of ray. Actually these men assert that polarized rays are emitted from objects which have equal wave-lengths with the nerves and with the magnetism of the earth, and that it is from the latter, especially, that vital energy passes to man in breathing. They also speak of a "screening" of these rays by bad conductors.

It is known also that electric rays are diverted by a good conductor and screened by it; now this occurs in the case of the earth rays when there is water or some other good conductor such as metal, coal, oil, etc. Above such deposits there is a lack of the radiations from the earth that are necessary for life, and the living organism is sensitive to this defect. The nerves contract and are subject to an unusual kind of agitation. The diviner's rod, which now behaves in a manner different from its behaviour when over other parts of the earth, helps to show the presence of these disturbances. When people pass over such portions of the earth, they become conscious of the absence of the normal radiations, and if they live above them permanently, become subject

---

[13] A. E. Becker, *Radiações maleficas do subsolo*, São Paulo, 1935.

[14] H. H. Kritzinger, *Todesstrahlen und Wümchelrute*, Leipzig-Zürich, 1929; F. Dietrich, *Erdstrahlen . . .? Ihr Wesen, ihre Wirksamkeit und wie wir uns von ihnen schützen können*, Villach, 1952.

[15] "Über neuartige Schwingungen der Wellenlänge 1-70 cm in der Umgebung anorganischer und organischer Substanzen sowie biologischer Objekte", in *Archiv für Entwicklungsmechanik der Organismen*, Roux, 1934.

to disease. All living organisms tend to be affected in such a situation; plants develop cancer and die.

For this reason certain apparatus has actually been designed in Germany, the purpose of which is to collect rays from other parts and to deflect them to the areas where they are lacking thus bringing health to the afflicted spots.[16] Theodore Czepl and F. Dietrich have been at much pains to trace these injurious subterranean watercourses and are thus rendering a great service to public health. Of late an entire literature has developed on this subject, particularly since the discovery of cosmic rays (see p. 191, note 14).

Up to this point we have been dealing with a purely physical phenomenon which has nothing to do with the occult at all, and actually some of the apparatus constructed, by Gay du Bourg for instance,[17] attains its results while dispensing wholly with the human element. The principle on which these contrivances work is that the conductivity of the air for electricity rises and falls according to the degree to which these rays are present or not. It would thus appear that the diviner's rod has really rendered great services to mankind. . . .

It must of course be noted that it is not the diviner's rod itself which indicates the existence of these subterranean treasures, but the man behind it, as indeed has been shown by Professor Calami of Placenza, who was a diviner himself. Professor Calami declares that he always had the feeling "that a current was rising through his legs, passed from there into his arms and so into his hands, where they moved the rod".[18] It was in this way that Colonel Heinemann (Bad Homburg v. d. H.) could disclose the presence of two strong courses of water in the Neunkirchner Höhe, which is very deficient in water. The water-diviner Dickmann from Springe did much the same on the old Rodenberg near Bad Neundorf. Fr Lacroix[19] tells us of the French priests Marmet and Baulit who discovered explosive mines hidden in the ground by the Germans during the first world war. Professor Bert Reese discovered Rockfeller's petroleum deposits; M. Boulenger discovered water for

---

[16] Cf. *Unterirdische Wasseradern und Wehrmeisterapparate*, by Fr Cyrillus Wehrmeister, St Ottilien, Bavaria, 1931.

[17] Feldmann, *op. cit.*, p. 29.

[18] Malfatti, *Menschenseele*, p. 126.

[19] *O Espiritismo* . . . , p. 141.

Brugmann Hospital in Jetter St Pierre; while Emil Jausé discovered petrol on the property of Princess Radziwill and the coal deposits of Count Potocki in Poland. M. Moineau discovered large sources of water with which it was possible to supply the city of Toulon, Count Beausoleil, who was imprisoned in the Bastille in 1641, was able to discover by means of his steel wand 172 deposits of metal which are in some cases still being exploited today. Another sixteenth-century water-diviner named Jacob Aymar was actually accounted a wizard because of the large sources of water which he discovered. Yet we know that all this was capable of an entirely natural explanation.

For all that, the effects of this practice may be very far-reaching. While such experiments are in progress the subject finds himself in a state of excessive concentration and absorption, so that he is almost bereft of his senses and is only a step removed from actual trance. Indeed this has been accepted as a fundamental principle among diviners. F. Dietrich writes[20]; "The significant change ... lies ... in the cutting out to the maximum extent of the surface consciousness, i.e. of cerebral thinking in favour of the subconscious or of the emotional life, in favour, that is to say, of being guided by the feeling of the heart and the solar plexus." It is very rare for a true diviner not to take the step into actual trance. When he is in trance we can observe all the usual phenomena associated with artificial sleep. In such cases the rod, being an aid to the trance, helps him to discover the number of a house, to discover a thief (as was done by the aforementioned Aymard, who could find criminals),[21] to diagnose diseases, discover treasure, and solve mathematical problems. In the final stage the actual divining rod is no longer necessary at all: the diviner simply observes the movement of his hand. This, however, really means that such people descend ever deeper into an unhealthy mysticism, with all the dangers for body and soul that we have already observed.

In this connection the following words by Fr Gemelli, O.S.B., director of the University of Milan, are well worth noting: "One often begins by just playing about with a rod, then one finds pleasure in it, and in the end one becomes an impassioned radiaesthetist. It is then very easy, particularly in a time of religious ignorance, to confuse the supernatural with what is not supernatural at all, but merely a caricature of the supernatural. Thus

---

[20] *Gyromantie, Grundlagen und praxis des Pendels*, Villach, Stadler, 1949, p. 9.

[21] Malfatti, *Menschenseele* ... , p. 133.

spiritualism is a caricature of the suprasensory, and it opens the door for superstition, and many are the nervous maladies that result."[22]

(C) COUÉISM AND CHRISTIAN SCIENCE

As has already been observed, the only form in which these rudimentary powers should be used is in healing disease. All doctors know how important a thing for his cure is the patient's confidence, and the Church herself teaches that the spiritual strength imparted by extreme unction sometimes brings with it the healing of the body, if in other respects the disease has not progressed too far.

But apart from this power under normal conditions, there are in the subconscious those purely spiritual powers of the soul which are remains of preternatural gifts. Sometimes these can achieve wonderful results. The philosophers Kant[23] and Feuchtersleben[24] already had some inkling of these powers, but it was the French schools, with Liebault and Coué at their head, which first constructed a system designed to aid the healing process by means of autosuggestion coming out of the subconscious.

Emile Coué (1857-1926), together with Baudouin, laid down the manner in which the body can thus be influenced and formulated two principles.

1. "Every thought strives towards its own realization"—a fact with which we are already acquainted. The sensory nerves carry a perception to the brain, which influences the motor nerves. The more often such sense-stimuli occur, the more complete the bridge between the two groups of nerves, the easier the automatic motion of the muscles and the readier the radiations which, according to some, they emit. "Cumberlandism", "muscle reading" and the phenomenon discussed below of the "thinking horse" are all based upon this fact. Coué made use of this in order to arouse the thought of getting well. It is unfortunately true that man can do little to influence his vegetative life. Coué therefore sought to exploit the subconscious, particularly in order to

---

[22] *Revista Ecclesiastica Brasileira*, 1942, p, 788.
[23] *Die Macht des Gemütes.*
[24] *Die Diätetik der Seele.*

overcome resistance, for in his view there is a second law which is almost the opposite of the first.

2. "The law of effort producing an opposite effect." When the will commands an act, then the reason judges whether such an act is possible, reasonable, useful, etc., and so by its doubts and reflections prevents the first law from being effective. For this reason Coué chose for his suggestions the state of incipient half-sleep during which the obstructive powers cannot so freely or so successfully take effect. There exist entire peoples whose mental processes are still comparatively free from the habit of reflection, and who are untouched by the conclusions derived from physics and the natural sciences; such peoples are more capable of extraordinary feats and miraculous cures than the civilized peoples, the possessors of the great and perhaps all too proud sciences. These last must be brought by artificial means to shut out, while in a state of sleep, all those doubts which a science, that professes to know all but in reality only knows half, tends to call into being; even so, they rarely get so far that the powers of their spirit can exercise dominion over the law of gravity or that of the conservation of energy, whereas the Indian succeeds in these things with an ease quite beyond the Westerner. "Whosoever shall . . . not stagger in his heart, but believe that whatsoever he saith shall be done; it shall be done unto him" (Mark 11. 23). The very words of Our Lord, besides their religious significance, acquire a meaning regarded merely from the natural angle.

To direct the powers of the body towards health in accordance with the first of the aforementioned laws, the most important thing is to obstruct the operation of the second law and cut out ratiocination and doubts. Coué seeks to attain this by means of acts of autosuggestion just before falling asleep, or immediately after waking, and advises the patient to repeat with great conviction the words "Every day and in every way I am getting better and better." His intention is thus to set in motion all the powers of the subconscious and so of the pure spirit with all the sovereign power of the soul over the body and by this means to control the automatic movements of the vegetative life, to direct the blood to the affected parts, also to heal them. It is said that he achieved astonishing results, though, as has been demonstrated here, they were all perfectly natural. The following observations by Brauchle are illuminating in this connection[25]:

> Natural sleep at night also is a state of subconscious psychic activity. Our dreams show the nature of our subconscious thought function. During sleep consciousness is extinguished. In the moment of waking it returns. The great correspondence between hypnosis and sleep is proved by the fact that each leads easily into the other. Thus it sometimes happens in hypnosis that the hypnotized person begins to snore during treatment; by this he shows us that he has slipped out of the hypnotic state into that of natural sleep, and this means that he has lost his rapport with the hypnotist. If such a patient is spoken to, he may perhaps not awake but resume contact with the hypnotist and the hypnotic state is re-established. Conversely it is possible—almost invariably with children, and quite frequently with adults—to transform the normal sleep of the night into hypnosis. The procedure is as follows: One approaches the bed of the sleeping person and whispers softly and slowly to him, but nevertheless with a certain emphasis, repeating whatever is said, if possible, several times . . . the sleeping person may not give any sign, nevertheless such whispers often work wonders. Heart attacks, thumb-sucking, stammering, bed-wetting and other propensities can thus be cured.

What matters then is our ability to awaken the patient's confidence and imagination and to mobilize his subconscious and purely spiritual powers, which then work on the body.

It is in the light of these principles that one must judge those superstitious practices which often have very good results because of the exceptional degree of faith which drives out all merely rational considerations. That is why a talisman is often effective, as are many other objects of superstition, simply because of the faith people place in them.

At this point we should also consider Christian Science which is attaining greater vogue than ever today. It is the publishers of the *Christian Science Monitor* who have for half a century been spreading among the people the "science" of Mrs Baker Eddy (1821-1910). The last named is accounted the founder of this religious movement, and her book, *Science and Health with*

---

[25] *Hypnose und Autosuggestion*, p. 47.

Key of the Scriptures, expounds the view that by becoming intellectually one with God the idea of disease disappears and health results.

In so far as there is an element of truth in any of this, it is founded on suggestion, and in particular on autosuggestion, that is, on ideas about health similar to those of Coué. Such ideas do no more than express the same truth in various forms, the truth that the soul has great influence on the body, though there is often in such cases an admixture of eclectic forms of piety which do more harm than good.

In this connection we should also refer to *Autogenous Training* (J. H. Schulz), and to Frankl's Logos-Therapy, both of which, like Couéism and Christian Science, can show a certain record of success. All this is in keeping with the general experience of psychotherapy. Furthermore, even doctors without religion, concede the extent of the influence of religion on bodily health. Thus the surgeon Sauerbruch in Berlin, Professor Dr Müller, Dr Jung in Zurich, Dr Allers in Vienna, all testify to the importance of religion for the health of the body. Dr Niedermeyer speaks of the purposive activation of spiritual powers.[26] Doctors even complain of the backwardness of certain circles in this respect: "In Goethe's day only a small number of people cleaned their teeth, and even this only occurred on an isolated occasion when the person concerned was taking a bath, and he would perform this function with a coarse brush. Our bodily hygiene has progressed a little since then, but our spiritual hygiene is still exceedingly backward, for our most profound spiritual hygiene has been neglected and even opposed, much harm being done by this to the people, while our purely worldly hygiene remains soul-less." If then the normal influence of the soul has such psychotherapeutic importance, how much greater the extraordinary influence that comes out of the subconscious. Nor is that influence purely negative, as in hysteria, it can definitely be positive, though it does not go beyond certain limits.

Nevertheless Fr Castelein reminds us that Rome requires something more than such apparently miraculous effects when it is a matter of canonization. It does not suffice that a wound should be instantaneously healed; the skin must be completely replaced and there must be no scars, while a microbic infection healed instantaneously must have reached a stage where even the

---

[26] *Linzer Quartalshrift*, 1937, 286.

most powerful hypnosis would not suffice to heal it. Cures that are effected at spiritualist seances, and assist the propaganda which helps that epidemic to spread, are founded on the firm and perhaps subconscious faith of the devotees. In such cases a definite use is made of the powers of the spirit, powers which have dominion over matter and the body. Even so we do not know whether this kind of thing is conducive to the benefit of the human race, or whether it may not lead to a catastrophe the consequences of which will not bear thinking about.

Most certainly these powers are also at work in the cures effected by the saints, and if such cures are greater than what can be effected by natural means, this is because religion calls powers into being that cannot exist without it. Certain doctors assure us that they have been able to call into being on some neurotic people something resembling stigmata, by means of suggestion; actually, however, these phenomena are mere pale shadows of true stigmata. Nevertheless the fact that cures are achieved by the unaided powers of the spirit-soul must make us extremely cautious in assuming on any occasion that a miracle has taken place, for a miracle is, after all, something that surpasses the merely natural and originates in the direct action of God. Miracles of course occur, for though much that was formerly assumed to be miraculous is accounted by us today as the natural manifestation of the spiritual powers of man, there are nevertheless certain limits of which medical science is itself only too acutely conscious, and this despite all its practice of suggestion, hypnosis and psychotherapy.

Genuinely miraculous cures, then, are something wholly distinct from the non-miraculous, though there will always be people whose whole outlook on life forces them to deny that such a distinction exists. As with occult phenomena, however, it is a question of simply examining the facts with an open mind, and of not coming to the enquiry with foregone conclusions. Such materialists as Dessoir, Baerwald and Lehmann of course proceed from the assumption that only that may be admitted which in their opinion accords with physical laws of nature; all else is rejected because such things just cannot be. Thus they will admit the existence of telepathy because, if necessary, they think they can explain it by some kind of physical radiation analogous to radio waves; but if they come across a case of clairvoyance, in which there has been no "transmitter", they promptly construct one, either by setting up the so-called "whisper theory" or by accepting the idea, if the supposed transmitter happens to be dead, of telepathic infectious matter being "sprayed" on objects. If none of this can be sustained, they again simply deny the facts.

This is the way in which the cures at Lourdes tend to be treated. Here people fall back on healing by suggestion, or if that explanation will not hold water, take refuge in the plea of ignorance, saying that the thing cannot "yet" be explained. A. Lehmann-Petersen[27] may be quoted as an example. We cannot, however, here deal at length with the medical discussion of the miracles of Lourdes. Many doctors, including such distinguished figures as Charcot and Bernheim, claim that there have been no reliably attested cures which go beyond what can be achieved by psychic treatment carried out under favourable conditions. The cures at Lourdes and similar places are said to have had their miraculous character attributed to them because people had not taken the trouble to investigate whether they were really concerned with some kind of organic damage or merely with a disturbance of nervous function (with so-called "functional" disease); the latter could be healed by psychic treatment, the former could not. The critics of such views have pointed out that an exact record is kept in Lourdes concerning every sick person that comes there, that the medical histories are attested by statements from the doctors who have previously treated the patient without success, and that no one is declared to be cured without a thorough examination. The whole material is available to any person who wishes to investigate the matter, and in the case of a cure, any doctor may examine the person concerned—and this has frequently been done. It must therefore be regarded as definitely established that cases of advanced tuberculosis, lupus (i.e. tuberculosis of the skin), malignant inflammations, etc., have in recent times been cured—in some instances instantaneously.

Yet the sceptic will not admit defeat. Here is a typical excerpt from the writings of Lehmann-Petersen, to whom reference was made above:

> Even if we proceed on the assumption that at least some of the allegedly miraculous cures have really taken place, this does not prove that anything in the nature of a miracle has actually happened. It is true enough that a doctor cannot cure such maladies as these by suggestion, but then he cannot create

---

[27] *Aberglaube und Zauberei*, p. 637.

the atmosphere of extreme suggestibility which is to be found at Lourdes and similar places, and which often borders on religious ecstasy. If such an essential condition is not present, the same results cannot be attained; therefore the assertion that it is not suggestion that achieves the miraculous cures has nothing to justify it. In most cases of the cure of organic disease we-are concerned, as already remarked, with tuberculosis of the lung, the skin (lupus), etc., that is to say with maladies where recovery may already begin to set in when the organism is assisted in its struggle against the disease by external and internal aids, the external ones being fresh air, sunlight and a plentiful diet, the internal ones tranquillity and the inner balance which religion can afford. It is therefore easy to suppose that the organism can master the disease when a greatly heightened suggestibility directs all the patient's available energy to that end. At present we know so little about the influence of spiritual activity on the bodily organs and functions, that it is premature to speak of miracles simply because successes have occasionally been achieved for which at the moment we have no actual explanation.

Now, on Lehmann's supposition, the extent of the degree of successful cures at Lourdes should be proportionate to the extent of the religious enthusiasm, but there is nothing to indicate this. Indeed, in 1914 the international Eucharistic Congress was held at that place, and unprecedented numbers of people streamed together there, the tide of joy and expectation rose particularly high, but there was not a single cure. The writer is far from denying that psychic factors have great curative influence, but these have their limits. That makes it all the more necessary to cultivate an objective approach when examining a cure, and that is precisely what the unbelieving physician, and the scientist who has determined in advance that miracles are impossible, cannot do. The following example makes this plain[28]:

> "How have you been healed?" a doctor once asked a girl who for four years had been suffering from a suppurating inflammation of the hip, due to cancer of the bone, and who a few days previously had suddenly been restored to perfect health. Her pains had disappeared together with subsidence of the inflammation. "Who cured me? The Blessed Virgin." "Oh," replied the doctor, "let's leave the Blessed Virgin out of it. Confess that you were assured in advance that you would be healed. You were told: 'Once you are in Lourdes,

---

[28] Donat, *Freiheit der Wissenschaft*, p. 294.

you will at a certain moment leave the bed in which you are lying.' That is quite a common sort of occurrence. We call it suggestion." The girl replied that this was not at all the way the thing had happened. The doctor ended by offering her money if she would admit that she had really been cured by suggestion, but the girl refused.

Ernst Häckel behaved in much the same way when H. A. Rambacher sent him Boissarie's book about the cures at Lourdes. He wrote to Rambacher (Donat, p. 295):

I am returning you herewith with many thanks Dr Boissarie's book on *The Great Cures at Lourdes*. The reading thereof, which greatly interested me, has served further to convince me of the colossal power of superstition, glorified into pious faith, of naive credulity that proves nothing critically and of infectious mass suggestion. It has also convinced me of the slyness of the clergy which exploits these things for its own advantage. The doctors who testify to the miracles and to the supernatural manifestations are partly uneducated and uncritical quacks, and partly deliberate swindlers who are in league with the power-hungry priests. Zola in his well-known novel has given the true picture of the grandiose swindle of Lourdes. Again many thanks for your kindly solicitude on my behalf.

ERNST HÄCKEL

We can learn much from the behaviour of this same Zola. I quote from Fr Donat (p. 295):

It should be known how the famous novelist behaved in regard to the facts of Lourdes. In the year 1892, at the time of the great pilgrimages, Zola came to Lourdes. He wanted to observe and then describe what he had seen. It was to be a historical novel, and time and again he had the statement repeated in the press that he would present the whole truth. In Lourdes all doors were open to him, he was admitted everywhere, was able to ask any questions he pleased and demand any explanations. A single incident serves to illustrate the manner in which he honoured his promise to tell the truth. On the 20th August, 1892, Marie Lebranchu came to Lourdes with an incurable affection of the lungs. She was suddenly healed and never had a relapse. One year after her cure she returned to the miraculous grotto, and the excellent condition of her lungs was again confirmed. But what did Zola make of these happenings? He lets the cured girl, when she first returns home, have a terrible relapse, "a brutal recurrence of the malady", as he calls it, "which remains the victor after all". The president of the Lourdes enquiry bureau introduced himself one day to Zola in Paris, and cross-questioned him. "How could you dare", he said, "to let Marie Lebranchu die? You know that she is as well as you or I." "What do I care?" came the reply. "I suppose I have the right to present my characters as I please, since I am their creator." Yet an author who wishes to exploit such freedom should not put it about that he proposes to write a historical novel that is factually accurate. Still less should other people see in such productions a "true picture" of Lourdes.

Fairly recently Dr Franz L. Schleyer subjected the cures of Lourdes to a critical examination[29] and made a searching study of 232 cases. Some of these were excluded because of the lack of a medical history, in others there was the possibility of a natural explanation, but 37 cases he was obliged to declare extra-medical and inexplicable. Medicine stands resourceless before advanced tuberculosis of the bone and lung, before the club foot and the pupil that is impervious to light, and the atrophied optic nerve. Yet in Lourdes these things have been the subject of instantaneous cures. Schleyer also discusses the case of Mile Lebranchu, who died in 1920, and declares this cure to be extra-medical.

When Häckel speaks of "uneducated and uncritical quacks" it is particularly apposite to refer to a recent French book by the Nobel Prize-winning physician Alexis Carrel whose notes are the foundation of the little book The Miracle of Lourdes (Stuttgart, 1951). He discusses the case of Marie Bailly who suffered from "tubercular inflammation of the abdomen in its final stages". Carrel was an unbeliever, and said to the person accompanying him: "I would gladly sacrifice all my theories and hypotheses if I could only witness so interesting and moving a phenomenon" (i.e. a miracle). He wrote of Marie Bailly when she was led to the bath: "The young girl has nothing more to lose, the death agony has already set in." Marie Bailly was suddenly healed. "A complete cure within a matter of a few hours—the dying creature with the blue face and the swollen belly and the wild pulse had been transformed into an admittedly emaciated but otherwise normal young girl."

---

[29] *Die Heilungen von Lourdes, Eine kritische Untersuchung*, Bonn, 1949, H. Bouvier & Co.

Carrel was later converted. Schleyer discusses this case and says that the disappearance of this malady is "hard to explain".

We may summarize as follows: It is possible that means will one day be found by which tubercular inflammation of the abdominal wall can be instantaneously healed; so long as such means are not available, we must regard such sudden healings of typhus, tuberculosis of the knee, "tubercular abscesses of ossal origin" etc., of which Dr Schleyer adduces 37 examples, as not being explicable in natural terms. It may well be that many diseases of psychogenic origin can be cured by means of hypnotism, Christian Science, Couéism and by popular healers in much the same way as this happens thousands of times at Lourdes without the thing being looked upon as a miracle at all by the bureau, but there is an essential difference between such occurrences as these and true miracles.

Winterstein[30] summarizes the matter thus:

> Miracles, if one concedes their existence at all, are unique "breakthroughs" of the order of nature brought about by divine intervention. It is its uniqueness that is the mark of the miracle, whereas parapsychology (which is "a science in process of development" [W. Ostwald] but not a religion) seeks in its own territory to discover regular sequences, that is to say laws of nature, and is not unsuccessful in finding them. As against this, I must reject another definition that treats miracles as natural phenomena which, owing to our limited knowledge, we do not yet understand (Wagner-Jauregg), for if that were accepted, the occult phenomena in general would all be miracles, as would indeed other manifestations of nature.

This general definition fits the actual facts very well. In Lourdes, for instance, the occurrence of cures is wholly incalculable and subject to no kind of regularity, for they fail to occur just when circumstances appear most favourable and vice versa, whereas magnetic cures, if they are carried out with care, are usually successful.

Some years ago the appearance of a certain Mirim Dajo excited much attention. This man, whose real name was Henskes Arnold, and who was born in Holland in 1912, presented himself to the doctors of Zurich, claiming the

---

[30] *Telepathie und Hellsehen*, p. 172.

quality of being completely invulnerable.[31] Actually he permitted them to stab him from the back with a round, very sharp dagger near the base of the spine, the dagger piercing right to the front and no bleeding was to be observed at the two skin wounds. With the dagger sticking fast in him he went up to the X-ray department on the first floor where X-rays were taken. These showed that the liver had been pierced, though the lung and kidneys had probably not been touched. There was, however, no bleeding when the dagger was withdrawn. Other scars caused by such dagger wounds were also observed.

Mirim Dajo was not under hypnosis, but was regarded as a fakir who kept his body extremely elastic by spiritual training, so that heart and aorta could escape the thrust when he was stabbed, and receive no serious injury. It is true that at the age of thirty-five he died from swallowing a 35-centimetre needle with a 2.5-centimetre head which had damaged the alimentary canal. The case of Mirim Dajo simply proves how greatly the body can be influenced by spiritual training, though this too has its limits. In a recent rather curious book[32] this "Fluidal Man" is represented as the victim of the doubters, the curious and the journalists, who always demanded the extraordinary, till at last the limit of nature's possibilities was passed and the man succumbed.

In conclusion, let it once more be made clear that the spirit-soul, acting on the body, can undoubtedly effect cures (as also illnesses) which surpass the normal and might thus be taken for miracles. This only shows that great caution must be observed before affirming that a miracle has taken place, particularly when diseases of a psychogenic character are involved of a kind that can be cured from the spiritual side.

Even if today we do not exactly know the limits up to which the effects of spiritual influence extend, an influence which can most certainly be strengthened by religious enthusiasm, we know nevertheless that there are provinces to which that influence does not extend; we know that not even the most powerful spiritual influence can straighten a club foot, or instantaneously make whole a broken bone. The power of the spirit-soul, as here described and discussed, may therefore be great indeed, but there are for

---

[31] See *Mensch und Schicksal*, 1948, p. 1, and *Schweizerische Medizinische Wochenschrift*, 1948, p. 352.

[32] Hans Malik, *Der Baumeister seiner Welt*, Vienna, 1949, p. 206.

all that limits to it. Beyond those limits lies the territory reserved for the miracles of God.

(D) Crystal-Gazing

One of the oldest ways of gaining access to the knowledge contained in the subconscious is so-called crystal-gazing, or crystalloscopy. The essence of this is that the person engaged on it fixes his gaze on some bright object such as a mirror, a bright sphere, stone or vessel, or on the palm of his hand which is filled with oil, water or ink, or again on to his finger nail, a piece of coal or a bright leaf; thus he falls into a hypnoidal state and projects into the object the telepathic experiences which he undergoes and the perceptions which he makes by clairvoyance. This is a very ancient practice, and one known to all peoples. Even in the Bible there is mention of the cup which Joseph had put into Benjamin's sack of corn the loss of which was immediately noticed at the court of Pharaoh, since the cup was one from which Pharaoh drank "and was wont to divine" (Gen. 44. 5). Numa Pompilius, Cagliostro and Marie Antoinette, as well as a number of men of learning, used this "manhole to the subconscious" (Tischner) in order to gain knowledge of things and happenings which were not cognizable by the senses. The bright objects play a part which is essentially that of a "visual stimulus" which can be assisted further by incense and suggestion; a kind of trance is thus brought into being which helps to produce the phenomena of telepathy and clairvoyance.

The Englishwoman Miss Goodrich-Freer (Miss X) has made many experiments in this field, and finds that about 30 per cent of all persons have good aptitude for it, though the degree and nature of endowment within that percentage differ very widely. With some people it appears suddenly, while with others it only develops gradually; some people see figures that move, with others they are immovable; some see the figures for a short time only, others can continue gazing at them for as long as they desire; sometimes the figures are as large as life, on other occasions they are so small that they must be examined with a magnifying glass. There are no general rules to be followed in learning or practising this skill, since in this regard every person is differently constituted.

Here is an example from the Orient, as recounted by the Englishman Theodore Besterman,[33] who has written the best monograph on this subject. A magician from Algiers took a child, drew a square in its hand that had certain signs in it, poured ink into the centre thereof, and told the child to look at the reflection of its face in the ink. Immediately the child did this he had a bucket of coals brought, threw a number of herbs in it and told the child to say when a Turkish soldier appeared. The child bent its head down, the bucket of coals spread a strong aroma, while the magician mumbled his incantations. When the child saw the Turkish soldier, it began to scream with fear, whereupon the magician set a small Arab servant in its place and went through the same procedure with him as he had done with the child. Soon the boy cried out, "There he is" (meaning the Turk), and described the man's clothing and how he was sweeping the place. Then came the Sultan upon a noble horse, etc.

This is a good case of visual stimulus increasing suggestibility. The child, put into a trance with the aid of a mirror-like surface and the scented smoke, saw everything suggested to it by the magician. Another example is given by the missionary Trilles, who explored among the wild pygmy tribes in the African forest together with Mgr Le Roy. When one day during their journey they found a tortoise for their supper—they were exceedingly hungry at the time—Le Roy said jestingly, "If the worst comes to the worst, we will add the head of our guide". The witch doctor in the neighbouring village had "seen and heard" everything in his magic mirror, although he knew no French, and repeated it all to the missionaries when they arrived, which greatly astonished them. When they asked the witch doctor about a despatch of goods that was coming, he took his mirror and told them exactly where it was at the time and when it would arrive. His information proved perfectly correct.

The things seen in crystal-gazing are not always the result of telepathy; they may be things which have been implanted in the subconscious and have been forgotten. Thus Miss X used the crystal to remember things which she had forgotten, or to find something that she had lost, such as the prescription of a doctor which she ultimately found among the letters of a friend. The "Seer of Prevorst" saw everything in a soap bubble, and could thus find lost documents or complete the dreams which in the morning she could no longer exactly

---

[33] *Crystal-Gazing*, London, 1924, p. 80.

remember; here a certain hypermnesia was at work. It is always the same region of the spirit to which we are transported whether in dreams, in trance or in any other state in which we withdraw from the life of the senses.

As already indicated, crystal-gazing may also be associated with clairvoyance. This occurs when things are seen of which no person in one's immediate surroundings can possibly have any knowledge. It occurs for instance when a fire on board ship is foreseen, or the results of an elephant hunt are predicted. Where there is apparent foreknowledge, we must assume that the process described earlier has come into action. Much is then inferred from circumstances that already exist but are unknown to the waking consciousness. Small differences between the thing seen in the crystal and the actual happening when it occurs merely prove that it is impossible to foresee things that depend wholly on the human will.

The pouring of molten lead on New Year's Day and the reading of tea leaves are popular pastimes that have a kind of affinity to the above, and indeed this form of "prophecying" may well be reckoned the most harmless of all those known.

(E) Spiritualism

The best known and most widely spread form of occultism is spiritualism. This cult not only contains most of the other forms of occultist practice, but is followed today by millions of people in all parts of the world. It is thus a great spiritual movement, whose foundation is the conviction that it can establish communication with the dead by means of mediums; for this reason it is also called "mediumism", though mediums are to be found in other forms. The peculiar thing about spiritualism is this, that though its devotees seek to have communication with the dead, they dare not do it immediately but seek to put an intermediary agency between the latter and themselves. These intermediary agencies are the mediums who in their turn make use of controls or controlling spirits, sometimes several at a time, in order to obtain the required messages.

The belief in the possibility of communicating with the spirits of the dead is very ancient indeed. There is hardly a people among whom it is not to be found. It exists among primitive peoples and existed among the peoples of antiquity. Among the civilized nations it comes as a reaction against a period of exaggerated rationalism and materialism. In ancient times necromancy was very widespread, and it was thus that men sought to establish communication with the dead. Already in Babylon they believed in ghosts that gave knocks; Herodotus and most Latin authors tell us of the conjuration of the souls of the dead; even the Israelites practised the art from time to time.[34] In order to suppress this superstition, Moses enjoined that those engaging in the practice should be stoned (Lev. 20. 27).

Tertullian, the great African apologist (160-240 A.D.), tells of materializations, calling up of the dead, trances and states of artificial sleep, of putting questions to talking tables (*phantasmata edunt defunctorum informant animas . . . somnia emittunt mensae per daemones divinare consuerunt*).[35]

Christianity caused this form of communication with the next world to drop, and St John Damascene (754), to quote but one example, makes no mention of it, despite the fact that in his *De Fide Orthodoxa* he speaks of the devil. It was only in the thirteenth century that, together with the witches, this form of demonomania appeared, and then it lasted right up to the eighteenth century, when it gave place to spiritualism.

Modern spiritualism had its beginning in the town of Hydesville, U.S.A., in the year 1847. In a family that had been ruined by alcoholism, the two daughters, Katy and Maggy Fox, heard knocks as though someone were knocking at the door. They began to ask whether it was the soul of some dead person, and received answers. Despite the fact that it was immediately obvious that the answers were incorrect—they concerned a person who was supposed to have been murdered and buried in the kitchen and the police found no signs of any of this—the relatives of the girls had the kind of business sense that could exploit the credulity of persons who attended the ensuing seances.

Certain men of science immediately declared that the knocks were made by the girls themselves, who actually confessed that they were the victims of the guile of their relatives; nevertheless the epidemic spread, and the "spirits" began to knock and manifest themselves everywhere. The two girls died from drink.

---

[34] Deut. 18. 11, and I Kings 28. 7.
[35] *Apol.* 13, Kösel edition, Kempten-Munich, 1915, p. 109.

In France a certain Léon-Hyppolite-Denizart-Rival (1869), later known as Allan Kardec, devoted himself to the spreading of spiritualism, the spirits having "revealed to him that, as Pontifex of this movement, he had a great task to fulfil in the founding of a new religion". Camille Flammarion and Victorian Sardon supported him in this work, the latter of whom "devoured books on philosophy, metaphysics and astronomy and directed the revelations of the spirits". Leymare actually started the photographing of spirits, though this was declared to be fraud by a French court; others effected cures and brought messages from the dead, meeting the wishes of their patrons in whatever way these might desire (*Mundus vult decipi*).

This was the course things had taken since Mesmer and Swedenborg in the eighteenth century. In the nineteenth century a regular epidemic of table-turning spread from America to England, and so to Europe, particularly to the Protestant countries. The American Andrew Jackson Davis (1826-1910) claimed to have seen in a cemetery the astral body of a dead person which was able to pass through the wood of the coffin, but not the iron door of the vault. It was thus held to be established that the astral body was something very insubstantial but still material. Allan Kardec assumed the existence of reincarnation, and thus encountered the opposition of the Catholic Church, while Davis particularly combated the doctrines of original sin, redemption and eternal damnation.

It is not difficult to understand the enormous spread of spiritualism; it was a counter-movement to the mechanization of life and to the tendency to deny the reality of human personality; and it also satisfied the desire to learn something about departed friends in the unknown world beyond. Spiritualism was also a natural result of the rejection of Christianity; faith in the Christian revelation would have given a knowledge of the secrets which men were trying to probe, though it would not have furnished the experimental proof which in an age of technics people are anxious to secure. So it was through the mediums that the dead began to speak, to knock and to write, and they did this so convincingly that even scientific men like Wallace, Crookes and Zöllner became weak and "believed"—until Hartmann, Janet and Myers drew attention to the subconscious. After that spiritualism lost more and more ground, particularly when the revelations from the beyond proved so very disappointing.

Our own attitude towards spiritualism must needs be different from that of its other opponents—the animists, for instance—and different also from that of modern science, for even when that science is not wholly materialist, it tends to reject spiritualism, either because it does not believe in the soul at all, or because it believes in a soul that is half material and therefore quite incapable of co-operating with mediums. Alternatively it rejects spiritualism, because spiritualism rests on assumptions that are entirely unproven.

As Catholics—and what is here written is written from the Catholic viewpoint—we reject spiritualism, not because it is *physically* impossible for the souls of the dead to perform feats of this kind—they are capable of that and of much more—but because it is not *fitting* that they should at a word of command be made to amuse us, simply in order to satisfy our curiosity or to serve as the object of scientific experiments like so many guinea-pigs to be vivisected. Souls are spiritual things, and thus *physically* far above human beings. They are for the most part filled with divine grace, and so carry the divine nature within themselves and are destined to enjoy the beatific vision; they are therefore "sons of God" and fellow-citizens of the angels and saints, whom one cannot easily visualize in the setting of a spiritualist seance. If they appear to man, they do so in a worthy form and for some high purpose on behalf of the kingdom of God upon earth and the salvation of souls. We do not therefore deny the possibility of their appearing as genuine ghosts, but refuse to believe that they would be mixed up with spiritualism unless it is proved that spiritualist practice attains that worthy form and is serving the rational purpose of which we have spoken.[36]

Another ground for our unbelief in this matter is the failure of spiritualist practice to establish genuine proof of identity with a deceased person, and we can but marvel that in the age of exact science people appear to remain so modest in their demands. We Catholics are not particularly concerned to prove that the dead do sometimes appear, yet that seems to be what chiefly interests such writers as Dr Emil Mattiesen, in his three-volume work *Das Persönliche Überleben des Todes*.[37] The same may be said of Camille

---

[36] See *Erkenntnis und Glaube*, March, 1952.

[37] Berlin-Leipzig, 1936.

Flammarion[38] or Dr Robert Klimsch,[39] who adduce a number of well-attested examples to prove their contention. We are convinced of the truth of this, and need no further persuasion. We are only too glad that people who do not believe in the existence of a soul or in an after-life should read such books as the ones referred to. Our chief concern, however, must be to enquire whether the occult phenomena which the mediums manifest at seances, and the "messages from the dead" in which those taking part so humbly believe, really emanate from the deceased persons concerned. It is precisely this that the writer denies, and he does so all the more readily because everything can be explained in terms of the spirit-soul.

There have, it is true, been men of science in the past who have spoken of the "unknown powers of the soul", and who felt able to explain a number of the phenomena in natural terms, yet sooner or later these encountered facts and phenomena, which drove them back on to the spiritualist hypothesis. This was the case with the Russian savant Alexander Nikolaievich Aksákow, who in his work *Animism and Spiritualism*[40] obstinately defends the spirit hypothesis against Edward von Hartmann's *Der Spiritismus*, despite the fact that he had elsewhere already spoken of the extraordinary powers of the soul. Similarly the astronomer Flammarion is at pains to recognize the extent of the psychic powers, but in the end we find him writing[41]; "At the same time it seems to me that the spiritualist hypothesis has as much right to be accepted as those already referred to, since discussions thereof have failed to impugn its validity." Scientists like Du Prel, Lombroso and Zöllner have also weakened. Frau Moser, who deals with this question in a most exhaustive manner and in an agreeably critical spirit, at least had the honesty to say that the best policy was to admit complete ignorance, since it was at present impossible to do more than set up theories that merely added to the confusion. "Hypotheses," she writes, "which merely cover a part of the field and only lead to the setting up of supplementary hypotheses, are things we can well do without."[42] She speaks

---

[38] *Rätsel des Seelenlebens*, Stuttgart, 1908.

[39] *Leben die Toten?*, Graz, 1937.

[40] Leipzig, 1919, German translation by Dr Gr. Const. Wittig.

[41] *Unbekannte Naturkräfte*, p. 370.

[42] *Okkultismus . . .*, p. 642.

much of the soul and even of the "omnipotence of the soul" but refuses to attribute to it a real spirituality, so that in the end she capitulates like the rest.

Even Tischner says that there are cases which cannot be explained simply in terms of the subconscious,[43] and quotes the following instance.

> A deceased person, Mrs Elisa M., once made a communication in a seance to Hodgson through Mrs Piper that on the previous day a relative of hers had died, a fact which Hodgson had just read in the morning paper. She stated that she had been at that person's bedside when he died, that she had spoken with him and repeated what she had said, mentioning the fact that he had heard and recognized her. Hodgson passed this communication on to a friend, and this friend was quite spontaneously told a few days later by a relative, who had been present at the man's death, that the deceased had in his death agony said that he could see Mrs M. and hear her and that she was telling him such and such things. All this corresponded exactly with what Mrs Piper had automatically written. Hodgson could have known nothing of all this.

It is inferred from this that Mrs Elisa M. must actually have appeared, and this was held to accord with the spiritualist hypothesis. Yet the argument is unsound. Let the reader again be reminded of our thesis of the spirit soul, which can apprehend everything to which it directs its powers of understanding, whether these things be thoughts or some other kind of fact. When it is a question of the former, science speaks of telepathy, when of the latter, of clairvoyance. Why then should so excellent a medium as Mrs Piper have been unable to visualize the scene while in trance, the scene in which a dying man appeared to be speaking with a dead relative? (N.B. It is possible of course that the relative in question might really have appeared if this would have assisted the cause of salvation, but there are other explanations. It is possible that the dying man, in his last agony—i.e. when the soul was nearly free from the body—merely imagined that he was conversing with his pious relative.) Alternatively Mrs Piper may have read it in the memory of that relative who was present while the man was dying, and now related the affair as though Mrs Elisa M. had appeared to her also. There would be no necessity for us to assume that there must have been a "transmitter"; that is to say that the dead person or the relative in question directly transmitted what the

---

[43] *Ergebnisse*, p. 175.

medium Piper "saw". Similarly we need not postulate a "soul-journey" or a "world subject" or anything else of that kind.

All the other difficulties raised by Frau Moser can be resolved in much the same fashion. Frau Moser seems particularly struck by the knowledge of languages which mediums appear to possess. The French scientist Richet recounts the following:

> A Parisian lady, Mme X, who had visions, practised automatic writing, and seems to have been endowed with second sight, continued over a number of years to write whole pages of Greek, doing so in a state of trance or semitrance this despite the fact that she had never learned the language. It all began with the appearance of a little man in a vision who called himself A. A. Renouard, and who turned out to be Richet's great-grandfather, a learned bibliophile but not a Hellenist. Mme X immediately, but quite erroneously, connected the idea of Greek with this vision. In her desire to learn that language, she acquired two little books which she later showed to Richet without any particular hesitation. These books seem to have been put aside, and the lady took no further interest in them. About this time Richet took part in a seance, at which Myers was present, and in the course of which Mme X for the first time wrote two simple Greek sentences. Others followed, mostly signed A.A.R. In the summer of 1900 a long complicated sentence was at last written which even Myers could not understand.[44]

How did the medium Mme X acquire this knowledge? It was easy to jump to the conclusion that she had got it from the little man who had appeared to her out of the next world. Yet after some searching, a French-Greek dictionary by Byzantios was found which contained these sentences, and from which Mme X—who had, after all, once occupied herself with Greek—read these same sentences with great difficulty by clairvoyance.

That mediums can achieve such "Book Test" feats has been experimentally demonstrated. The medium is given an instruction to pick out mentally a certain book in a bookcase, in a distant room, and to turn to such-and-such a page and say what is contained thereon. If this can be done, why should not Mme X have been able to read these sentences without the mediation of a dead person? In such a case there can be no question of the intelligent use of a

---

[44] Moser, *Okkultismus*, p. 379.

foreign language. Frau Moser herself states that "there is not and cannot be such a thing as really speaking a foreign tongue which one has not learned" (p. 333). Should such a thing occur, then this would indeed be proof that preternatural intelligence was at work, as will later be explained.

Similarly the fact that a person enters into the way of life, character and most intimate experiences of one who is dead does not prove that the deceased person has actually appeared, it merely shows that a good medium can "see" and "read" (one usually speaks of "tapping") the thoughts and memories in the subconscious of those attending the seance, and even of others, and can give public expression to them, whether in writing or by the spoken word, or in some other way. That the mediums themselves believe that a spirit is speaking through them has no bearing on the question, for the mediums do not know in their upper consciousness what powers or knowledge they possess in the subconscious. Artists often stand speechless before their own creations, as did Richard Wagner before his Tristan, being quite unable to understand how he had written such a thing. The best proof, however, that no soul from the next world has ever appeared to spiritualists is that nothing new about that next world has ever been revealed, and some kind of revelation might surely at one time or another have been expected. Moreover a medium can imitate the writing and characteristics of living persons quite as successfully as it does those of the dead.

It may well be asked why mediums always associate their communications with some other person, and why, since these derive from their own subconscious, they do not treat them as coming from themselves. It has, however, already been said that the acts of cognition performed by the subconscious have a dreamlike quality and are often devoid of any real sense; if they are to be worth serious attention, they need direction and some point around which the ideas they contain can be organized. This is what happens when some indisposition of the body influences our dreams and guides them in a certain direction; the same applies to hylomantic objects, to the suggestion practised by those taking part in a seance, to the personality of the hypnotist, and this is also the function which the idea of the dead person performs. All these things serve to direct the subconscious thoughts, or rather the subconscious knowledge, along a certain definite course.

Here we find the answer to another question that is frequently asked, namely how the selection takes place between the different "radiations" that act upon the medium. Leaving aside the fact that we reject its supposed "radiations", the determining factor is again the guiding object or influence to which the medium is subject, though chance plays a large part in this, since the judgments are quite arbitrary and incalculable.

That dead persons are quite superfluous for the delivery of these "messages" is shown by the story earlier related by Fr Castelein, and there are few examples that enable us to recognize so clearly the identity of the directing intelligence.

But the same thing applies everywhere. It is not some dead person (nor is it the devil) who is the originator of the "revelations" at seances; indeed, a medium once actually bore witness to what really happens. When asked where his knowledge was acquired, "Out of the silly thought-box of your own brains", was the answer: i.e. not from the dead. "We ourselves", it was stated openly to Flammarion, "are the more or less conscious authors of our productions", and this is true despite the fact that mediums are usually convinced that they have their knowledge from "spirits", or at any rate find it interesting to associate their revelations with the names of spirits. Actually, as we have seen, these names only serve as a kind of fixed point around which their dreaming can be organized for guidance and direction. Or are we really to believe that Asmodeus, Leviathan, Christ, Mary, Homer and Augustine make an appearance just to say "good morning"?

It used to be constantly stated that an entirely uneducated medium completed Charles Dickens's unfinished novel *The Mystery of Edwin Drood*, and was able to imitate the mode of thought, the style and even the spelling mistakes of that author. This, it is always said, could only happen if the spirit of Charles Dickens himself was dictating the thing word for word. Nevertheless a fragment was found among Dickens's papers which proved that the author had planned the work entirely differently. The medium's achievement was nothing more than a brilliant product of her trance and was similar to that of Mrs P. Curran in St Louis. Mrs Curran wrote hundreds of poems, parables, aphorisms, stories, long and short novels and dramas, which, she claimed, were dictated to her by the spirit of a certain Patience North, the daughter of a weaver in Dorset in the seventeenth century. These productions were remarkable for their knowledge of the people, the history and geography of the place, and constitute a striking achievement of the subconscious; they typify the acts of knowledge made in dreams, under hypnosis and, for that matter, in artistic creation generally.

In cases like these, it is not beings from the beyond who provide the knowledge the medium displays, but simply the medium's own spirit which sees and reports the facts intuitively and by clairvoyance. In this connection I must again refer to the phenomena connected with Mrs Piper,

> who [Frau Moser tells us] had an incredible degree of positive knowledge concerning hundreds of dead persons, their acquaintances, relations and all the circumstances of their life, a knowledge the accuracy of which often came to be confirmed in the most roundabout way—on occasion even from other continents. This knowledge in the course of time assumed dimensions that made it seem miraculous on that ground alone, a miracle, among other things, of sheer memory, for there was never the slightest confusion; and even years afterwards when her visitors called unannounced. Invariably the same messages were received concerning things which sometimes lay as much as a century back in the past and of which the visitors were proved to know nothing, and could indeed have known nothing.[45]

All that was at work here was the abnormal faculty of clairvoyance with which this worthy inoffensive middle-class woman had been endowed.

So far therefore no phenomena have come to light which require the activities of spirits for their explanation. All can be explained by the subconscious faculties of the spirit-soul, though naturally those who do not recognize the existence of the latter must then confess their complete inability to furnish an explanation at all.[46] But the spirit-soul and its faculties of clairvoyance explain everything in a manner that is in no way forced. On that assumption we can understand how "tables teach us things which could not possibly be known and which surpass the limitations of human faculties",[47] for they are guided by subconscious faculties, with the result that lost objects (keys, rings) are found, criminals discovered and diseases diagnosed. What

---

[45] Moser, *op. cit.*, p. 538.
[46] Moser, *op. cit.*, p. 642.
[47] Moser, *op. cit.*, p. 585.

remains most noteworthy is that no knowledge has ever thus been vouchsafed which some living human being somewhere did not possess. The spirits, for instance, have never told us the contents of a letter by a dead person, which no other person had ever read. Indeed the spirits of the dead have never told us anything, which shows that they have never intervened at all; nor has any medium ever won any of the many prizes for genuine scientific achievement.

(F) Ghosts and Hauntings

Many people have racked their brains to find an explanation of the so-called spook phenomena or of the hauntings that occur in certain places. The phenomena are of course most varied and must be explained in varying ways. Sometimes mere hallucination, often collective hallucination, is at the bottom of it, a hallucination which is almost infectious, so that all who hear about the phenomena profess to "see" them.

It would nevertheless be a mistake to attempt to explain everything in these terms, for often there can be no doubt as to the reality of the phenomena, especially when they are also seen by animals, when horses start and snort, and dogs bark or run away terrified. There are certain houses which are definitely haunted, and there are spook phenomena which are tied to a certain person. These last fall into the same category as the physical phenomena associated with mediums; they are like dreams come alive, and therefore irrational and confused; they cease when the person concerned has gone away, or when the subconscious of such a person has been influenced and dispossessed of the dream-figures, as described above.

It may now be asked how such dream-figures that have, so to speak, come alive, become so real that they can even be seen by animals. The general sense of our thesis here permits us to reply that we must concede to the spirit-soul the power, among others, of influencing matter; modern nuclear science teaches us that matter can be converted into energy (loss of mass) and vice-versa. This is not a new creation of matter, but a transformation, the power to effect which even the strictest theology permits us to ascribe to creatures. Certain creatures therefore must be held to be endowed with this faculty, and a number of spook phenomena can thus be explained.

These spook phenomena correspond to the apports and telekinetic phenomena of spiritualism. A passage from Fr Gastelein should be noted here (p. 201):

> We must be even more careful [he writes] in assuming that a medium can produce phenomena of levitation, can move objects without touching them, lift tables, influence scales from a distance, etc. It is true that serious men of science, who are anything but credulous, admit this, and we should have to admit, if these things are so, that a nerve-stream can at the command of the will produce certain effects at a distance. Such a thing would have to be most carefully observed and examined, but is not absolutely contrary to a rational psychology.

There is no need to fall back on this dubious nerve-stream which can allegedly produce effects at a distance, but for the existence of which we have no proof at all. We need go no further than the writer's "spiritual" explanation which ascribes certain rudiments of angelic powers to the soul, even when it is connected with the body, powers which it once possessed in full. It is really not difficult to explain the facts on that basis; all the more so, since theology itself, with its teaching on pure spirits, on our first parents, and on mysticism old and new, has suggested it.

In L., a village in Upper Austria, the following occurred during the war: a farmer had two sons, Alois and Joseph H., both of whom had been called up for military service. The latter had a considerable affection for the maid, Barbara H., and had gone back to the colours with a heavy heart after his leave in 1943, because he had a premonition that he would never return.

The farmer himself was in prison because he was suspected of being a monarchist. He was released in November, and on his first night at home, all the doors suddenly stood open and the electric light suddenly went on. It was later ascertained that this was the exact hour in which the son Joseph fell on the Russian front. From that moment onward, spook phenomena began to take place in the house. The crockery began to move on the hearth and fell to the ground, but did not break, nor were the contents spilled. There were knocks on the walls so loud that they could be heard in the neighbouring house 20 metres away. Brooms and other objects flew through the air, the cider-press fell over, though again nothing was broken, and so did the full chaff-cutter, without spilling any of its contents.

The parish priest of the place, W.P., to whom we owe this account, was called; he blessed the house with the canonical blessing, but was compelled himself to observe how brooms fell at his feet, while a sharp knife which was torn out of the maid Barbara's hand fell on the floor near him. In the night the maid herself saw the dead Joseph, who asked for her prayers, which she thereupon most conscientiously made. By advice of the Bishop, she was then put into another house, whereupon the phenomena ceased. When she afterwards returned, they began again afresh.

In July, 1944, the maid said that on the 15th August Joseph would enter heaven, and in point of fact from that date onwards everything was quiet, and the disturbances did not return.

Here are all the elements that we expect to find when "spook" is attached to a particular personality. The maid was naturally anxious about the safety of her young man, and by second sight saw the hour of his death, and this knowledge expressed itself in a kind of dream symbolism by the turning on of the lights and the opening of the doors. All the spook phenomena were designed to arrest attention, as happens in cases of hysteria, and were indeed dreamlike, nonsensical expressions of the maid's subconscious. It was in a dream, too, that the maid saw her young man, who however told her nothing whatever about the war, but only something which out of her own sphere of knowledge she projected into him. When the priest went through the stable during the maid's absence, nothing happened. When she returned, she said to him, "Go through it again. You'll see." The priest did so, whereupon all the phenomena described above occurred again, and he saw how a little forage basket went rocking across the court, and how a broom was pushed along. She believed that the dead man had been released from purgatory through her prayers, and this belief was strong enough to capture her subconscious, so that nothing occurred after the 15th August.

People have hit on the idea of hypnotizing persons who are associated with spook phenomena and of suggesting to them, while they are under hypnosis, that the spook should cease, whereupon it actually does cease.[48]

---

[48] See Moser, *op. cit.*, p. 845.

The most confused and also the most intensive of all these somnambulist activities was that of the "Seer of Prevorst" (Fredericke Wanner, whose married name was Hauffe 1801-1829). Her story was set down by the amiable doctor and poet Justinus Kerner (1786-1862), Strong natural aptitudes were in this case heightened by magnetic treatment, so that an unusually high level of achievement was attained. "Somnambulism", it has been written, "was almost her permanent state, so that even in her waking hours she was never truly awake in the full sense of the word" (Du Prel). The magical and, as we should today say, superstitious signs and amulets which she employed seem, as with true magicians, to have served only to heighten the power of suggestion used for the purposes of healing, as in the healing of the mentally infirm Countess von Maldeghem. The same seems to have been intended of her sun circle in relation to her life circle, as also of her intercourse with the spirit world. (It is by no means impossible that people in a somnambulist state, that is to say in a state when the spirit-soul is operating, really "see" spirits which are not merely the creations of their brain, since animals also react to them in a peculiar manner by sweating and snorting, all the more so if such a vision has a serious purpose, namely that of bringing about the redemption of the person concerned.

It is in connection with this general set of ideas that we should here refer to J. I. Kant's *Dreams of a Ghost-seer elucidated by the Dreams of Metaphysics*, Friederich Schiller's *Der Geisterseher* and Arthur Schopenhauer's *Essay on Ghost-seeing and Matters Connected Therewith*, ghost stories in which the idea already vaguely operates that the human soul is the real cause.

It is true enough that there is still a residual category to explain—that of spook phenomena attached to a particular place, where it is impossible to establish any connection with any living individual. In such cases as these, which are very rare, I have no hesitation in assuming, that the apparition is really that of a departed soul, particularly when a serious purpose may be inferred, when for instance the soul is expiating some guilt, or has come to give warning or comfort, or to ask for our prayers—things which God might well permit.

After all, the writer did not reject the possibility of a genuine intervention of souls in occult phenomena, such as those of spiritualism, or deny that the dead might be capable of producing the manifestations in question. He merely affirmed that it was not fitting that they should do so, and that there was a natural explanation for all these things. Of course the notion that such phenomena may actually be caused by a departed soul will alienate those who reject the whole idea of a survival after death or the existence of the soul. With these last the writer does not propose to enter into further controversy. His philosophy of life is already decided.

There was a well-authenticated story of the reappearance of a dead person in the life of St John Bosco. The latter had agreed with his friend and fellow student Comollo that whichever of the two died first was to give the other some indication concerning the state of his own soul. Comollo died on 2nd April, 1839, and Don Bosco now waited for some message. In the night of the 3rd-4th April (after the funeral) Don Bosco sat sleepless on his bed in a room containing twenty other theological students.

> Midnight struck and I then heard a dull rolling sound from the end of the passage, which grew ever more clear, loud and deep, the nearer it came. It sounded as though a heavy dray were being drawn by many horses, like a railway train, almost like the discharge of a cannon. . . . While the noise came nearer the dormitory, the walls, ceiling and floor of the passage re-echoed and trembled behind it. . . . The students in the dormitory awoke, but none of them spoke. . . . Then the door opened violently of its own accord without anybody seeing anything except a dim light of changing colour that seemed to control the sound. . . . Then a voice was clearly heard, "Bosco, Bosco, Bosco, I am saved." . . . The seminarists leapt out of bed and fled without knowing where to go. Some gathered in a corner of the dormitory and sought to inspire each other with courage, others crowded around the prefect, Don Giuseppe Fiorito di Rivolo; thus they passed the night and waited anxiously for the coming of day. All had heard the noise and some of them the voice without gathering the meaning of the words. I sat upon my bed and told my comrades that they had no cause for alarm. I had clearly understood the words; they were "I am saved." Some had also understood them as clearly as I had done, and for a long time afterwards there was no other subject of conversation in the seminary.[49]

---

[49] See Joh. B. Lemoyne, *Der ehrwürdige Diener Gottes Don Johannes Bosco*, I, Munich, 1927, pp. 226-230; Dr A. Ludwig, "Postmortales Erfüllen eines Versprechens", in *Zeitschrift für Parapsychologie*, 1931, p. 336.

So ends Don Bosco's account.

Another case in which we have no ground for doubting the actual appearance of the deceased is the case related in *The Proceedings for Psychical Research,* V, 36 (1927), pp. 517 ff., under the title "The case of the Will of James Chaffin". James L. Chaffin was a North Carolina farmer, who had four sons. He made a will in 1905 in which he made his third son, Marshall, sole heir to all his property. In 1919 he wrote with his own hand another will, according to which he left his property to all four children. He hid the document in an old family Bible, folding into a kind of pocket the pages containing the 27th chapter of Genesis (Jacob replaces his brother Esau). He also sewed in a note into the inner part of an overcoat of his with the words: "Read the 27th chapter of Genesis in father's old Bible."

The farmer died in 1921 and the property passed to the third son, as the 1905 will, which there were no grounds for challenging, had provided. In 1925, however, the second son, James Pinkney Chaffin, began to dream of his father. The latter appeared to him several times, and on the last occasion was wearing the overcoat in question. In that particular dream the father said: "You will find my will in the pocket of my overcoat." On the next day a search was made for the coat, which had already been appropriated by another brother named John, and in the lining, which had been sewn together again, the vital piece of paper was discovered. Again, in the presence of witnesses, the Bible was duly found, in the drawer of a writing-desk in a room which lay somewhat apart. It was already in such a decayed state that when they took it out it fell into three pieces. In one of these parts, which was picked up by a neighbour, the will was discovered.

So that there should be no calling in question of the testator's intention, the property was taken over by all the brothers together. What had happened was that a father, who perhaps had had too much pressure put on him by one of the children, made a will in the latter's favour and had then changed his decision. He had, however, wanted to avoid trouble, and so had hidden the will in the manner described in the hope that it would soon be found. When the finding of the will was delayed, his soul began to feel the need of hastening that finding, which gives us a rational ground for the manifestation concerned.

It is possible that, actuated by such reasons as these, souls really do appear from the next world and create visible effects to identify themselves, as Bruno Grabinski tells us in his book *Spuk und Geistergeschichten Oder Was Sonst?* (1920, 4th edition, 1952). Nevertheless, as Professor Feldmann[50] makes plain, such accounts should always be accepted with caution, though there are always people with an insatiable appetite for strange tales, and superstitious people who will read of such things with interest.

(G) Hylomancy (Psychometry)

As we have seen, the subconscious is active according to the degree that the upper consciousness is put out of action. Translated into the terms of theology, this means that the spirit-soul of man, which since the Fall leads only a troubled life, can assert itself only by loosening its connection with the body, that is to say by becoming to a certain extent body-free. It becomes wholly free of the body in death, but partially attains that condition in sleep, which is the brother of death. Yet what we see in this state of semi-freedom from the body is a mad confusion of dreams, which is generally devoid of any sense whatever. Dreams receive some kind of meaning, as we have seen, when someone suggestively directs them.

Something similar to what occurs in natural sleep takes place in the various states of artificial sleep, which are somehow directed by telepathy and rapport, and can thus in certain circumstances be made to serve man. One particular form of such direction is to be found in hylomancy, a thing for which there are several other names, which vary according to the conceptions and phrase predilections of the person concerned. The American physiologist and anthropologist Professor J. R. Buchanan, who was the first to examine the phenomena concerned, called it "psychometry", a name that many people reject, though it has to some extent established a place for itself. Others used names such as "pragmatic cryptaesthesia" (Richel), "paramnesia" (Oesterreich), "relative retroscopy" (Tartaruga), "retrospective metaesthesia" (Fischer), "clairvoyance into the past", etc. The writer believes that we should stick to the term hylomancy, by which he understands the faculty of obtaining

---

[50] *Okkulte Philosophie*, p. 37.

extraordinary knowledge by touching a lifeless object, and in this process the lifeless object has no other function than to direct the subconscious.

This implies a rejection of the conception of Dr G. Pagenstecher, who after years of research[51] found the solution of the riddle in the so-called "impregnation theory". The essence of this theory is that the lifeless objects in question have been artificially influenced and then radiate impressions of light, sound and smell on to the person in trance. Nevertheless it was proved that the success of his experiments was due to telepathy, for the knowledge possessed by the medium never went any further than that possessed by those present, and the idea that "the material thought-images ... were impressed on some part of the brain, perhaps as some kind of microphotographic print betrays a crass materialism compared with which Büchner is a positive innocent".[52]

Yet another explanation is that of the American medium Mrs Piper, who with the aid of a hylomantic object was able to tell a number of details that were known to nobody concerning the life of a departed person—a fact that certainly justifies us in inferring abnormal powers. It seems certain, however, that she derived many things from the subconscious of those present, and even from that of absent persons, while we have no means of testing the validity of the rest. Mrs Piper herself ascribed everything to the spirits, the spirit-controls, of which she had many. In particular her spirit "Dr Phinuit" jabbered quite inordinately, but there was never anything in the way of a real revelation.

People rack their brains as to the precise significance of the hylomantic object. Yet it has already been explained. It merely serves to establish the rapport and acts as a guide, so that not only telepathy, but also clairvoyance ("telaesthesia"), may become possible. A few examples will illustrate this.

There is much excellent evidence of such psychometric phenomena where hypnotized persons and mediums have been able to give information concerning certain objects with which they manage to establish some kind of connection.

A medium is given a medal that has been awarded to a soldier for bravery. The medium then gives an exact description of the battles in which the medal

---

[51] *Geheimnisse der Psychometrie oder Hellsehen in die Vergangenheit, Gegenwart und Zukunft*, Leipzig, 1928.
[52] Moser, *Okkultismus*, p, 537.

was won. When given another medal, which has not as yet been awarded to anybody at all, the medium gives an exact description of the textile mill in which the ribbon had been woven.

Fr Gerhard Binnendyk, C.SS.R., sent his family in Amsterdam an Onca tooth which he had obtained in Minas Geraes and had carried about with him on many travels. A medium in Holland, who did not know the good father at all, was able to describe his appearance and his experiences on his pastoral journeys (Lacroix, p. 142).

Raupert tells that a medium was able to give an account of his (Raupert's) whole life by merely holding an envelope with Raupert's address on it.

A priest in Czechoslovakia was able to diagnose diseases if he received the outline of a patient's hand traced on a piece of paper.

Another was able to indicate water and mineral deposits if furnished only with a sketch map of the district, or when passing over it in a balloon.

The examples related by Tischner[53] seem mostly to depend on telepathy, for there was always somebody other than the medium possessed of the knowledge which the latter revealed. One can really only recognize as genuine examples of hylomancy those where the facts were not known to any other person.

In March, 1914, an old man aged eighty-four was found to be missing from Château Givry (Dep. Cher, in France), and intensive search failed to find him. The steward of the estate sent a scarf out of the old man's cupboard to the scientist Osty, in the hope that the latter would be able to find the missing man by means of a medium. The medium in question, Mme Moret, gave such full information about the old man (who actually was dead), and about the place where his corpse was to be found, that the search succeeded by reason of her help. Here are all the factors that go to make up a genuine case of hylomancy. The impregnation theory clearly breaks down, for the scarf was hanging in the cupboard and the dead man was in a distant wood; neither does telepathy or hypermnesia provide an explanation, since nobody knew of the place where death had overtaken the old man. Here we are obviously concerned with clairvoyance guided by a hylomantic object.

---

[53] *Ergebnisse*, pp. 175 ff.

In another case the medium Emma was able to disclose what had happened to a payment made to a bank, when the payment had gone astray. All she asked for was "the papers", i.e. the letter in which the notes had been sent. She then put herself into a trance and saw how through negligence the notes had been put aside with a lot of other papers. After a search the notes were found among some papers that had not been used for years, and would perhaps have remained unnoticed for years to come. The notes were found wrapped up and in a certain room exactly as the medium had described.

(H) Hypnosis

There are several stages in the process of setting our bodily senses in the background. They range from natural sleep right up to the morbid twilight states and artificial trance; in all of these the soul becomes partly free of the body and can do things which would be impossible in the normal state of consciousness. There is, however, always one difficulty—the phenomena are so arbitrary, so incalculable and so confused, that it is necessary for them to be purposively directed by some dominant idea or some guide. In hylomancy we saw how the use of some lifeless object served to guide the powers of knowledge. The really perfect form of such guidance of the unconscious and subconscious powers, however, is only to be found in hypnosis, in which the will of the hypnotist, which moves in the reaches of the upper consciousness, appears as authoritative for the hypnotized person. The essence of hypnotism is that it is an artificially induced sleep brought about by means of suggestion by another person. This suggestion can be strengthened by magnetic stroking (it is also possible by ever-deepening hypnosis to pile one hypnotic state on top of the other, so to speak, each state having its own memory, though the waking state is remembered in all). The hypnotized person then is *en rapport* with the hypnotist, and in this condition exactly fulfils his will.

The first thing to note about hypnosis, then, is that it induces the kind of sleep which makes subconscious spiritual activities possible, and that this state is induced artificially by means of suggestion. To make such suggestion possible, the senses are acted on, as by fixing the attention on some bright object, by soporific music, by incense or by inducing that pleasant feeling that arises by the reordering of those small quantities of electricity that are to be found on the surface of the body; that is to say, by the stroking that induces animal magnetism and so influences the nerves—much as blowing on the subject helps to wake him up. Animal magnetism is thus not something essentially different from hypnotism, but one of the practices that help in the suggesting of sleep. The most important element, however, is the rapport by means of which the subject remains in touch with the outer world and is guided both physically and mentally. It is precisely this that is so mystifying to the materialist enquirer. "Hypnosis", says Freud, "is, so to speak, a mystical expedient. Its mechanism is inexplicable to me, and I can understand as little as others why one person should be a good hypnotic subject while another cannot be hypnotized at all." If we recollect what was said above about the suggestibility of pure spirits, we will see that this matter of the rapport falls in with the same set of ideas.

Being thus in contact with his subject, the hypnotist is able to release the powers of that subject's spirit-soul. Where it is a case of simple suggestion, no failing of sensory perception can be observed, though the attention is already directed in a particular way, but it is undeniable that people are more amenable to suggestion, as Couéism clearly shows, when the sensorium begins to grow dim and the soul thus becomes free to receive impressions from without. In this condition it can also establish direct contact with the soul of another, receive that other's thoughts and combine them with the experiences that lie dormant in the subconscious. Proceeding from there, it can excite the actions of the body and influence it to an extraordinary degree. The body then performs involuntary motions, and experiences irresistible likes and dislikes, even in its vegetative Life, which normally does not stand under the direction of the will.

In hypnosis all this is intensified, the sensorium disappears completely, the mental connection with the hypnotist becomes perfect. Insane persons resist such connection, but nervous and hysterical people enter quite readily into it; in the main all persons are capable of being hypnotized, though they generally display some resistance to the first attempt; once they have been hypnotized, however, they lose this power of resistance. On this many moralists base their condemnation of hypnotism, in so far as by reason of it men lose their freedom of the will for ever. This is so great a good that men have no right to part with it, particularly since, once lost, it can never be wholly recovered.

Hypnotism moreover is harmful to health, deprives man of the use of his reason, and subjects his will to that of another who may misuse his power by suggesting sinful and criminal modes of conduct, for although it is well established that a hypnotized person will not commit acts that are entirely contrary to his moral nature, nevertheless even this form of resistance can be broken down under repeated hypnotism.

This being the case, hypnotism can hardly be justified except with strong reservations, though most moralists seem to take a fairly liberal view of the matter.

This much then is clear. In hypnosis a cutting out of the senses takes place and there is direct intercourse between two spirits, of whom the one influences the other, but through suggestion and not noopneustically.

If we are to evaluate hypnotism correctly, we must have a thorough acquaintance with its phenomena, which have been observed for a considerable time and are well attested. All seem to argue the activities of a spirit, and some say that this spirit is the devil. Yet that spirit is not the devil, but the human soul in a state of partial freedom from the body. We can, however, infer from what the human soul achieves on these occasions, how great were the powers of the first human beings and how vast were the consequences of sin. That thought is bound to strike us when we observe the astonishing things that the poor remnants of that endowment can achieve.

Let us then proceed to a brief examination of the characteristics of the hypnotic state of the senses.

(i) Activities of the Senses

In our normal state, the senses receive material impressions, send them to the brain, where through the activities of the soul these sense perceptions are released. In hypnotism the procedure is the opposite; the impressions and perceptions occur as the hypnotist orders the soul to receive them, and as the latter in its turn orders them from the senses. If the soul orders anaesthesia to take place, the senses receive no impressions at all, even when they are duly excited. The skin may be slashed, the nose bored through, noises may be made, and the subject given ammonia to smell, even surgical operations may be performed without the hypnotized person feeling anything. If on the other hand the hypnotist, and through him the soul, orders hyperaesthesia, then the hypnotized person can see things a long way off, can see through opaque objects, can see things with the naked eye that normally can only be seen under a microscope,[54] can pick out the gloves of a particular person by their smell from among thousands of others, and can do many other things that "seem to remove all limit from its capacities" (Baerwald).

Sense perceptions under hypnotism may be changed and become illusory; the subject eats onions and takes them for apples and vice versa, and in the latter case tears appear in the subject's eyes. The subject may find that a rose has a nasty smell and delight in the delicate aroma of things that actually have a nasty odour. He or she may also become blind—completely so, or on one side only, and everything can in a moment be changed into its opposite. Innumerable experiments have been made which clearly prove that it is the soul which, under the hypnotist's influence, gives its commands to the body, while the body makes the desired perceptions, even though they correspond to no reality whatever.

(ii) The Motor Nerves

The power of the purely spiritual will is clearly shown when a person is laid across two chairs in such a manner that only the head and the heels are supported. Normally nobody can remain in that position, but under hypnosis a person will remain in it for as long as may be desired, even when heavy weights are laid on the body.[55] We see here the force of purely spiritual power which is capable of moving the largest bodies without any difficulty. It is also the motor nerves which are set unconsciously in motion to produce raps (though the cause of raps is often quite a different one) or to play pianos, to walk or pass food through the bowels—even blood can be caused to leave the veins in this manner, as will be shown below.

---

[54] Moser, *Okkultismus*, p. 219.
[55] Cf. Schneider, *Das andere Leben*, p. 114.

(iii) The Vegetative Life

We have no direct influence on our vegetative life, nor can we consciously control our digestion, an inability which many of us have cause to regret; everything here proceeds automatically. Nevertheless in hypnosis the case is different, for in that state it is possible to lengthen the pulse or the breathing, to accelerate the digestion, to regulate the flow of the blood, so that hyperaemia appears at some point on the skin which then becomes red and begins to blister. Contrariwise, the hand may become cold when the appropriate suggestion is made.

> Thus pulse and heart, body temperature and bowel activity, can all be influenced in a most far-reaching manner by suggestion, the secretion of saliva and of the breast gland can be regulated both quantitatively and even qualitatively, the composition of the gastric juices may be changed so that they exactly suit various types of food suggested, such as milk, bread, meat, etc., while a reddening may be produced and strictly controlled over unlimited portions of the skin, the whole process often taking no more than a few minutes. Equally indisputable is the influence that can be exercised on bleeding, and in much the same way the physiological effects of such drugs as adrenalin, atropin and pilokarpine can be counteracted by counter-suggestion under hypnosis.[56]

"Blood-speaking" can cure bleeding. The Russian peasant Rasputin, called "The Holy Devil" by Filöp Miller, was summoned to do what he could for the son of the Tsar Nicholas II, and asked to still his blood, for the Tsarevitch suffered from uncontrollable bleeding. Rasputin was always successful.

It is, however, inaccurate to place the stigmata of the saints in this category, as Frau Moser does, since such persons did not receive the stigmata under hypnosis, nor did they, for that matter, desire them. Moreover genuine stigmata remain permanently and may even involve the formation of new structures, as, for instance, the nails in the case of St Francis of Assisi.

---

[56] Moser, *op. cit.*, p. 211.

(iv) The Power of Imagination

It is plain that the basis of all these illusions of the senses is the imagination, which is activated by the various ideas. The subject experiences the sensation of heat or cold, has a bad or a pleasant taste in his or her mouth according as such tastes are suggested. Imagination also sharpens the memory on which all that is seen and heard is impressed. A soldier writes something on a piece of paper under hypnosis. After a time the paper is taken away from him and an unwritten sheet is substituted for it. The soldier does not notice this, but nevertheless reads out all he had written on the original sheet, even correcting the mistakes he had made. It is not the eyes that read in this case, but the spirit, the soul in a state of semi-freedom. When the subject wakes up, all memory of what has been done by him or her is utterly lost (amnesia), for that extraordinary power has only been at work in the subconscious, and the normal consciousness has known nothing of it. In the hypnotic state the subject can of course display an extraordinary memory and great mental powers (hypermnesia), giving evidence of knowledge not possessed in the waking state at all.

(v) Hallucination

When we spoke of the illusions of sense we mentioned hallucination, that is to say, perceptions that are false in so far as there is no corresponding sense impression from an external object. In hallucination the senses appear, as has been said, to perceive something that is not there at all, whereas the term illusion is applied to the perception of a real object that has been misinterpreted. We suffer from such hallucinations when we hear voices that do not actually exist. This principally occurs during illness or in sleep. Above all, however, hallucinations occur under hypnosis as has already been made plain. Apart from those experiments which are little more than games, such as making the subject take red for white, see big as little and distant things as close at hand, making the subject hear birds singing when actually bells are ringing, mistake salt for sugar, ammonia for the smell of roses and water for champagne (actual drunkenness ensuing from the supposed champagne), etc., etc.—apart from such playful experiments as these, there are a number of others that can be made. The subject can for instance be persuaded by suggestion that he or she is an entirely different person. This does not mean that the sense of substantial identity of the ego is lost but merely that the accidents of its behaviour are forgotten. It may for instance be suggested that the subject is a girl, in which case that subject will lower the head and bring out a mirror; if it is suggested that the subject is a general, that subject will give military orders; if the suggestion is that the subject is a priest, eyes are raised to heaven and the motions of reading the office are performed; and the same subject will begin to go about on all fours, if the suggestion is made that it is a little dog.

Nor does this represent the limit of the power of hallucination. The hypnotist can suggest the most extraordinary and even dangerous lines of conduct, which are then carried out, but without any difficulty and without any show of resistance. When the suggestion is made that the subject should steal, poison a rival or shoot somebody (with a pistol that the subject erroneously believes to be loaded), then the command is automatically obeyed—often with a great deal of premeditation, note being taken of all the circumstances and a fictitious alibi invented. Admittedly investigators have not quite made up their minds whether the hypnotized persons really may be said to commit these crimes, or whether in actual fact they know perfectly well that the crimes they are expected to commit are nothing more than "laboratory crimes".

There is really only one thing of which we can be certain; it is that, as we have already seen, people of good character resist criminal suggestions. It was suggested, for instance, to a certain person that he should put sugar into a friend's cup, after having previously been told that the sugar was poison. Then the same person was ordered to steal a watch. The person carried out the first instruction but not the second, saying, when questioned, that there was no harm in putting sugar into somebody's cup, even if it was said to be poison, but that it was a crime to steal.

It would appear that even under hypnosis a residue of free will and morality remains, or, to put the matter psychologically, the influence of law and morality, together with the awareness of the will of God, are stronger for the soul, even in its state of extreme suggestibility, than the suggestion of a hypnotist.

But the power of hallucination goes yet further in posthypnotic or retroactive suggestions. The former are commands which are given under hypnosis but are carried out in the waking state. It was suggested to an old sergeant that in three months' time he would find the President of the Republic in the doctor's house and that the President would give him a medal. After exactly three months the old man appeared at the doctor's house and bowed to one side, although nobody was actually there at all, uttering the words: "Thank you, your Excellency."

In retroactive hallucination, it is suggested to a person that they have seen or done this, that or the other. After waking, the subject quite honestly declares this to be the case, although the facts are quite different. Again it is the soul to which these suggestions have been made and which now dictates conscious acts out of the subconscious.

(vi) Healing

The only real benefits brought about by hypnotism are perhaps the cures that can be effected by it. Apart from anaesthesia in surgical operations, hypnotism used therapeutically can also cause the nerves and veins to obey. Coué built up his system on this, as we have seen, and we may illustrate the fact by a few examples.

A girl of twelve who limped because of a diseased knee was hypnotized, the suggestion being made under hypnosis that she could walk normally. When she woke up she was cured. For the most part it is hysterical contractions that are healed under hypnosis. A smith had injured a muscle while bending iron; he was now lame and could hardly sleep because of the pain. He was twice hypnotized and the pains disappeared.

Under hypnosis sick people can see inside their own bodies, can declare the position of a foreign body, which can then be removed[57]; also the nature of the necessary medicines can be discerned. One is strongly reminded of those people among the ancients who could diagnose and find the cure for illnesses in dreams. Thus, within certain narrow limits, "medical occultism", if the term is rightly understood, must be recognized as having a certain validity. There are indeed great possibilities here for mankind, if the hypnosis can be

---

[57] See Moser, *op. cit*., p. 596.

made deep enough for correct impressions to be obtained under it. It is, however, precisely here that there is some insufficiency, so that for the present people prefer to rely on the medical science of the conscious mind.

That the soul has a great influence upon the body is proved by many experiments. Tarchanoff knew a student who could deliberately slow down his heart beats or, if required, speed them up, or enlarge the pupils of the eyes. One of Schleich's patients could raise the temperature of her body to 42 degrees centigrade; another could put himself into a state resembling that of death and remain in it for hours at a time. His body would become ice-cold, his face pointed and grey, the eyes glassy, the heart would stand still and there would be no sign of pulse or respiration. From this state he could arouse himself at will. After such experiences as these, one can well give credence to the reports that Yogis let themselves be buried for six weeks and then rise again from their graves.[58]

Into this category we must also put such things as the charming of warts, the effect upon a child of some disturbing sight experienced by the mother during pregnancy, etc., etc.—it is always the power of the soul over the body, a power that is in a special degree released in hypnosis.

(vii) Spiritual Phenomena

The spiritual phenomena may all be described in terms of telepathy and clairvoyance, which are effective in hypnosis in proportion to the depth or otherwise of the hypnotic state, and to the strength of the rapport between hypnotist and subject.

We are here not concerned with "Cumberlandism" or "muscle-reading"; that is to say, with the reading of thoughts by means of the little involuntary muscle movements which accompany every thought according to the ideomotor law. These are on occasion even intelligible to animals, as was proved by Krall[59] with his horse Zarif, which could even solve mathematical problems. The horse of course only gave the answers (by tapping its foot) when these were known to some person present and it noticed that person's involuntary muscular movements when the correct number of taps had been

---

[58] Cf. Wiesinger, *Nach Manilla*, pp. 92 ff.
[59] *Zeitschrift für Parapsychologie*, 1926.

made—whereupon it stopped tapping. This is something perfectly natural, and therefore need not be dwelt on any further here. Here we are dealing with the genuine reading of thoughts, and with purely spiritual influences exerted at a distance.

One phenomenon that has been extremely puzzling to investigators is the hypnotized person's ability to measure time, and his awareness of time, although this seems explicable enough on our own thesis as a natural consequence of the spiritual state into which the subject is put by this peculiar kind of sleep. There are many people who can wake at a desired time out of natural sleep without any alarm clock, if they make up their minds to do so. This phenomenon can be observed in hypnosis in a heightened degree. Charles Townshend, writing in 1844, drew particular attention to this.[60] He states that he has never known true somnambulists miss the exact moment when they were to remind the "magnetizer" to wake them, despite the fact that on waking they were completely unable to say what the time was. The most extraordinary thing of all, however, is that even post-hypnotic commands are obeyed at a particular moment of time which has often to be arrived at by calculation; for instance, the subject is told to carry out a particular task in 3300 minutes and is normally quite incapable of translating this into hours. Such people are often quite unable to memorize the long rows of figures used in such experiments, let alone to convert them. "Here all connection with mere analogies is suddenly broken off", says Janet. "We make a sudden leap and find ourselves on the borderland of the mysterious powers of animal magnetism." Whoever does not believe in a spiritual existence and all the special powers that are germane to it will find that all this is quite unintelligible, for here the theory of suggestion offers no explanation, in so far as the hypnotists themselves are often unable to make the calculations concerned, and even make mistakes. The spirit-soul, however, does not need to depend on any calculations; it sees the facts intuitively, and a certain period of time is a fact like any other. Indeed, here the question expands as Frau Moser says, "to the problem of problems, to the problem of the human soul", to the problem of the body-free spirit-soul that is distinct from all matter.

---

[60] *Facts in Mesmerism*, p. 142.

(I) Diabolical Possession

We have already said enough to show that the various occult phenomena discussed all admit of a natural explanation and that modern philosophy and psychology point the way to it. But this does not mean that the actual spirit world may not have an influence on the visible world of creation, or that we must as a matter of principle reject any such idea. On the contrary, if we can say of the rapport that there is a mysterious connection between the hypnotist and his subject and that the former more or less directs the sensual and spiritual life of the latter, then it is only logical to assume that the actual spirit world, if we adopt the point of view of the theologians and accept its existence, can exercise an influence on man. If we assume that, then we have to reckon with the possibility of so-called possession, i.e. the taking possession of a human being by a demon, and if the data of the faith or historical reports tell us of such happenings, we may look upon possession as a scientifically established fact.

It is admittedly difficult to distinguish possession from many other morbid conditions of an occult kind, since the symptoms are often very similar, but there are certain things that enable us to distinguish between the two. There is first of all the theological fact that Christ himself repeatedly spoke of possession and commanded the evil spirits to "depart" from out of certain men, a thing that cannot be explained as "accommodation" to the beliefs of the time (Semler), since such a thing would not be consistent with the holiness and truthfulness of the Saviour. In any case, psychology and medical science know of no such prompt cure effected by the simple speaking of a single word.[61] This last was some time ago clearly demonstrated by Frau Dr med. Katharina Knur,[62] and the psychiatrists Krafft-Ebing and Kräpelin have confirmed it in their books on psychiatry, which have gone into many editions.

Indeed, nearly all modern psychiatrists have reached this conclusion. Thus the neurologist Dr Alfred Lechler writes[63]:

---

[61] Cf. Wiesinger, *War die in der Heiligen Schrift berichtete Besessenheit blosse Geisteskrankheit?*, Dissertation, Schlierbach, 1911.

[62] *Christus medicus?*, Freiburg, 1905.

[63] *Zur Frage der Besessenheit*, Neubau, 1948, p. 234.

There is no doubt in my mind concerning the occurrence of actual possession, even in our own day, though such a thing is admittedly rare. I myself have seen a number of cases in the course of my practice which could not adequately be explained in terms of psychology or psychiatry. In all these cases I waited for a long time before diagnosing possession and invariably tried to see whether some other explanation would not fit the facts, but no such explanation was to be found.

The psychiatrist D. Walter Schultze writes in similar terms in his *Evangelische Theologie*.[64] For this reason the Church has rightly created exorcists as a special degree of Holy Order among her ministers, although cases of genuine possession are extremely rare, and she herself reserves the right to judge whether a particular case is one of possession or not; each case must be examined to determine whether it is merely a case of pathological schizophrenia, or something due to preternatural influence. For the transition from one to the other is gradual and often almost unnoticeable, so much so that many scientifically trained observers claim to see the influence of a spirit where we ourselves still believe that purely natural causes are at work.[65]

Certainly cases such as the following, which was reported by Wilhelm Auffermann and was widely circulated in the European press, must be reckoned as borderline cases. In the South Italian town of Catanzaro, on the 13th February, 1936, the body of Giuseppe Veraldi, a man of twenty, was found underneath the bridge, and it was thought that he had thrown himself into the river with the intention of taking his own life. Some three years later, on the 5th January, 1939, the seventeen-year-old peasant girl Maria Talarico passed this bridge in the company of her grandmother, being on the way to an agricultural course of instruction in the town. Suddenly the girl stopped, gazed attentively at the shore, collapsed and appeared to lose consciousness. When she had been taken home she said to her mother in a rough man's voice: "You are not my mother. My mother lives in the wooden hut, and her name is Catarina Veraldi. I am Pepe." She then asked for wine and cigarettes, took a piece of paper, and wrote on it in the dead Giuseppe Veraldi's handwriting, and began to play cards with the people who were there, calling them Toto,

---

[64] 1949, pp. 151 ff. See *Zeitschrift für kath. Theologie*, 1950, p. 479.

[65] E.g. Tischner, *Ergebnisse*, p. 175.

Elio, Rosario and Damiano. It was remembered that these were the names of the dead man's friends—Toto had in the meanwhile emigrated to South America, She told how these friends had on that fatal occasion put sugar, salt and poppy seed into his wine and made him drunk; how then they had beaten him and dragged him to the bridge. When Pepe's mother arrived, the girl said to her in Pepe's voice: "My friends murdered me; they threw me into the river bed, then as I lay there they beat me with a piece of iron and tried to make the whole thing look like suicide." An examination of the police report made three years previously confirmed the possibility that this might have been the manner of death. The girl, who appeared to be endowed with some kind of clairvoyance, made further statements, then she tore herself away and ran to the bridge, from which she threw herself over the parapet, crying out, "Leave me alone! Why are you beating me?" and then remained lying in the exact position in which Pepe had been found. Suddenly, after the dead man's mother had asked him to leave the girl, she returned to her normal state and stood up.

Twelve years later a letter came from Tucuman in the Argentine, from a certain Luigi Marchete (probably the aforementioned Toto, since Elio was dead, while Rosario and Damiano were still in the neighbourhood), making Pepe's mother his sole heir and stating that he, Marchete, was the murderer of her son, he had beaten the man over the head with a piece of iron found in the river, because Pepe had been pursuing his wife Lillina, and the injuries had proved fatal. The other three had been accessories. Marchete had fled to the Argentine with false papers, had made money there, but had never had a quiet conscience, and now asked for forgiveness. Thus what this peasant girl in her abnormal spiritual state had declared concerning Veraldi's death was confirmed.

Was it the dead man himself who spoke through her? The unusual circumstances of the case, the suddenness of the trance in a perfectly healthy peasant girl, its length and its sudden cessation at the request of the dead man's mother, the serious purpose behind it all, which was to pin responsibility on to the murderers—all seem to point in that direction. As against this, no previous case is known where the possession of the body of one person by the soul of another who was dead has been proved, nor is there any mention in Revelation of anything of the kind.

Some cases of possession were collected by Dr Justinus Kerner,[66] by Dr C. A. Eschmeyer[67] and by Joseph von Görres in the fourth volume of his *Christliche Mystik* (Regensburg, 1842). For a century, however, there have been no further such collections; indeed, the cases are very rare, and even then should in many instances have been more carefully scrutinized than has actually been the case.

The evangelical pastor Johann Christof Blumhardt in Möttlingen, Württemberg, had experience of such a case, which is described by T. H. Mandel in his *Der Sieg von Möttlingen im Lichte des Glaubens und der Wissenschaft* (Leipzig, 1896); this case, however, was included among the purely physical phenomena by Moser,[68] together with the manifestations surrounding the little son of Professor Thurys Freund, and Professor Barrett's Florrie and Angelica Cottin. Both Mandel, however, and H. Freimann[69] accept it as a case of possession.

Because of the similarity of the symptoms, it often happens that doubt must for a long time prevail whether there may not be a natural explanation for certain phenomena, or whether they must necessarily be interpreted in terms of preternatural influence. For instance there is still no certainty whether between the years 1632 and 1639 the nuns of Loudun near Poitiers were possessed, or whether they were merely suffering from some infectious form of neurosis. The Jesuit J. von Bonniot[70] and Dr Charles Hélot[71] are of the former opinion, though experience recently gained might well lead us to question this. Most certainly the Church has declined to commit herself,[72] and it will in any case be difficult to arrive at a decision now, since the documents often flatly contradict themselves. For instance, we are told at one point that Sister Clara not only spoke Spanish and Italian, but also Greek, Turkish, and even Tupinambasic (the Tupinambas are an Indian race in Brazil), while

---

[66] *Geschichte Besessener neuerer Zeit*, Stuttgart, 1834.

[67] *Konflict zwischen Himmel und Hölle, an dem Dämon eines besessenen Mädchens beobachtet*, Tübingen and Leipzig, 1837.

[68] *Okkultismus*, pp. 711 ff.

[69] *Teufelaustreibung in Möttlingen. Wahrheitsgetreu erzählt von solchen die dabei waren*, Osterwald, Stuttgart, 1892.

[70] *Wunder und Scheinwunder*, Mayence, 1889, pp. 363-398.

[71] *Névroses et Possessions Diaboliques*, Paris, 1898. pp. 467 ff.

[72] Curtius, *Hochland*, 1925-6, p. 64.

Claude Quillet, an eye-witness, says: "I noticed that they (the nuns) only answered questions that were put to them in Latin to the extent that certain words were intelligible to them which happened to be much the same in our own language. When certain sentences were framed, however, or expressions used which contained no words which were similar to their equivalents in our own tongue, they remained silent."

We must therefore really confine ourselves to comparatively modern cases which can or could be checked. A case of possession, or rather of obsession, that occurred quite recently is reported in the *Benediktusbote*[73]:

> Because of the war a childless family had moved from the Rhineland into a little village on the Chiemsee in Upper Bavaria and occupied two small rooms. The man, a civil servant, was a Protestant; the wife was a Catholic. They took in a thirteen-year-old foster-child called Irma. Since the child's character was not such as to make them inclined to adopt it, they took in a second, four-year-old child called Edith and adopted it. After a year, actually in 1946, the latter succumbed to an indescribable fit of rage. So serious was the attack that the child was taken to the doctor who prescribed cold compresses. But the child began to deteriorate in character; it began to give impertinent answers in a voice that was not its own at all, using very telling phrases, despite the fact that it could as yet barely speak its own tongue correctly. Also it became visibly thinner, became dirty and ugly, and performed the functions of nature in the room, which began to be full of urine and excrement. The family began to undergo a period of terrible trial, lasting from June, 1946, till February, 1947. Everything was befouled, food was spoilt or disappeared—which in those days of food shortage was a very serious matter; the little girl bit her foster mother's fingers so badly that for six weeks she had to wear a bandage. A number of other things besides food began to disappear—keys, for instance. Heaps of filth and pools of urine appeared under the eyes of the occupants of the rooms, and that in such quantities that they could not have come from a grown-up, let alone from a small girl, despite the fact that the small girl in question boasted maliciously that they had.
>
> Since there was already suspicion of demoniac influence, a miraculous medal was hung around the child's neck, whereupon the child's health was completely restored. She said that "it" no longer whispered into her little head to do this or that. Now the other girl, Irma, became the target for the

---

[73] Reisinger, Wels, 1950, pp. 130 ff.

unwelcome attentions. Her clothing became full to a quite horrible extent of nasal discharge and a yellow slimy mass that looked as though it had come from some sick animal was all over the crockery. Petrol was poured on to the herrings, the husband had the rolls snatched away from him, and it was no longer possible to keep anything safe at all. The mayor and the parish priest were informed, but to the dismay of the couple, refused to give any credence to their story.

After this an exhaustive report was sent to the Archbishop's Secretariat at Munich, a reply being received that "there certainly were such things as demons and that the possibility of demoniac influence had to be reckoned with, and that the faith definitely taught as much", while a learned specialist in this field wrote: "Whoever actually sees this reaching in of the spirit world into the natural one, and whoever has actual personal experience of it, cannot possibly doubt the existence of that other world. Such a man will indeed think twice before letting the demon get him into his clutches for all eternity."

However, the affliction continued. While the husband had his accounts in his hand, having just made them up, they were cut in pieces, and the girl Irma received razor cuts on the hands and head and her heavy pigtails were cut off. The hardest blow of all for the family was that the villagers began to object to them, and demanded their expulsion. Only their landlord, a woman, had pity on them, although she herself had suffered a good deal because of them.

At this juncture the family heard of the holy cross in the Benedictine monastery at Scheyern, and told old Fr Stephen Kainz of their terrible predicament. The good Father sent some little blessed crosses, and blessed the family from a distance with a fragment of the true Cross, which had been venerated at Scheyern since the twelfth century. From that moment all was quiet.

When the two people heard, however, that another family of evacuees was being similarly pestered, they advised this family to seek help in Scheyern, whereupon, as had been expected, all the trouble promptly ceased—only, however, to begin afresh, as though by way of revenge, with the original family. Now paper was burnt everywhere, food began once more to disappear, or was rendered unfit for consumption, and the little girl's hair was cut off. Again an appeal was made to Scheyern, whereupon in February, 1948, everything became quiet.

It would indeed be hard to find a natural explanation for such happenings, even though we seek most liberally to apply the idea of suggestion and spook, for all who were living at that place were healthy and their participation was purely passive: further, only religious means were effective in curing the evil.

A particularly well-authenticated case of possession in modern times is that of two children from Illfurt, near Mulhouse in Alsace, who manifested the symptoms of possession in 1865. The children, Theobald, aged ten, and Joseph, aged eight, came from the respected family of Burner, which numbered seven members. Fr Sutter's book, *Satan's Power and Works on Two Possessed Children*, written in 1921 from authentic documents, has been translated into a number of languages, including Indian languages and that of the Ewe negroes.

> The boys began without any visible reason to turn around rapidly, while lying on their backs, to "thrash" the bedsteads and break them up; then they would remain for hours lying apparently lifeless; soon after this they developed an insatiable, wolfish hunger, their bellies began to swell, their legs began to intertwine like flexible withies, so that nobody could untwist them again. Then there appeared to them a hideous being with a duck's beak and with claws and feathers. Theodore threw himself madly upon it and pulled out feathers which lay about and gave off a loathsome stink. This occurred twenty or thirty times, in the presence of hundreds of people. The feathers, with their hideous smell, left no ash behind when burned. Sometimes the boys were lifted up from their chairs and hurled into a corner; on another occasion they felt a pricking and tickling all over their bodies, and fetched incredible quantities of feathers and seaweed from out of their clothes, and this occurred however often their shirts and clothing were changed.
>
> One of the most remarkable things about all this was that the children flew into violent rages and began positively to rave whenever any blessed objects were brought near them, and would eat nothing when, without their knowing it, a little holy water had been mixed with their food. They would also cry out in a rough man's voice, and would only stop when told to go on crying as much as they liked for the glory of God.
>
> After the doctors had tried all they could without success, the parish priest was called, who took pity on the poor tortured creatures and was anxious to bring some comfort to their parents who were almost in despair. The children, who had been well brought up with due regard to morality, found abusive names for all holy and consecrated objects, knew of things not taking place in their presence, and answered in French when they were asked questions in

Basque. The devils did not want to go back to hell; they gave their names and answered the priest's questions.

The children were taken to the hospital, where they were for a time more quiet. They were now deaf; also they avoided coming near any consecrated or religious object. At length an episcopal commission was appointed to examine the matter, which made a report in preparation for the exorcist. When Theodore was brought into the church so that the exorcism might be proceeded with, he trembled all over his body, developed a fever, foamed at the mouth and spoke blasphemies. When the priest recited the exorcism "I command thee to depart from here" the devil spoke from the child, saying, "My time has not yet come, I am not going." When the priest further recited "In the name of the Immaculate Conception", the boy called out in a deep bass voice, "Now I must yield", and fell down as though he were dead. After an hour he came to, rubbed his eyes and looked at all the people about him in astonishment. He knew none of them, although for four years they had constantly been about him. The only people he knew were his parents; his hearing returned, however, and he was the same well-behaved, decent boy that he had been before, simply four years older.

Some weeks later Joseph was similarly cured and by the same ceremonies, and continued thereafter to live a normal life. The whole picture of the condition of these children is different from that of the ordinary states of madness or of trance. The fact that the children were healthy to begin with, as indeed was the whole family, the sudden occurrence of the abnormal happenings, the impotence of the doctors and the hospital authorities, the stinking feathers and the seaweed, which all could see, the strange loathing for and fear of consecrated objects, the inexplicable hatred against everything connected with religion, and finally the manner of liberation, all argue a preternatural cause, though the apparent endowment with clairvoyance and the knowledge of languages are normal occult phenomena.

There are other recent cases, such as that of the two Kaffir girls in the Mission School at St Michael, near Umzinto in Natal, who were successfully exorcised by Dr Delalle, the bishop of Natal. There are various accounts of the story, and some booklets[74] were published which were translated into other

---

[74] *Gibt's auch heute noch Teufel?*, by Fr Wenzel Schöbritz, C.SS.R., 5th edition, Reimlingen, Bavaria.

languages, appeared in various German ecclesiastical publications, and were the occasion of much controversy when published in the *Kölnische Volkszeitung*. There seem to have been faults on both sides. On the one hand, little purpose seems to be served by the use of such expressions as "with burning shame"; on the other hand, proofs were adduced to substantiate genuine possession which were in reality no proof at all. People should really keep their heads on occasions of this kind, for knowledge of languages, levitations and knowledge of hidden things occur among the ordinary phenomena of telepathy and occult powers in general, so that the number of people who witnessed these things is really irrelevant. There may here or there have been a hallucination, but in the main there is no reason to doubt that the phenomena occurred, since the testimony of a large number of witnesses agrees about them. Also the burn in the underclothing was undoubtedly genuine, and there is no point in bringing up heavy artillery against it.

What principally strikes one, and what distinguishes these happenings chiefly from normal occult phenomena, is that the abnormal conduct of the girl Germana commenced after she had committed herself to the devil in writing, that she recognized and feared holy objects, and that finally the "disease" only lost its hold at the bidding of the exorcising words of the bishop.

It follows from what has been said here that the Roman Ritual's definition of the characteristics of possession requires some modification in the light of modern science. One of the signs of possession enumerated in the rubric is: "the making and understanding of long speeches in tongues which are unknown to the possessed person". This seems a reliable sign, in so far as there is no known case to date of a person in a trance uttering an ordered discourse in a tongue that was unknown to him. Whenever mediums have uttered words in a tongue that was unknown to them, they have merely read sentences by clairvoyance in some book or said something which, because of hypermnesia arising in the trance, they remembered out of the past. There is no recorded case of an ordered dialogue with question and answer in an unknown tongue taking place in a trance. If therefore this ever should occur, we would have to infer possession. The *understanding* of unknown tongues, however, is not a certain sign of possession, since in ordinary occultism there is such a thing as an understanding of the processes of pure thought, in whatever language they may find their expression.

Further, the rubric speaks of "having knowledge of hidden and distant things". This, however, is a symptom which we can no longer rely on in view of the facts of telepathy and clairvoyance. Other parts of the rubric, such as that where it speaks of "putting forth powers that go beyond age and nature", are equally inapplicable; for we have already noted cases of heavy objects being lifted up at seances and caused to float through the air, to the astonishment of those present.

The eighteenth-century theologians Ferraris and Brognoli name other symptoms, such as "attention to questions and commands which are only made inwardly", but today, when we know of the fact of mental suggestion, such phenomena also must be disregarded. The case is very different when people react in an unusual way to the *exorcismus probativus*, or when persons who are normally of good character are suddenly seized by an incomprehensible hatred of all holy things, when their hatred suddenly burns against dedicated persons and against near and dear relatives, or when they become incapable of uttering holy words, or incapable of prayer, or of using holy things such as relics or of making the sign of the cross. By and large, however, one should see the picture as a whole and form one's judgment from the totality of the symptoms, and not from a few isolated facts which happen to find their counterpart in the ordinary processes of occultism, and even in quite ordinary nervous derangements. It is because the "discernment of spirits" is so difficult, that the Church counsels the greatest caution and reserves the application of exorcism to herself, suspending the priest who prematurely resorts to it.

Most people, when the subject of preternatural influence comes up, fall into one of two extremes; they either see the devil everywhere and help to develop that mania on the subject that has done so much harm, or they simply will not listen to any talk of diabolical possession or of the world of spirits and angels at all. It is the same as in the case of miracles. Some see miracles everywhere, others simply refuse to accept them at all. Some will quite prematurely declare that a miracle has occurred, others take the line that all science would be at an end if "such break-through of the closed causality of nature were ever to be assumed".

The truth lies in the middle. Just as we Catholics are in no way urged to engage in the mass construction of miracles, so, under the guidance of the

Church, we are extremely hesitant to assume the existence of diabolical possession in any given case. Nevertheless we are taught to accept the possibility of such interference on the part of the spirit world, while the facts of occultism, in hypnosis for instance, teach us the psychological mechanism used in such interference. Through the superabundant grace of redemption, however, such cases of invasion by evil spirits are extremely rare.

It would appear that the time is past when serious medical science could relegate *a priori* the possibility of possession to the realms of fable and superstition. As the above examples clearly show, doctors whose professional attainments must be taken seriously are convinced of its reality; they occasionally discuss such cases, but dare not as yet treat of them in writing, though that may be because they think that once diabolical possession has been definitely established, the case no longer pertains to their department at all. The day will come, however, when people will discuss such cases from all the different angles from which discussion is possible, from that of theology, of medicine and of philosophy, and this too will redound to the salvation of mankind.

V

SEARCHINGS BY MANKIND TO ATTAIN TO THE CONTEMPLATION OF SPIRITUAL TRUTH AND TO TRANSCEND THE MATERIAL

Neoplatonism, Theosophy, Yoga, Cabbala and Astrology

If our solution of the mysteries of spiritualism is correct, and if there are indeed in man spiritual powers which are the remnants of preternatural gifts, then it should hardly surprise us if these remnants were manifest fairly frequently (and not only at spiritualist seances) and if we could find traces of them long before the knocks of Hydesville, and this, in point of fact, is precisely what we can do. We have already spoken of the ancient necromancy, and here we may include all pythonesses and seers, magic healers, wizards, augurs, druids, dwarfs and water-spirits, all of whom used to ascribe their powers to gods or demons, for nothing was as yet known either of the soul or of divine revelation, a knowledge of which would have explained whence these powers came. The important thing to note is that all these phenomena had one thing in common. They occurred in a state of derangement when the senses were no longer functioning normally *(unter "Verrückung" der Sinne)*. This "taking leave of one's senses" was achieved either through the fumes that arose from the abysses of Delphi, or by means of soporific music, violent dances, intoxicating drink, salves or by other mysterious devices. Even today there are still serious attempts to attain new knowledge, new powers, ideas and help which are all based on the existence of these rudimentary gifts, though usually such cults bring complete mental disintegration in their train and achieve no useful result at all.

In the light of these observations let us for a moment survey the first of such efforts, the cult called Neoplatonism, which has found its imitators in modern Theosophy, Anthroposophy and in the oriental Yoga cult and in Hinduism.

When we spoke of the connection of soul and body we sided with Aristotle against Plato who more or less tore human nature in twain. If we desire to amplify and complete this judgment on the two princes of philosophy, we might well call Aristotle the philosopher of nature and Plato the philosopher of the preternatural, since his teaching on the origin of ideas reminds us of preternatural, infused, or innate ideas.

Plato was born in the year 427 B.C., and became a pupil of Socrates (470-399 B.C.), who taught that virtue was a form of knowledge. Plato wrote down his teacher's thoughts in the dialogues, though these no doubt contain much that is original. In the *Phaedo* he expounded the doctrine of ideas. It is not the individual sense impressions that bring us true knowledge, but the thinking in ideas, for it is only ideas that exist. The perceptions of our senses only communicate the appearances of the things of this world, and these are always transient and have only a relative reality dependent on the degree to which they partake of the ideas. It is in the latter that the eternal reality resides which only reason can recognize.

The first place among the ideas is taken by that of "the Good", which is God himself, the condition and origin of all else. Souls too are eternal. It is only because of certain less good qualities that they must be united to a body until such time as they can return to their original incorporeal existence (cf. Wiesinger, *Zur Bedeutung Platos Heute*, Wels, 1949).

It is the task of man to strive towards moral perfection by remembering the ideas he has once seen. Sense perception can help, but the important thing remains the immediate contemplation of the ideas. This doctrine was accepted and continued by Plato's pupils of the Academy, who strove ever more to contemplate truth directly by spiritual contemplation up to the time when the Neoplatonist Ammonius Saccas (175-242 A.D.) and his pupil Plotinus (205-270) worked out a coherent system. Their aim was to defend Hellenistic philosophy against the oriental sects, and they began to toy with religious speculations. Plotinus tells us in his books (he wrote fifty of them) that he was able by direct contemplation to know the nature of his own soul and of God. He also constructed a theology with Christian elements which was later used by St Augustine. Plotinus by great efforts achieved something approximating to a mystical sleep, during which his partly body-free soul was able directly to perceive suprasensory truths.

We have spoken of Neoplatonism as the first of these cults. In strict accuracy, however, it should be stated that Gautama Buddha (560-480 B.C.) had earlier achieved something very similar by means of continuous contemplation, and had imparted this art to his pupils. These spiritual transports were so delightful to him that he looked upon the life of the senses as mere suffering, from which, as he said, we must save ourselves by denying our will to exist, and thus enter Nirvana. Actually this contemplation and dreaming of spiritual things in an ascetic mysticism is the essence not only of Buddhism, but of the whole of Hinduism; for the latter is a religion of dreams and suprasensory experiences. Today the Yoga cult teaches a kind of forced contemplation achieved by means of mortification, breathing exercises, rhythm and fasting, the object being to attain union with the absolute. "Our soul is a little light which seeks to unite itself in Nirvana with the great fire-God."

It should be noted, however, that the manner in which the fakirs seek to disencumber themselves of their bodies is different from that of hypnosis and of the repose of Buddha, for it occurs by means of mortification and breathing practices, the latter of which brings about a not inconsiderable degree of carbon dioxide poisoning, and this in its turn causes a diminution of the surface mental processes. It also leads to extreme emaciation and to a general disappearance of the power of sense perception. The soul thus becomes free for suprasensory knowledge and action. Through such practices and training the fakirs reach a stage where they are able to discontinue breathing and can allow themselves to be buried alive for half an hour, or even for six hours, or for weeks or even months; they can lengthen the rate of their pulse, can walk on fire without being burnt. This is in accordance with the words of the Bhagavad Gita: "O my soul, no weapons can cut you nor can the fire burn." They even assert that they can prolong their life for centuries.[1]

That the partly body-free soul can act on the body is, as we have seen, a fact, and this action can be increased according to the measure of the freedom from the body; the soul can thus act outside of the body, and can become

---

[1] Cf. Wiesinger, *Nach Manilla*, p. 91.

aware of distant objects and of suprasensory truths. When Westerners encounter such "miracles" they tend to be dumbfounded by them and not infrequently start practising the cults concerned. This was the case with the Russian Helena Petrowna Blavatzld (1831-1891), who together with Colonel Henry Steel Olcott (1830-1907), a Buddhist philosopher, used oriental philosophy to found Theosophy, a cult that became well known and widely practised in the West.

Like Neoplatonism, Theosophy seeks by means of contemplation to attain a direct knowledge of God even in this world, a contemplation which is the result of certain "immanent acts of human nature". Actually we know that these "immanent factors of human nature" are the purely spiritual faculties of the soul; we know their origin, their history and their dangers, which are evident enough in Theosophy.

To complete the story we should add that the Englishwoman Annie Besant (1847-1934), Blavatzki's successor, continued the latter's work in the direction of occultism and introduced into the system, among other things, certain Christian ideas as well as certain oriental pseudo-mystic elements concerning rebirth and the transmigration of souls (metempsychosis). She legally adopted the Hindu boy Krischna-murti, who was to be the "master and saviour of the world", but who later denied his messianic mission.

> As among all other races there was present in the Indians the spontaneous conviction, arising from a vague halfconscious unreasoning intuition, that the soul is in its essence a spirit, and as such, can have an existence divorced from the body. Unconsciousness, dreams and ecstasies seemed to offer confirmation in terms of actual experience that such divorce could take place. As against this there stood that other fact, namely that the soul in this world is actually bound to the body. Its existence under these conditions is not in accord with its spiritual nature, and its final goal must be that independent purely spiritual existence which it will enjoy when it has left the body; that will constitute its ultimate perfection.[2]

It is true that neither Theosophy nor Anthroposophy touches the depths attained by Indian thought, and that at times they really do no more than trifle in a mischievous manner with the credulity of their adherents, but they bear

---

[2] Mager, *Mystik als Lehre und Leben*, p. 248.

witness to an innate longing on the part of all peoples for some direct connection with the purely spiritual.

Some words of Fr Mager are here extremely apposite:

Whoever has worked his way into the psychology of peoples [writes Mager] will become ever more vividly conscious that something great, real, exalted and true was vaguely apparent to the spirits of them all. Yet though such awareness may have had all the power of a force of nature, it still tends to remain dim . . . and those who experienced it did no more than attain to the portal which led to a new and independent world, the world of the soul separated from the body and of an infinite personal God. At that point sheer exhaustion caused them to break down.[3]

Ideas very similar to those of Theosophy inspired Dr Rudolf Steiner when he designed his system of Anthroposophy. To some extent he set himself in opposition to Theosophy and expounded his doctrines as the products of his own mind. Again we may quote Fr Mager:

All the knowledge which, in his hoverings and wanderings through and over the different departments of learning, he tasted and snatched at, he managed with an uncanny skill and with a delicate spiritual illumination to weave together as threads into a single unity. Greek mythology which he learned at his *gymnasium* provided him with Atlantics, Hyperboreans and Lemurians, and he did some borrowing from the oriental mystery religions and from the Gnostics and Manicheans, The primeval fog of Kant-Laplace served him as a model for his spiritual primeval world, which by condensation and fission releases all beings out of itself. He lodged as a transient guest with biology, chemistry, geology, physiology and experimental psychology, and for a time the history of philosophy also had its effect on him. He went to school with the Cabbala, with occultism and spiritualism. He read the books of the New and of the Old Testaments, and for a long time, and with a considerable talent for getting at the inwardness of what he read, he studied Goethe. For most of the time, however, his little builder's hut stood on Indian soil, where he used the building materials prepared by neo-Indian philosophy for his own

---

[3] Mager, *op. cit.*, p. 250.

constructions. In the whole edifice of Anthroposophy there is not a single stone that has not been broken loose from some other building.[4]

In the centre of his thought, however, there stands, not God, but, in accordance with the anti-transcendental trend of the age, man: "Man is the summit and perfection of the universe. God is at best only a function of his development."

It is true that one sometimes has the impression that all these witty and playful combinations are only the product of the dreaming and discursive fantasy of a somnambulist, who from the depths of the subconscious traces connections which at first sight seem astonishing but which ultimately present themselves to us rather as the vague intimations of a misguided spirit than as truths arrived at by any process of exact thought. Again let us hear Mager:

> It is my profound and well-founded conviction that Steiner's Anthroposophy cannot be characterized otherwise than as the systematizing of the hallucinations of a misguided spirit into a coherent world picture.... Though Steiner may be continually speaking of the progress of thought towards self-consciousness, and of the contemplation of pure spirit, nevertheless his conceptions must be distinguished essentially from the Hegelian idea of the consciousness of the self, and from the contemplation of Plotinus or Buddha—to say nothing of the contemplation of the Christian mystic.[5]

Naturally enough Steiner's adherents take a very different view of him. These hold that "his life work is the conscious continuation and perfection of the way of Goethe, and is thus the fulfilment of the deepest longings of the modern European spirit". It seeks the suprasensory world, but being inimical to every kind of mediumistic approach (*alien medialen abhold*) strives to reach it only by the road of science. As against this it is stated that Steiner shows the means by which the powers of suprasensory knowledge that slumber in man can be released and raised to body-free consciousness.[6] It was not Steiner's intention, it is claimed, to set himself against Christianity; he was

---

[4] Mager, *Theosophie und Christentum*, pp. 42 ff.
[5] Mager, *op. cit.*, p. 46.
[6] O. I. Hartmann, *Wir und die Toten*, Kienreich, Graz, 1947, pp. 35 ff.

merely adapting spiritual knowledge to the modern age, so that people who stood aloof could once more be won over and interested in higher things. In order to succeed in this, he would have needed to give a clearer demonstration of the connections between his own teaching and Christianity with its belief in God. Such is the opinion of the Anthroposophist convert Bernard Martin.[7]

It is, of course, to Steiner's credit that he deliberately set his face against the crude materialism of his time and attempted to spiritualize the natural history, chemistry, physics and medicine of his time and to raise them on to a higher plane. He sought to do this with the aid of the sheer immensity of the knowledge which an inspired intuition enabled him to accumulate—a fact which made a profound impression on many seeking souls. That much of his thought loses itself in mere dreamy abstractions is due to the above-mentioned circumstance that the purely spiritual powers in modern man have been atrophied and that for this reason no really significant and serviceable cultural edifice can be erected on them. As the mystics must always be orientated by the tenets of the Faith, if they are not to fall into the aberrations of quietism, so the culture of the spirit must never wholly divorce itself from the firm foundation of the senses, if it is not to run to seed in fruitless dreaming.

Even among the Anthroposophists there are striving and searching souls, who must be taken seriously, and that is indeed something which the present writer is only too anxious to do. Yet their whole behaviour is but a confirmation of the present thesis, and they should really themselves recognize that the powers of the soul which we have here described make but an insecure foundation on which it is dangerous to build, unless there is far-reaching support and confirmation by the senses. For all that, we Christians should search our consciences and see whether we do not tend to pay too little attention to the spiritual powers of genuine mysticism and so let many people of real spiritual depth drift away from us. That is something which we should always bear in mind, even while rejecting, as we must necessarily do, the whole movement as it presents itself to us today.

Most certainly the Anthroposophic movement represents the ultimate point reached by the degenerate culture of the West that is so far removed from God, even as Plotinus represents the final point of Hellenism, and

---

[7] "Was ist Anthroposophie?" in *Stimmen der Zeit*, Vol. 145, 1949, p. 109.

Buddha the final flower of Indian culture, but in this present case the ultimate point is on a comparatively lower level. It is lower in precisely that degree that our distraught Western culture is something lower than the spirit of Hellas or than this Indian repose of spirit. Anthroposophy really represents nothing more than a sudden flicker of the hungry spirit-soul, a desperate striving to break through the limits of the bodily and to press forward to the purely spiritual. Yet such movements of the soul grow ever more ineffective. They were strongest with Buddha, and in his case the whole surroundings, the climate, the human type and the whole Platonic-Indian philosophy assisted the process. The present-day trends of Hinduism, Fakirism and Shankar-philosophy, as exemplified by Rabindranath Tagore, Animanonda Brahmabandav, Saddhu Sundar Sing and more lately by Paramhanza Yogananda,[8] are weak excrescences from this gigantic work. The same thing can be observed in Neoplatonism. It contrived still to arouse the enthusiasm of the Church Fathers, but today it has hardly more than mere historical relevance. So it is with Steiner. His defenders and adherents come nowhere near the eminence of their master.

It is not my purpose to evaluate these various theories which, as we have seen, are a mixture of occultism with pantheistic, evolutionist. Christian, Buddhist and Hinduist ideas, the character of which depends on the particular school where the founders and adherents of the philosophy in question happen to have made their studies, nor is it a matter for surprise if the esoteric quality of these doctrines sometimes threatens the psychic equilibrium of their followers, for we know that such doctrines are the product of a partial derangement (*Verrückung*) of the spirit; indeed, this applies to all the variants of occultism, which are all systems in which artificial dreams are at work, systems in which knowledge and historical fact are held in contempt, until everything ends in pure madness.

As to the Yogis, the Western mind, preoccupied as it is with technical development and with all manner of scientific enquiry, has no aptitude for the kind of concentration which the Yoga cult demands. Orientals are different; they have for thousands of years had an entirely different kind of hereditary endowment and live in a climate more conducive to dreams and meditations.

---

[8] *Autobiography of a Yogi*, New York, 1948.

They are indeed Platonic natures, who can only with difficulty accustom themselves to the philosophy and syllogisms of Aristotle, but they show a higher development in those purely spiritual faculties which in the West only make their appearance in the darkness of spiritualist seances or during actual mental disturbance.

One conclusion there is that we must fasten on as we hurriedly survey these world ideas which are to be found in every place: it is that they derive from an irrepressible longing, from a natural and passionate desire for those preternatural gifts which became useless by sin. These gifts were not intended as something contrary to nature, but as a support and perfection thereof. Today, after the Fall, man can only quench this most understandable desire for them by winning back, by the power of grace in true mysticism, something of that which has been lost. Apart from mysticism, there remains only artistic creation, in which also resides the grace of God and in which the shrewd observer can also see fragments of those erstwhile angelic powers. These last, however, can only produce great world cultures with the aid of the corporal soul expressing itself in science and technical achievement. The highest form of culture comes into being when Plato and Aristotle, wisdom and science, culture of soul and technical skill, are joined together in the right proportions, and in those proportions seek to conquer the world for the upward ascent of man.

What Theosophy, which has grown on Indian soil, is to the Christian West, the Cabbala seeks to be upon the national soil of Judaism. The name comes from the Hebrew *Cabal* (=to receive) and signifies a secret doctrine, derived from ancient Jewish literature, by means of which a man can influence nature through a certain mystical use of letters, perform miracles and attain all manner of magical results. It is really not worth the trouble of going into this system in any detail, since most of the interpretations involved are forced, artificial and have about them the foolish and even nonsensical quality of a dream; cures that have been ascribed to this agency can probably be explained by auto-suggestion—when, that is to say, they have been other than merely illusory.

Much the same may be said about astrology, which declares that the position of the stars enables man not only to foretell the weather, but to read human destiny as well. It is, of course, true that cosmic rays can, by their interference, influence electromagnetic action within living cells; indeed, there are some who contend that the very origin of life on earth can be explained by these rays[9]; it thus "no longer appears completely absurd that a cell should have come into being under the sign of a particular constellation" and in this way the illusions of astrology receive something like a scientific foundation. Nevertheless astrology has for thousands of years never progressed beyond certain dark intimations; it is an old superstition that goes back to the time before Christ; it has on several occasions been condemned by the Church, but it has nevertheless, since the first world war, revived as a substitute for genuine religious practice, particularly in Theosophist, Anthroposophist and occultist circles. These ridiculous, artificial and equivocal theories should be rejected out of hand, though they often fascinate the great uneducated masses, to whose blind faith they owe the influence they exercise, for the horoscopes which astrologers produce are framed in such general terms that they fit any situation, and if, after any particular event, the interpretation is padded sufficiently, they can be quite startling. One hears stories of people who put their whole faith in horoscopes which have been drawn up for them, and who then aver that all has turned out as shown thereon. One hears of such cases as that of a person whose horoscope was drawn up under the sign of Leo, and who was then informed by some learned man that on his birthday the sun was in Piscator, whereupon that person had a new horoscope drawn up, which fitted the facts even better than that drawn up under Leo. The whole thing is so elastic that one can read anything into it, and one can well apply the words of Pico dell a Mirandola which he uttered in the fifteenth century: "Astrology is the corrupter of philosophy; it soils medicine and puts an axe to the roots of religion. It robs men of their tranquillity and fills their minds with disturbing images; it turns the free man into a slave. It cripples men's energy and throws them forth on to a sea of misfortune."[10]

---

[9] Cf. Lakhovsy, *Das Geheimnis des Lebens*, pp. 205 ff.
[10] In Fischl, *Christliche Weltanschauung*, p. 248.

VI

MYSTICAL SLEEP

[In mystical sleep God uses the mechanism of the human personality described in this book, and in the highest forms of the mystic life brings about something like the condition enjoyed by our first parents. When this occurs, both the spiritual and the corporal elements of the soul again function together and the one need no longer be put out of action in order to liberate the other.]

We have now seen that, with the exception of genuine prophecy, of "free" spooks that are bound neither to a person nor to a place, and of genuine possession, occult parapsychological phenomena must be regarded as a rare development of our own spiritual life, a life that has its basis in man himself and in his spirit-soul. We need not therefore take refuge in unproven "radiations", still less in supposed spiritualistic or diabolical, let alone supernatural-divine interference. Even prophecy, spooks and possession must be kept within the strict sense of their own definitions and treated as exceptional things. Prophecy, for instance, must not be confused with mere shrewd anticipation of the future, an anticipation based on causes already existing and containing their consequences within themselves. Free spooks, again, must not be identified with spook phenomena that are bound to an abnormally endowed person, or with such as can be explained by collective hallucination, nor must genuine possession be predicated in the case of those varied manifestations that people with possession on the brain tend to diagnose as such. We must confine ourselves strictly to such well-attested facts as do not admit of explanation in terms of parapsychology. Everything else admits of a natural explanation, either in terms of some physical force of an electroid or magnetoid character, or of those abnormal spiritual powers which we encounter in our investigations into the occult powers of the subconscious. Those abnormal powers have here been shown to be nothing other than the spirit-soul in action, and the sooner this is recognized, the sooner we shall be able to effect a synthesis between modern science and the inferences to be drawn from theology.

In my examination of this matter I have been able to show that the subconscious was amenable to a progressive guidance of its uncontrollable powers by external agencies, ranging from hylomantic objects to a suggested idea, and from an ordinary hypnotist to a demon, by agencies, in fact, which pass through the whole hierarchy of creation. Our business is now to draw the conclusion and to see that the soul is kept open to the influence of its Maker, for though the latter has power over all creation, he has nevertheless made his guidance and taking possession of the soul depend on certain conditions, namely on the effects of the Redemption, by which our original state of innocence is restored. This is the process that takes place in the true mystical life.

When I speak here of mystical sleep, I do not thereby wish to imply that this is the essence of the mystical Life, or a necessary transition to the higher stages of that life. It is only the most generally trodden way, and one in which the external relationship with other abnormal states of the soul is particularly clear. For the mystical life, has only an external connection with the phenomena so far described, but it nevertheless represents the progress and fulfilment of an elemental urge in human nature to establish a relationship with God that cannot be attained by our natural powers. The powers possessed by man before sin were lost, and the misfortune for human society was incalculable, but man still retained a dual characteristic.

Firstly, there remained to man his soul as such, with all its powers and faculties, though it was now constrained within the bounds of his physical body. Yet originally that soul by a special grace of God should have preserved purely spiritual powers that transcended the physical, and by means of these should have been able to sustain, rule and perfect the body's powers and so keep that body sound and immortal, and regulate its appetites. But that soul was confined through sin within the limits of the body, and was weakened in its spiritual powers, as has been shown. Nevertheless, the soul remained—it lived.

There was also an urge and a striving on the part of the spirit-soul to tear itself away from the body's embrace.

> There is a feeling innate in man and in all peoples [writes Mager], which is incapable of conceptual definition, that the moving and animating principle within us, the soul, is something independent, reaching out beyond the bodily

life and its demands into the infinite. It is as though the soul ever instinctively strove to assert, against all attempts to equate it with our bodily life, its essential spirituality and immortality. In this spontaneous and usually unconscious protest of our human nature against the equation of the soul with the material, there also breaks through an instinctive awareness that body and soul are things of an opposite nature. The soul in its elemental urge towards pure spirituality feels itself constrained and hindered by the body and by the things of sense. They seem to be almost its mortal enemies. Since, however, it cannot simply disencumber itself of the body, it seeks to repress and limit the latter's desires and demands to a minimum. Purifications, expiations and castigations of all kinds are intended to make of the body an obedient instrument for the soul.

As men are by nature aware of the spirituality and immortality of the soul, so with equal directness and instinctiveness they feel the presence of a being in nature which is itself beyond nature and, though it animates nature, is not itself nature but a spirit. God and the soul are both spirits. Their natures are related. It is true that man contrives on occasion to reject God purely intellectually when he professes to proceed from the point of view of the scientist pure and simple, and to deny him; but no one will ever be able to eradicate from the human breast that dim but yearning perception of a spiritual, supermundane and infinite being; and it is this being that the soul seeks to approach. It seeks direct contact with him, and it is here that the material, the body, puts itself obstructively in the way. Again we see that antagonism to the material, to the body. The strongest methods are devised for the elimination of the body and of the life of sense, so that the soul may be released from all its entanglements in the body, and fly freely forth into the world of the spirit.[11]

There thus originated numerous attempts to regain those powers that had been lost by man, sometimes by honest striving after a form of self-preparation that was far-seeing, scientific, and wholly in accord with nature. Buddha, at the end of the culture of India is a case in point, as is Plotinus at the end of that of Greece. At the end of Western culture we have Steiner. There has, of course, always been magic, for magic never wholly dies.

But man never gets further than the gateway, "the threshold of a world behind whose doors eternal life lies hidden. Through those doors he could not

---

[11] Mager, *Theosophie und Christentum*, p. 13.

pass. When he reached them he collapsed and the ancient world collapsed along with him."[12] "A connection between God and the soul that was really a union between two persons was never attained. Yet it was only such a connection that could assuage the deepest longings."[13] Without power and without resource, mankind stands there in this mood of Advent with its longings and its cries. One has exactly the impression that the very latest developments are pointing once more to Christianity, in which the longing of mankind throughout the ages might at last find its satisfaction.

> When Christ was already upon earth [writes Mager], the representatives of the people sent messengers from Jerusalem to John the Baptist with the question whether he was the Messiah. He denied this and said, "Already he stands in the midst of you and you know him not." Our own time, so full of longing and searching, turns to Theosophy, Anthroposophy and other doctrines to find redemption. Yet the solution of all our riddles has been standing in the midst of us for two thousand years; for two thousand years there has been standing in the midst of us the assuagement of all our longings, the consummation of all our aspirations.[14]

Christ has brought us redemption; not only has he restored to us the supernatural good of sanctifying grace, he has also brought us the supernatural idea, in the sense that the way is once more open for us into the realm of mystic remembrance, to a union of love with the pure spirit, with God. It is the way taught by the Christian mystics.

> Christianity is in its innermost being essentially mystical, for it proceeds from the fact that there is a direct connection between spirit-soul and God. The activity of the soul as a pure spirit is mystical, an activity that goes hand in hand with the elimination of the corporal-sensual and of the functions of the corporal soul. If we say that the essence of Christianity is mystical, it follows logically that we should conceive of all baptized persons as mystics. Yet the mere fact that the Christian accepts in the Faith the truths of Revelation by no means implies that that inner transformation has already taken place within him by which, even when it is still in the body, the soul is raised up to

---

[12] Mager, *op. cit.*, p. 18.
[13] Mager, *op. cit.*, p. 83.
[14] Mager, *op. cit.*, p. 84.

the independence of a pure spirit, without thereby loosening its connection with the body. Since the goal of the Christian life and the direction in which it acts lies along the same road as that trodden by the mystics and the saints, there is no gainsaying that Christianity does strive to free the soul from that confinement to the body to which original sin has relegated it and to train it for the freedom and independence of a pure spirit.[15]

St Paul distinguishes between the corporal and the spiritual soul, between the *homo psychicus* and the *homo pneumaticus*. Naturally St Paul recognizes the essential unity of the soul, but as Aristotle distinguishes between the three functions, the vegetative, the sensitive and the spiritual, so there are again two groups within the intellectual soul; the first, those of the corporal soul which works by means of the body; and the second, which as a pure spirit unites with the pneuma, God, and thus is designed to achieve union with God, though in the reverse order from the "processions" in the Holy Trinity. The Father begets the Son, and the Holy Ghost proceeds from both; so the soul must first unite with the Holy Ghost, and it is only through him that it obtains sanctifying grace, the sonship of God. "According to the fathers there corresponds to the outward movement of the divine persons a return one, in which the Holy Ghost, by his entry into our souls and his enduring work therein, leads us upward to union with the Son and through him with the Father."[16] With the mystics it is not knowledge, still less an inquisitive search for knowledge of hidden and secret things, that takes the first place, but love, which leads the spirit-soul into ever closer union with God.

"In baptism by the Spirit (as the Scriptures call the baptism of Jesus, to distinguish it from the baptism of John the Baptist) the love of God is poured out into our hearts through the spirit of God which dwells within us."[17] In this manner the pneuma, the spirit-soul, rises to a new life. We are here not concerned with a mere renewal, but, to use St Paul's words, with a new creation in the full sense of the term.[18] Spiritual processes now take place which never existed, nor could have existed, before. That is why St Paul designates himself and his community as *primitiae spiritus*, as the first to

---

[15] Mager, *op. cit.*, p. 93.
[16] Scheeben, *Mysterien des Christentums*, 1912, p. 165.
[17] Rom. 5. 5.
[18] II Cor. 5. 17; Gal. 6. 15.

whom this life of the spirit-soul has been vouchsafed. That in this granting of the divine spirit we are concerned with real operations of the soul is shown us by the story of primitive Christianity where the fullness of the divine spirit could be perceived by all. At that time outpourings of the spirit were looked upon as recognizable signs of the rebirth within. Thus Christianity is the only religion which builds up on the facts of an independent spirit-soul in man, one spiritual God in three persons, and an immediate union between the two. Let it again be emphasized that Christianity with its new-creative redeeming activity begins at just that point where the old theosophies had ended in exhaustion.[19] What therefore distinguishes the mystics is "an experienced knowledge of God through love".

To this goal man attains first of all by his own efforts, by means of which he reaches at least the first stages of the mystical Life. Poulain[20] mentions four such stages, vocal prayer, meditation, affective prayer and the prayer of simplicity, all of which can exist side by side or follow one after the other. The prayer of simplicity is the highest stage that can be reached by means of ordinary grace, a stage which even the natural mystic can reach. What is beyond this belongs to the mystic life proper, which is also spoken of as being infused, and is different from all other kinds, requiring, as it does, a special and unique grace on the part of God. This is a very brief statement of the doctrine commonly accepted today of the mystical gifts of grace.

This is not the place to enter into the controversy between Saudreau, Lamballe, Dimmler, Garrigou-Lagrange and Lercher on the one side and Poulain, Richstätter and Mager on the other, as to whether the mystical life is or is not essentially different from the preliminary stages that lead up to it. Mager, however, does seem to be right when he says that the grace bestowed by God in this state is not essentially different, but that the acts performed by man in the mystical state are quite different, being acts of the spirit-soul. We wish here to develop this idea somewhat further.

Three or four stages are again recognized in this infused mystical life: the prayer of quiet (imagination still retains its freedom), the prayer of union (with ecstasy), the prayer of spiritual betrothal and marriage.

---

[19] Cf. Mager, *op. cit*, p. 89.
[20] *Handbuch der Mystik*, Herder, 1925.

It is clear from what has been said that the most important thing for the ascent of the various stages of the mystical life is love, and it is here that we can find the solution of the riddle why none of the worldly philosophers have attained to such knowledge of God by direct experience. They lack the key, which opens the treasury of God's grace and so alone gives the special power required to rise to the highest stages. Neither the Platonists nor the other philosophers knew love; still less do the modern theosophical, anthroposophical or occult systems know it. Further, the mystical life cannot be forced upon anybody, as Fr Surin, S.J., sought to force it on the superior of Loudun, the unfortunate Jeanne des Anges (Mme de Belciel).[21] Here also we have the answer to the question whether the soul can, even in this life—that is to say, during its sojourn in the body—act as a pure spirit.

> If primitive Christianity and tradition both bear witness to the fact that there is such a thing as a direct experimental perception of the working of grace and of the Spirit within the soul, then this is only conceivable or possible psychologically on the assumption that the soul can act, and does in point of fact act, as a pure spirit. It is only thus that we can explain the declarations which all mystics make unanimously, namely that they can in their mystical experiences actually contemplate God and his attributes, the Holy Trinity, etc. We can well understand that this so-called mystical contemplation is not the same as the contemplation of the blessed in heaven. It is the same kind of knowledge as, according to Catholic doctrine, is possessed by the departed soul in purgatory, when it is not yet healed of all the wounds incurred during its association with the body. As long as the soul in its mode of being is still imprisoned in the body, the apprehensions of the spirit-soul cannot be direct, but only partially so. Hence possibilities of error arise for the mystic, and the possibility of a degeneration of even the grossest kind. A man enjoying mystic contemplation can still never dispense with the Faith, or with the norm established by the Church's teaching office. When the soul in its mystical experience acts as pure spirit-soul, then there is nothing inexplicable about the various secondary phenomena of the mystical life such as visions, voices, etc. It seems unnecessary for me to add that a soul which under the influence of the divine spirit gradually frees itself from its entanglement with the body, and from its union therewith, is raised to the manner of activity of a pure spirit,

---

[21] Henri Bremond, *Histoire littéraire du sentiment religieux en France*, Bloud et Gay, Paris; see *Mystische Hochflut im 17. Jahrhundert*, by E. R. Curtius, Hochland, 1925-6, p. 61.

and experiences, knows and loves, God in an incomparably higher fashion. We can only form a very imperfect idea of the joys and happiness, the tortures and the night of the soul that go with the life of mystic contemplation. The mystics call the joy of contemplation an anticipation of the joys of the blessed, and the tortures an anticipation of purgatory.[22]

The mystic's union with God does not lead to the beatific vision, but because it is born of love, and love strives for perfect union, the soul is sorrowful for so long as union is not perfectly attained as with the souls in purgatory.

> Admittedly in the dark night of the soul the presence of God is experienced, but it is experienced as a purifying force, and for that very reason as something painful. That is why it is for the soul as though God were very distant, which is precisely what the souls in purgatory feel. Opposites are on the same level of being. If indeed the soul is in that state in which it directly experiences God's working in itself, then the feeling brought about by separation from God is of the same degree as the feeling aroused by his immediate presence. Hence the dreadful torture. For this is indeed the suffering of a pure spirit.[23]

The sufferings of the mystics are greater than any bodily suffering. St Teresa once complained to her Saviour of these sufferings, and the Saviour replied: "That is how I treat my friends." Whereupon St Teresa rejoined: "No wonder that they are so few." The suffering is that of the soul that is still separated from God, and its longing for more perfect union in the beatific vision. Only there is perfect happiness to be found.

It also becomes clear, however, that the soul can indeed function as a pure spirit, though it can only do this by disencumbering itself as far as possible of all that pertains to the body. Hence the need for mortifying the senses, a process that has no other purpose than the repression of the bodily.

> If we subject to psychological analysis the means that are supposed, on the ground of general experience, to lead to the mystical life, we again find that they have no other object than gradually to lead the person concerned to an activity that is that of the spirit-soul and nothing else. In that measure in which

---

[22] Mager, *Mystik als Lehre und Leben*, p. 51.
[23] Mager, *op. cit.*, p. 225.

they eliminate all that pertains to the corporal soul, they enable the spirit-soul to assert itself. Vocal prayer that stands at the threshold of the way which turns a man from the outward to the inner life, is still saturated with elements of sense which permeate the imagination and make up its concepts. Even in so-called meditation the corporal soul still plays a very large part. The soul immerses itself in the truths of revelation, which present themselves to it as things of the outer world. The purpose of such meditation, as it moves from one truth to another, is to make those truths into motives of action. The will is to be powerfully stimulated. The waters of the soul are to be brought into motion. After protracted practice it is easy for the soul to obey the higher impulses and set itself thus in movement without prolonged meditation. This is the phase of affective prayer. The part played by the corporal soul steadily diminishes. The movements of the soul become deeper and reach right down into the purely spiritual. Then only the smallest of impulses is required to bring the soul into movement on its own account. This is the so-called prayer of simplicity. Without meditation, a single simple truth acts so powerfully upon the soul that it remains in movement for a whole day. Here the assistance of the corporal soul is reduced to a minimum. From time to time there is an experience of that nearness of God of which previous mention has been made. With this we reach the point where the element of the corporal soul withdraws completely and the mystical life of the spirit-soul begins.[24]

The degree of the elimination of the corporal soul is in this instance greater than in sleep, but less than in purgatory, and this may well be one of the reasons why the acts of knowledge performed during sleep are of less consequence. This elimination of the corporal soul proceeds by stages. In the "prayer of quiet" the imagination is still active, nor will the soul have as yet been able fully to free itself from its operation.

The mystical Life [says Father Mager] is life indeed, and life is development from the imperfect to the perfect. Mystical development takes place, according to our mystics, in certain distinct stages. In the initial stage, that of the prayer of quiet, God and the soul still confront one another at a certain distance. True, the soul already feels the irresistible magnetic power which God exercises upon it. It burns with the desire to approach God more closely and to lessen the distance between him and itself. In direct self-awareness the

---

[24] Mager, *op. cit.*, p. 172.

soul becomes conscious of hindrances and inhibitions, imperfections and impurities which make it impossible for a more intimate union with God to be achieved. The soul still suffers too much under the leaden weight of the body and its effects. There ensues an agonizing condition—a night both of the senses and of the spirit, as it is called in the mystical literature of Spain. What is happening is that an inner transformation of the soul is taking place. God and the soul are approaching one another. All this is of course mere pictorial imagery. It vaguely symbolizes what occurs, but does not describe it.[25]

It is in the prayer of union that the ecstasies occur, which are a complete cessation of sense perception. St Augustine describes ecstasy as follows: "When the soul's attention has been completely diverted from the senses of the body and utterly torn away from them, there follows that state which one calls ecstasy. Then a man sees nothing, whatever bodily objects may be present, even though his eyes are open, nor are any voices heard." Somewhat later he speaks of ecstasy as "a condition in which the soul is more withdrawn from the bodily senses than it is in sleep, but to a lesser degree than in death".[26]

Ecstasies, however, only last for a time, and are essentially negative; they are merely a help, or rather a necessary presupposition, if purely spiritual activity is to take place. In the prayer of union the last fetters fall away. In the preliminary stage, the prayer of union (when it occurs) is preceded by the prayer of quiet. Also when it ceases it passes back into the prayer of quiet, and it is only after this that the normal state reasserts itself. Later the prayer of union occurs without there being any transitional stage that leads up to it, and it becomes intensified to such a degree that the soul seems drawn to God, embraced by him, veritably snatched away by him, so much so that the mystic feels that soul and body have actually parted. A positive rent appears to occur between them. The soul loses all consciousness of the body, of space and of time. This condition comes so suddenly into being and with such a degree of power that the body becomes rigid and is sometimes actually drawn upwards together with the soul. This is ecstatic prayer, the condition of ecstasy. St Teresa has given us marvellous descriptions of the bodily changes that take place on its approach.

---

[25] Mager, *op. cit.*, p. 166.
[26] St Augustine, *De Genesi ad litt.* 12. 12; see Mager, *op. cit*, p. 298.

In the mystical life, ecstasy plays the part of a normal but not indispensable organic connecting link. There is no need to speak of it as extraordinary, let alone as miraculous. In it that process reaches its culminating point, which we have already observed, the process by which the soul is lifted out of its imprisonment within the body, and can thus function as a pure spirit, the functions of the corporal soul being for the time eliminated. The separation of body and soul cannot go further than it does in ecstasy without bringing about actual death.

Mystics are very far from designating ecstasy as the culminating point of the mystical life; indeed, it does not pertain to the essence of the mystical life at all; there are mystics who never experience ecstasy—St Augustine, for instance, and St Gregory the Great; also ecstasy is experienced by persons who are still immersed in the natural mysticism of the pagan philosophers. Indeed, ecstasy is for many mystics simply the result of the weakness of their bodies, which are so overwhelmed by the sudden snatching to himself of the soul by God, that all semblance of life seems to leave them. The body must in such cases first accustom itself to the soul's new mode of activity. For others, on the other hand, ecstasy is definitely an end to be desired. Poulain in his *The Graces of Interior Prayer* speaks of it as the third stage of the mystical life.

This dualism between soul and body, which attains so radical a stage in ecstasy, is something imperfect and unfinished, a fact that the soul when in ecstasy quite clearly recognizes. The obstructive effects of the body are still too strong within the spiritual soul, which is confronted by the need of a new cleansing and purification. This is the final and most terrible night of the soul. In it the last wounds are cauterized and healed—the wounds inflicted by original sin on the soul in respect of its union with the body. It is only now that the ultimate bonds that hold back the soul are relaxed. Now, in the words of St John of the Cross, God permeates the soul as heat permeates air. Heat and air both tremble in a single motion, despite all the distinctions between them they have become one in this common motion. This intimate penetration of God and the soul is called by the Spanish mystics "spiritual marriage" (matrimonio espiritual).[27]

---

[27] See Dr M. Waldmann in *Lexicon für Theologie und Kirche*, art. "Parapsychologie".

In spiritual marriage, the mystical experience becomes a permanent condition, which lasts without interruption throughout the day and is only interrupted by sleep. The mystic can now undertake any other kind of activity and give it his full attention, and the psychic law that attention cannot be directed to two things at once is suspended. There is now no cutting out of the functions of the corporal soul—yet despite this we have before us to a most marked degree that very thing which was to be observed in the prayers of quiet and of union, namely the free activity of the soul as a pure spirit independent of the body. The element of imperfection which was still present in the prayer of union and the prayer of quiet, in so far as in these all activity of the corporal soul had to be eliminated—that element has now disappeared; the harmony between body and soul has been completely restored. The soul has now ceased to be the slave of the body; the chains have been completely broken; the body, which had once been unable to endure the reversal of the accustomed relationship, has now become the obedient servant of the spiritual soul. What the theologians call the *fomes peccati* has at the same time been extinguished. External objects and bodily impulses no longer determine the end and purpose of human knowledge and will and so the self-realization of the soul; they are now only the means to effect the spiritualization of the soul, and so to make it more receptive of God's working in it. The mystics agree that in this state of spiritual marriage the soul knows God not simply as the absolute or as the creator and sustainer, the giver of eternal blessedness, but as God in three persons; they see him in fact as the triune God—in so far, of course as creatures standing outside the beatific vision can do this.[28]

"A remarkable thing in the state of spiritual marriage," says St John of the Cross, "is that when it occurs the senses again exercise their full function. In the previous stages the mystical state is only momentary, and during it sense-activity is suspended. But in the perfect state of spiritual marriage the sensual part of man is so adjusted to the spiritual that it can continue its activity even though that wholly different form of knowledge which is contemplation is actually functioning."[29]

From all this it is sufficiently clear that all the phenomena of occultism and parapsychology (until we actually come to genuine prophecy and the

---

[28] Cf. with all this Mager, *Mystik als Lehre und Leben*, pp. 167 ff.
[29] St John of the Cross, in Mager, *Mystik als Lehre und Leben*, p. 378.

appearance of phantoms which are not tied to any person or place) are explicable in terms of a very rare condition of the human soul and that they need not be interpreted in spiritualist terms or in those of the diabolical or, for that matter, of the supernatural or the divine. A very important point is that we should distinguish between ecstasy and trance, for they are "polar" psychological opposites, as like and unlike as genius and madness. Maximum tension of a power of the corporal soul—even an intellectual power—leads to ecstasy, while maximum relaxation from all such activities leads to sleep and, under certain conditions, to twilight states, trances, etc. What St Paul says concerning the speaking with tongues (I Cor. 14), the thirty-year theological and ecclesiastical battle against the ecstasies of the Montanists, St Thomas, Cardinal Cajetan in his commentary on the latter's *Summa*, Benedict XIV in *De Beatificatione* III, c. 49—all bear witness to the fact that the main criterion between the mystical life that is truly supernatural and divine on the one hand, and the mysticism of natural philosophy and in particular that debased mysticism (*Aftermystik*) which is a phenomenon of parapsychology on the other, lies precisely in this essential difference between ecstasy and trance.

We must also draw a distinction between the phenomena of religious (Catholic) parapsychology and the true Catholic mystical life; Katharina Filljung of Biding near Metz (1848-1915) and even Theresa Neumann may be cited as examples of the first, while Mother Salesia Schulten, the Ursuline of Osnabrück (1877-1920), may be chosen as a classic example in our own day of the genuine mystical Life in its highest and purest form. According to Richstätter (*Lexicon für Theologie und Kirche*, ix. 353), "her writings are among the most valuable things in the whole mystical literature of the world". To the other cases, however, we may well apply the words of Cardinal Cajetan in his commentary on the *Summa Theologica* (II-II, q. 173, a. 3, ad 4) that a condition in which memory and consciousness have disappeared is out of harmony with what is laid down by St Paul (I Cor. 14, 32): "The spirits of the prophets are subject to the prophets." We can certainly say that the phenomena connected with Theresa Neumann do not fit into the traditional pattern—which of course is in itself no ground for rejecting them. She is a blessing for all the people of Germany, who should be duly grateful.

Speaking generally, one may say that visions, voices, stigmata and levitations are secondary and inessential things which should be treated with great caution, since the element of illusion is very prone to enter into them. To be able to say when such things are something other than mere phenomena of parapsychology (to say nothing of the delusions of the devil) is a science on its own account.

I found it impossible to refrain just now from describing the true phenomena of the mystical life in the words of the master of that subject, Fr Mager. Mager is almost the only contemporary writer who speaks of the purely spiritual soul, describing its activity as beginning when the senses are withdrawn, but who also insists on the essential difference between the true mystical life and all other states of the soul, especially natural mysticism and, still more, pseudo-mystical tendencies. These thorough-going studies of the mystical life help to confirm the writer's thesis, particularly against Castelein and Lepicier, who will never accept a purely spiritual activity on the part of the soul and so must, at any rate in Lepicier's case, ascribe all occult phenomena to the devil.

It is the task of Christianity to overcome the consequences of original sin, and that in the fullest sense; in the mystical states there is a restoration almost of the state enjoyed by Adam in Paradise.

Let us, however, turn back to Fr Mager:

> It would therefore appear [he writes] that such contemplation—at least this seems to be the conclusion we can draw—is a *modica participation,* a measure of participation in the angelic mode of knowledge, which means that the human soul here functions as a pure spirit. Even if we assume that the part played by mental imagery has been reduced to a minimum, our human mode of cognition could never, not even in the least imaginable degree, become a participation in the *cognitio angelica,* the "angelic mode of knowledge"—any more than the most delicate organization of minerals, though it may simulate the coarser forms of plant life, can turn itself into a plant. Yet for all that the chemical prerequisites in a plant are of the same kind as in a mineral compound. If, however, this mystical contemplation is rooted in the soul's activity as a pure spirit, there is nothing so very extraordinary in the fact that it should feel the nearness of God, have an experimental perception of God, behold the Blessed Trinity, etc. These things become matters of course; they

are an essential part of that *cognitio media* which, according to St Thomas,[30] Adam enjoyed while still in a state of innocence.[31]

This is the state to which St Benedict sought to lead his monks and to which he refers as *oratio pura*.

St Ignatius also seeks to create in his *Spiritual Exercises*, the conditions for the true mystical life, as Fr Richstätter points out,[32] through great purity of soul, love of the Saviour and the desire to participate in his sufferings, by his rules for the discernment of spirits, by directing to prayer from the heart and the production of contemplation.

Fr Mager insists elsewhere that

> the mystical life does not imply anything unusual or exceptional that is reserved for specially privileged people. Rather is it a part of that great transformation that must take place in man as he approaches his final perfection. It begins at that point where the soul, still bound to the body, begins to function as a pure spirit, that is to say independently of the body. It means therefore the spiritualization of man, a withdrawal within himself, the attainment of independence, by his purely spiritual part, the re-establishment of the spirit in its original sovereignty over the body.[33]

To form a clearer understanding, however, of the psychic processes involved in all this it would be well to examine such figurative concepts as those of the "night of the soul" and "passive purification". In general the mystics tend to speak of two such "nights of the soul"; the first occurs at the beginning of the prayer of quiet, when the senses begin to be withdrawn and the processes of logical reasoning begin to cease. Up to this point the person concerned had been in the habit of cooperating faithfully with grace to practise meditation, and make resolutions for the future conduct of life. This now becomes impossible, and the fear which this inability engenders produces the feeling of being in a state of spiritual dryness and emptiness, a thing which

---

[30] St Thomas, I, 94, a. 1.
[31] Mager, *Mystik als Lehre und Leben*, p. 209.
[32] *Die ignatianischen Exerzitien und die mystischen Gebetsgnaden*, pp. 33 ff.
[33] Mager, *Mystik als Lehre und Leben*, p. 171.

causes intense suffering until there has been complete adjustment to this new way of the following of Our Lord.

The other night of the soul begins when at length it succeeds in utterly breaking through the bounds of the sensual-bodily and stands, as it were, face to face with the purely spiritual, with God, Three in One. In this state the soul recognizes the holiness of God, and—when it looks at itself—its own unholiness and sinfulness. No very grave faults may be involved, but even quite small transgressions now seem to be immeasurably terrible things which render it unworthy of the proximity of God. Such souls now regard themselves as the greatest sinners in the world—and this is no mere phrase to them, but bitter earnest, and they are filled with sadness and shame at the thought of it; the whole force of their being draws them irresistibly towards God, and yet they tend to draw back through a sense of their unworthiness. Their condition is very like that of the poor souls in purgatory, who are aflame with the love of God and desire to see him, but may not do so till they have performed the full measure of their penance—this is indeed the real nature of the suffering in purgatory, and what the soul of the mystic experiences is really something very like it. It is suffering of this kind that drew from St Teresa the words quoted a few pages back.

Alongside these nights of the soul we have the so-called "passive purifications". As the soul contemplates the holiness of God, the resolution is formed in the subconscious to be holy and to avoid this or that imperfection in order to be less unworthy of God's presence. When the soul returns to the life of sense, these resolutions that are embedded in the subconscious spread their effect into the ordinary life of the person concerned, the actual psychical mechanism being the same as that which permits purely hysterical thoughts to dominate the body throughout a lifetime. In the case of the mystic, the result is that he is simply no longer capable of falling into the faults in question; he is in fact in a very similar condition to that of a man who has been hypnotized, and afterwards performs "post-hypnotic" acts without really knowing why he does so. In this manner "the last wounds are cauterized and healed".

Thus at every stage of the mystical life we encounter states which become quite intelligible to us if we compare them with those parapsychic phenomena which were described in the preceding pages, while these phenomena in their turn sustain the general theory that has here been advanced. Although the psychic mechanism is the same, we are nevertheless dealing with two radically different sets of things. Ecstasy, for instance, which is really a mystical sleep, not only affords cognitions of a much higher order than the artificial sleep of hypnosis, but is actually the latter's polar opposite, and the mere fact of a certain psychic parallelism should never induce us to treat the two phenomena as being of the same order. There is a whole world of difference between them, both as to purpose and cause. Yet it is with this same fundamental mechanism of the soul that grace works and God leads on the soul in a manner adapted to its nature.

The mystical graces of prayer represent the highest stage of spiritual knowledge and are, in the words of St John of the Cross, "a heroic effort to pass beyond our human nature into the realm of pure spirit"; nevertheless the mystics warn us against striving to attain these states for their own sake, since they involve an abnormal form of spiritual life. "It is best to reject all this out of hand and without enquiring whether the origin be good or evil."[34] To desire visions and voices is a sign of childishness; ecstasy itself is a weakness (St Teresa); and similar warnings occur in the midst of dissertations on the highest mystical states. It is true that some mystics have a different view. For St Bernard, for instance, ecstasy was a thing definitely to be desired; it was a foretaste of eternal happiness. It is not a purely negative thing, an emptying, a paralysis of the physical, but rather something positive, a wholly new form of being and existence.[35]

Enough has been said above about the results of original sin and the danger that the experimental "derangement" of the spirit may become chronic. Speaking purely psychologically, therefore, the same general principle applies even to the experiences of the mystic life. Though it is certainly our duty to co-operate with the graces of God, it would nevertheless be rash to overlook the dangers involved in cutting out our normal sense life while we are still on earth, dangers that can only be eliminated in the mystical life that is truly led by God and guided by his grace, but which are ever-present in the baser forms of mysticism.

---

[34] St John of the Cross, cf. Fr Penido, O.P., in *Revista Eccl. Brasileira*, 1941, p. 441.
[35] See Dr Robert Linhardt, *Die Mystik des hl. Bernhard von Clairvaux,* Munich, 1923, pp. 231 ff.

It is not the writer's intention to pursue these ideas any further, or to write a general theory of the mystical life. All he has sought to do is to sketch in the general features of that life, the real nature of which is known to comparatively few people, and so to furnish further proof for the central idea of his thesis. For if such states as those described occur in the mystical life, then there must be a certain aptitude or predisposition to them rooted in human nature itself, as also supernatural grace itself finds in man the *potentia obedientialis*. Such aptitude, unfortunately, only rarely bears fruit; for one thing, it is only possible for it to do so within the Catholic Church, in which alone the full benefits of the Redemption are to be found, and with them the potentialities originally possessed by Adam. Moreover, even within the Catholic Church it is rare for the true mystical states to be achieved, partly because these depend upon the free granting of grace by God, and, apart from that, it is all too rare for men to undertake the labour of mounting the first steps in the mystical life; their love and readiness for sacrifice are too weak for that.

For that very reason, however, they are all too ready to join the heathen in treading the paths of the occult and indulging themselves in pseudomysticism, and to dissipate their energies in magic, spiritualism and theosophy, to their own physical and spiritual ruin. Such a thought was indeed uttered by Bishop Keppler,[36] when, confused and deeply shocked by the very horror of it all, he witnessed the antics of the dancing dervishes. What was the purpose of the performance that he so vividly described? Surely it was nothing less than the despairing cry of the immortal soul for union with God. The true mystical life is unknown to such people; hence these aberrations. The same might well be said of occultism as a whole. It occurs most frequently in those places where Christianity is unknown or known insufficiently, above all where the Christian way of life is not followed. "*Aemulamini charismata meliora*" (I Cor. 12. 31)—"Be zealous for the better gifts."

---

[36] *Wanderfahrten und Wallfahrten im Orient*, p. 138.

www.ingramcontent.com/pod-product-compliance
Lightning Source LLC
Chambersburg PA
CBHW061215070526
44584CB00029B/3840